Pitt Press Series

TACITUS

CORNELII TACITI

DE VITA

IULII AGRICOLAE,

DE ORIGINE ET MORIBUS

GERMANORUM

T0371556

TACITUS

CORNELII TACITI

DE VITA

IULII AGRICOLAE,

DE ORIGINE ET MORIBUS

GERMANORUM

EDITED BY

J. H. SLEEMAN, M.A.

FORMERLY FELLOW OF SIDNEY SUSSEX COLLEGE, CAMBRIDGE,
PROFESSOR OF CLASSICS IN THE UNIVERSITY OF LONDON

WITH TWO MAPS

Cambridge :
at the University Press
1933

CAMBRIDGE
UNIVERSITY PRESS

University Printing House, Cambridge CB2 8BS, United Kingdom

Cambridge University Press is part of the University of Cambridge.

It furthers the University's mission by disseminating knowledge in the pursuit of education, learning and research at the highest international levels of excellence.

www.cambridge.org
Information on this title: www.cambridge.org/9781107486591

© Cambridge University Press 1914

First edition 1914
First published 1914
Reprinted 1923, 1928, 1933
First paperback edition 2015

A catalogue record for this publication is available from the British Library

ISBN 978-1-107-48659-1 Paperback

PREFACE

IN view of the vast amount of labour expended by
generations of scholars upon the *Agricola* and the
Germania of Tacitus, it is hardly possible nowadays to
propound novel, yet sane, interpretations of the numerous
difficulties which they contain. The present book at least
disclaims any attempt to accomplish such a feat. It merely
endeavours to put together in a convenient and handy form
what is necessary for the understanding of these famous
monographs, avoiding, so far as possible, long discussions
of doubtful and often indeterminable questions and attend-
ing rather to the practical needs of student and teacher.
So many English editions of the *Agricola* are now available
that an apology seems almost needed for adding another to
the list; but the *Germania* has been less frequently edited
in this country, and recent archaeological and palaeo-
graphical discoveries have provided a certain amount of
new matter for the elucidation of both treatises.

At the outset I would refer to the inestimable debt
which, in common with all students of Tacitus, I owe
to Mr Furneaux. His editions of the *Agricola* and the
Germania may fairly be said to supersede all previous
expositions of these works, and they are long likely to
remain the standard commentaries, especially on the
linguistic side. The editions of Wex, Kritz, Draeger,

Zernial, Schweizer-Sidler and other German scholars I have constantly consulted, but Furneaux seems always to sum up what is best in them, and thanks to the soundness of his judgment seldom gives an unconvincing explanation. I desire to make the fullest acknowledgment of what my notes owe to Mr Furneaux. I wish also to express my indebtedness to Mr H. M. Stephenson, who has previously edited these treatises in the Pitt Press Series, to those indefatigable Tacitean scholars, Messrs Church and Brodribb, and, among more recent English and American editors of the *Agricola*, to Professor Flamstead Walters, Mr J. W. E. Pearce and Professor D. R. Stuart. I have several times quoted Mr W. H. Fyfe's translation. Dr Schanz' *Geschichte der römischen Litteratur* has been of great help to me in preparing parts of my Introduction.

Since Mr Furneaux wrote, the discovery of new manuscripts has led to some amendment in the texts of the treatises, particularly in that of the *Agricola*, though unhappily several of the greater textual riddles still remain unsolved. In this connexion scholars owe a deep debt of gratitude to Professor Cesare Annibaldi, who has so carefully edited and criticised the text of E, and to Professors Leuze and F. F. Abbott, who have recorded the readings of T. I have found Paolo Fossataro's critical edition of the *Agricola* most useful.

In recent years excavation has thrown a good deal of light upon Agricola's operations in Britain, and it is to be hoped that further work with the spade will increase yet more our knowledge of his campaigns. For what we already know we have mainly to thank Mr Curle, Dr Macdonald and Professor Haverfield, my debt to all of whom, particularly the last named, will appear sufficiently from my notes. For British antiquities I have constantly consulted Dr Rice Holmes' great work, *Ancient Britain and the Invasions of Julius Caesar.* For German archaeology and ethnology my main sources have been Dr E. Schwyzer's invaluable edition of the *Germania* (based upon that of Schweizer-Sidler) and the writings of our eminent English authority, Professor H. M. Chadwick.

The maps inserted in the present volume are new. In preparing them I derived much assistance from the maps of Britain and Germany in Mr Murray's series and from the map of Germany in Schwyzer's edition, as well as from the geographical disquisitions of Professor Chadwick in his *Origin of the English Nation.*

My obligations to other writers are, I trust, adequately acknowledged in the notes. In conclusion I desire to thank Professor Summers for so often putting his great knowledge of Silver idiom at my disposal and giving me his opinion on difficult passages ; Mr H. L. White for assistance in scientific and other matters ; and the officials of the University Press not only for correcting many errors but also for suggesting a number of extremely valuable improvements in my notes.

J. H. SLEEMAN.

SHEFFIELD,
August, 1914.

S.   *b*

CONTENTS

INTRODUCTION

§ 1. *Life of Tacitus.*

Our information about the life of Cornelius Tacitus is somewhat meagre. There is uncertainty even as to his name. Ancient authors generally call him Cornelius Tacitus without a praenomen, in accordance with a practice which became common in the first century A.D., of describing persons by gentile name and cognomen alone. Sidonius Apollinaris[1], a writer of the fifth century, and certain late manuscripts speak of him as Gaius, but the name Publius given him by Codex Mediceus I, a manuscript of the highest authority, is generally accepted as correct[2]. The place of his birth is unknown[3], the date can only be conjectured. Pliny the younger[4] mentions him as a close contemporary, —the two are *aetate propemodum aequales,*—but adds that he himself was still quite a youth when Tacitus had already made his name as an orator. Pliny was born in 61 or 62 A.D. Tacitus[5] describes himself as having been *iuvenis admodum* in 74 A.D., the dramatic date of the *dialogus de oratoribus,* and we know that he was quaestor in or about 80 A.D., the earliest legal age for the tenure of that office

[1] *epp.* IV. 14 and 22.

[2] An inscription found at Mylasa in Caria, describing Tacitus as proconsul of Asia, was at first thought to be decisive in favour of the name Publius, but the original editors of the inscription seem to have misread certain letters.

[3] The tradition that he was born at Interamna (Terni) arises from the fact that his namesake and admirer, the Emperor M. Claudius Tacitus (275 A.D.), was a native of the place. Its inhabitants built a tomb in the historian's honour, which survived to the latter part of the sixteenth century, when it was destroyed by order of Pope Pius V because of Tacitus' hostility to Christianity (Furneaux, *Ann.,* Vol. I. p. 5).

[4] *ep.* VII. 20. 3.   [5] *dial.* 1.

being 25. So we may fairly conclude that 54 or 55 A.D. was
the date of his birth. His father is identified by some with
Cornelius Tacitus, procurator of Belgic Gaul, whose son was
personally known to Pliny the elder[1]. The identification is
chronologically probable, and anyhow the procurator is
likely to have been a relative of the historian. That he
came of good family is shown by his whole political and
social career.

In his youth, according to the fashion of the time, he
devoted himself to the study of oratory. The Ciceronian
manner of his first work, the *dialogus*, lends some slight
plausibility to the suggestion that he, like his friend the
younger Pliny, was a pupil of Quintilian, the leader of the
Ciceronian reaction. We know from his own account that
he attached himself to Marcus Aper and Julius Secundus,
the leaders of the Roman bar in Vespasian's time, and
prosecuted his forensic studies with all the enthusiasm of
vouth[2].

In 77 A.D., when about 23 years of age, he was betrothed
to the daughter of the consul Agricola. He married her
perhaps early in the following year, immediately before his
father-in-law was appointed to Britain[3]. His official career,
as he tells us himself[4], began under Vespasian, probably in
79, the last year of his principate, and was continued under
Titus (79–81) and Domitian (81–96). Under the Empire
the *cursus honorum* was generally (1) military tribunate, a
subordinate legionary command, (2) vigintivirate, a civil
office with police, judicial and other functions, (3) quaestorship, (4) aedileship or tribunate, (5) praetorship, (6) consulship. According to the generally accepted view, Tacitus
held one or both of the first two minor offices under
Vespasian; he was quaestor and *ipso facto* member of the

[1] *N. H.* VII. 17. 76.   [2] *dial.* 2.   [3] *Agr.* 9. 7.
[4] *hist.* I. I. 4 *dignitatem nostram a Vespasiano incohatam, a
Tito auctam, a Domitiano longius provectam non abnuerim.* Some
think that *dignitatem...incohatam* refers to the quaestorship, not to
the minor offices mentioned above. If Tacitus was quaestor in 79,
he cannot have been born later than 54.

Senate in 80 or 81 under Titus, and tribune or aedile in the early years of Domitian's reign. In 88 he was praetor and a member of the priestly college of the *quindecimviri sacris faciundis* who had charge of the Sibylline books. In this dual capacity he assisted at the celebration of Domitian's Secular Games[1].

After his praetorship he was absent from Rome for four years[2] (89–93), doubtless as governor of a province. This could not have been one of the senatorial provinces, to which appointments were made for one year only. It was perhaps an imperial province of the second rank, for instance Gallia Belgica, where he might well have acquired his interest in German peoples and customs. When Agricola died in 93, he was still absent from Rome[3], but he returned the same year. He received no more promotion from Domitian, but remained a silent spectator of the horrors of the tyrant's closing years. The memories of this dreadful time have coloured his whole outlook upon history. In 97 he was consul under Nerva, and in this year delivered a funeral oration over the aged Verginius Rufus[4], who as legate of upper Germany twenty-nine years before had crushed the revolt of Vindex. In 100 he and Pliny at the solicitation of the African provincials successfully prosecuted their extortionate governor Marius Priscus. In speaking of the trial Pliny mentions the peculiar dignity of Tacitus' oratory[5]. The last biographical fact which we know of Tacitus is that about 112 A.D. he was proconsul of Asia[6], thus attaining to one of the highest and most important administrative posts under the Senate's control. His death is supposed to have occurred soon after the accession of Hadrian (117 A.D.).

---

[1] *ann.* XI. 11. 3.   [2] *Agr.* 45. 5.   [3] *Agr.* 45. 4.

[4] Pliny, *ep.* II. 1. 6 *laudatus est a consule Cornelio Tacito ; nam hic supremus felicitati eius cumulus accessit, laudator eloquentissimus.*

[5] Pliny, *ep.* II. 11. 17 *respondit Cornelius Tacitus eloquentissime et, quod eximium orationi eius inest,* σεμνῶς.

[6] See p. ix, note 2.

Eleven of Pliny's *Letters* are addressed to Tacitus, but they do not throw much light upon the historian's personal characteristics. In one[1] Pliny prophesies immortality for Tacitus' *Histories* and hopes that he may find a place in them. Two[2] which describe the eruption of Vesuvius in 79 were written in response to Tacitus' request for an account of the death of the elder Pliny, a victim of the catastrophe. In a letter to his friend Maximus[3], Pliny tells with infinite satisfaction an anecdote of Tacitus, which better than all the dry details of biography makes the man live before us. At the games in the Circus Tacitus was sitting next to a Roman knight, who after some learned conversation asked him, "Are you an Italian or a provincial?" "You know me," said Tacitus, "from my writings." Whereupon the stranger replied, "Are you Tacitus or Pliny?"

§ 2. *Tacitus' literary career.*

Tacitus' career as an author fell mainly in the reign of Trajan (98–117 A.D.). His first work, the *dialogus de oratoribus*, an inquiry into the causes of the decline of oratory, professes to reproduce a conversation between eminent literary men, at which he had been present in his youth. Its periodic structure, and lively, copious and even redundant style, are distinctly Ciceronian and probably reflect Tacitus' early oratorical training under masters who, like Quintilian, thought that 'to admire Cicero greatly was to have made good progress.' The date of the appearance of the *dialogus* is much disputed. There are internal objections to assigning it to the reigns of either Titus or Domitian, and recent critics incline to the belief that it was written and published after Domitian's death, i.e. in 97 or 98 A.D. If this view be correct, it is very remarkable that within a few months Tacitus produced works so entirely different in style as the smoothly flowing Ciceronian *dialogus* and the terse, epigrammatic

[1] VII. 33. 1.   [2] VI. 16 and 20.   [3] IX. 23. 2.

Agricola and *Germania.* Still we must remember that
contemporary taste demanded different manners for history
and for oratory[1], and we must look for the antecedents of
Tacitus' historical style not in the *dialogus* but in Sallust
and Virgil, in Curtius and other writers with marked Silver
characteristics. The words *vel incondita ac rudi voce* in
c. 3 of the *Agricola* suggest that the historical work upon
which Tacitus was then engaged was his first attempt in an
unfamiliar style.

The *Agricola* and the *Germania* can be definitely assigned to the first year of Trajan's principate, 98 A.D.[2], the
former, as is suggested by its introduction, appearing earlier
than the latter. While composing the *Agricola* Tacitus
was already engaged on a history of the reigns of Domitian
and Nerva[3]. Subsequently he somewhat altered the scope
of his work, and probably at intervals between 104 and
109 A.D. published his *Histories*, covering the years 69–
96 A.D. Of the 14 books into which the *Histories* seem to
have been divided, 1–4 and part of 5 are extant. Tacitus'
latest and most remarkable work, the *Annals*, or, to give it
its original title, *ab excessu divi Augusti*, deals with the
reigns of Tiberius, Caligula, Claudius and Nero (14 A.D. to
Jan. 1st 69 A.D., where the *Histories* begin). The work
comprised 16 books, of which 1–4, part of 5, 6, 11–15 and
part of 16 survive.

§ 3. *The Agricola; its contents, purpose and characteristics.*

The *Agricola* opens with some observations upon biographical writing and in particular its dangers and practical
extinction during the tyranny of Domitian. Even under
the happy auspices of Nerva and Trajan Tacitus has to
lament a widespread hostility to good men which compels
him to ask indulgence for offering to the world a biography

---

[1] See Pliny, *ep.* v. 8. 9, and Schanz, *Gesch. der röm. Litt.* 2 Teil,
2 Hälfte, p. 295.
[2] See *Agr.* 3. 1 note, *Germ.* 37. 2.   [3] See on *Agr.* 3. 3.

of Agricola (cc. 1-3). He then plunges at once into his subject, narrating Agricola's parentage and early life, his education at Massilia, his military apprenticeship in Britain under Suetonius Paulinus, his marriage with Domitia Decidiana, his quaestorship, tribunate and praetorship (cc. 4-6). Next we hear in somewhat more detail how he espoused the cause of Vespasian, commanded the 20th legion in Britain, governed Aquitania, was elevated to the consulship and appointed to the governorship of Britain (cc. 4-9).

At this point occurs a long interlude, occupying about a sixth of the work and comprising a description of Britain (cc. 10-12) and a sketch of its conquest up to the time of Agricola (cc. 13-17). This interlude serves as an introduction to the most important chapter of Agricola's life, his successes in Britain. He signalises his arrival about midsummer by defeating the Ordovices and reducing Mona, though his troops were expecting no further operations that year (c. 19). Then follows an account of his equitable government and administrative reforms, his strategic skill, and his efforts to Romanise the country, together with a brief military sketch of the Roman advance northwards, a reference to Ireland and Agricola's designs upon it, and a description of operations against the Caledonians, who after some indecisive fighting combined for a final effort to repel the invaders (cc. 19-27). Here the thread of the biography is again interrupted by an account of the mutiny and subsequent adventures of a cohort of Usipi (c. 28). The artistic purpose of this interlude is to emphasise Agricola's crowning achievement, the slaughter of the Caledonians at Mons Graupius, by definitely marking it off from the preceding narrative. Before the battle Calgacus, the Caledonian general, and Agricola address their troops (cc. 30-34). The battle is then described in some detail (cc. 35-37). A summary of the results of the victory, an account of Agricola's withdrawal into winter quarters and a brief reference to the circumnavigation of the north of Scotland by the Roman fleet, close this section of the *Agricola* (c. 38).

The third part of the biography begins with Agricola's recall by Domitian who was suspicious of his success. Though awarded the usual triumphal honours, he was coldly received by the Emperor and sought to avoid further suspicion by living in retirement (cc. 39–40). Even so, his enemies constantly whispered accusations against him into the Emperor's ears (c. 41), and, acting apparently on an imperial hint, persuaded him to decline the offer of the proconsulate of Asia or Africa (c. 42). His death in 93 A.D. excited general sympathy, which was increased by the rumour that it was due to poison. While refusing to commit himself to a definite statement that Agricola was poisoned by Domitian's orders, Tacitus does his best to leave the reader with an impression of the Emperor's guilt (c. 43).

Agricola's personal characteristics and worldly circumstances are then briefly touched upon. He is shown to have deserved the epithet 'happy,' in that he died at the height of his fame and prosperity and was spared the sight of Domitian's worst atrocities (cc. 44–45). The *Agricola* closes with a magnificent apostrophe to the dead and an assurance that he will live for ever in the hearts of men (cc. 45–46).

Much has been written about the purpose of the *Agricola* and the precise kind of literary composition to which it belongs. It is certainly to be regarded as what it professes to be, 'the life of one who has passed away,' 'a work intended to do honour to Agricola,' 'an expression of filial regard.'[1] Had Tacitus been in Rome at Agricola's death, in accordance with custom he would doubtless have delivered a funeral oration over him. As he was absent, five years afterwards he wrote a biography. But though the work is primarily a biography, in places it diverges into history, as in the description of Britain and the earlier stages of its

---

[1] See 1. 4, 3. 4. Cp. 46. 4. See Schanz, pp. 298 ff., for excellent summaries of the views which have been held as to the literary form and purpose of the *Agricola* and the *Germania*.

conquest, the episode of the Usipi and the elaborate account
of the battle at Mons Graupius.

Gudeman[1] calls the *Agricola* a biographical encomium, a
species of composition belonging to the γένος ἐπιδεικτικόν
(*genus laudativum*) and developed out of the panegyric,
especially the λόγος ἐπιτάφιος (*laudatio funebris*). He shows
from Menander, Hermogenes and other Greek rhetoricians
that the encomium was naturally divided under six heads,
(1) introduction, (2) the hero's parentage, birth and education, (3) his personal characteristics and pursuits, (4) his
achievements, (5) a comparison of him with others, (6) epilogue. It cannot be said that the *Agricola* harmonises very
well with this scheme. Agricola's 'personal characteristics'
have no separate section to themselves but appear at intervals
throughout the work, though Gudeman insists that the
majority of them are mentioned in the chapters immediately
following the 'education,' and that they are identical with
those which the Greek authorities name as indispensable to
the hero of a biographical encomium. The presence of the
geographical excursus in close proximity to the 'achievements' of the hero Gudeman explains by the fact that
Agricola was the first to conquer Britain completely and
so to win a thorough firsthand knowledge of the land and
its people. The greatest weakness in Gudeman's theory is
that there is no 'comparison with others' (σύγκρισις). The
account of previous British governors certainly cannot be
regarded as such, and the isolated phrases quoted by Gudeman (e.g. *quae vel incuria vel intolerantia priorum*, c. 20. 1)
do very little to supply its place. Gudeman in fact, while
pointing out interesting analogies to the orthodox Greek
encomium, has not succeeded in bringing the *Agricola*
within the four corners of that species of composition.

Some, like Andresen, have argued that Tacitus had by
him at Agricola's death an account of Britain and its
conquest, already written for his contemplated treatise on

---

[1] See the introduction to his German edition of the *Agricola.*

Domitian's reign, and that he subsequently worked part of
this material into a biography. But there is nothing to
show that Tacitus had planned a historical work as early
as 93 A.D., nor is the *Agricola* so incoherent a collection of
snippets that it needs any such hypothesis for its explanation.
If the episodic and more or less irrelevant features of the
Agricola require defence, parallels may be found in Sallust's
Catiline and *Jugurtha*, the plans of which Tacitus probably
had in his mind when writing the *Agricola*. All three works,
for instance, have introductions, accounts of the early life of
the chief actors, digressions and episodes (cp. especially the
description of Africa in *Jug.* 17–19), long speeches and full
narratives of decisive battles[1]. An additional reason for the
Agricola's excursions into history may perhaps be found in
Tacitus' admitted concentration upon historical studies at
the time of its composition.

For Tacitus to write a biography of Agricola was in
some respects a difficult and delicate undertaking. When
the work was composed, an extremely bitter feeling prevailed
in senatorial circles not only against Domitian but against
all who had served under him, and this both the biographer
and his hero had done. Tacitus was praetor and governor
of a province under Domitian (see p. xi). Agricola had
been his faithful general in Britain, and when recalled in
85 A.D., instead of revolting against the tyrant with his four
victorious legions, as he might well have done, he meekly
obeyed the summons[2]. His subsequent life of retirement
in Rome, with its one object of avoiding the Emperor's dis-
pleasure[3], would naturally be regarded with some contempt

[1] See Furneaux, p. 16, where a good summary of the resemblances is given. There is one important difference, that neither of
Sallust's treatises has epilogues.

[2] See on 39. 4.

[3] With Agricola's withdrawal from affairs cp. Seneca's conduct
after his dismissal by Nero. "Seneca thanked him, the usual end
of an interview with a despot. But he entirely altered the practices
of his former greatness; he kept the crowds of his visitors at a distance, avoided trains of followers, seldom appeared in Rome, as

by the more uncompromising members of the senatorial opposition, who admired a Rusticus or a Senecio[1]. These hostile prejudices explain Tacitus' appeal for indulgence in c. 1. 3 and his outburst in c. 42. 5: "Be it known unto those whose custom it is to admire lawlessness that even under evil emperors there can be great men, and that obedience and submission, when accompanied by industry and energy, may attain to as high a degree of distinction as many have attained by dangerous paths but with no benefit to the state, winning fame by an ostentatious death."

Tacitus gives us to understand that it was only by the exercise of extreme caution that Agricola was able to escape the consequences of Domitian's hate for so long as he did. It is not easy to avoid the suspicion that in order to clear Agricola's reputation from the taint of servility and cowardice Tacitus may have exaggerated the Emperor's hostility to him and the necessity of his withdrawal from public affairs in the interests of his own safety. However that may be, the evidence that Agricola's death was due to poison administered by the Emperor's order must have been of the slightest. Tacitus has no material on which to frame a definite charge. He makes up for the lack of it by giving play to his almost diabolical faculty of innuendo and thereby manages to leave us with perhaps a worse impression of the Emperor than a direct accusation would have created. Some authors have gone so far as to maintain that the *Agricola* is in essence an apology for its hero and implicitly for its author. This view clearly overemphasises one aspect of the work. Still the *Agricola's* apologetic vein is strong enough to suggest that it may have caused some distortion of historical perspective.

though weak health or philosophical studies detained him at home." (*Ann.* XIV. 56, C. and B.'s Trans.)

[1] See on 2. 1, 4. 4.

§ 4. *The Germania; its contents, purpose, sources and value.*

The *Germania* is divided into two main parts, the first (cc. 1-27) being a general account of the country and its customs, the second (cc. 28-46) a special description of particular tribes. Beginning with the boundaries of Germany, the origin and characteristics of its inhabitants, its climate and products (cc. 1-5), Tacitus proceeds to a comprehensive survey of German institutions, embracing war, political and religious usages, the *comitatus*, houses and villages, clothing, marriage, rules of succession, the blood feud, habits of intemperance, food and drink, gambling, status of slaves and freedmen, land tenure and agriculture, and burial customs (cc. 6-27). In the second or special part he gives brief accounts of the separate nations of Germany, emphasising in each case the peculiarities which distinguished them from other Germans. He first deals with the German and non-German tribes of the Rhine frontier and then with those of western and north-western Germany (cc. 28-36). The mention of Rome's ancient enemies, the Cimbri, leads to a digression on the stubborn resistance which the Germans had offered to Rome for more than two centuries (c. 37). Next the various tribes of the Suebi are described, first those of central Germany, then those to the south, which are enumerated from west to east along the line of the Danube, and lastly those of the eastern and north-eastern districts, including Scandinavia (cc. 38-45). The book concludes with an account of the tribes of doubtful race on the eastern frontier and a reference to fabulous peoples beyond (c. 46).

From the above summary it seems clear that the purpose of the *Germania* was simply to describe the geography, ethnography and social condition of Germany. Being occupied, as we know, with a work of contemporary history, Tacitus naturally studied a country which was bound to

figure largely in it[1], and we may imagine that as the results
of his researches increased in bulk he decided to work them
up into a separate monograph and issue them independently
of the larger work.   The circumstances of the moment may
have helped him to this decision.   Germany at the time was
attracting a large measure of public attention.   The Emperor
Trajan, who had been at Cologne when Nerva died, was
still away in the north, strengthening the frontier defences
and attempting to establish friendly relations with German
tribes.   Rome, always alive to the northern danger, realised
it all the more keenly owing to the Emperor's prolonged
absence.   Hence the time was particularly appropriate for
the appearance of a work on Germany.   Led by these
considerations, many scholars, notably Müllenhoff, have
argued that Tacitus' purpose in writing the *Germania* was
not ethnographical and sociological, but political, that he
intended to represent the Germans as Rome's most formidable foes, to justify Trajan's defensive measures and to show
that they required his active supervision on the spot.   Now
the *Germania* contains only two 'political' passages, one,
the famous prayer in c. 33, that "among the nations of
Germany may endure if not love for us, yet at least hatred
for each other, since, while the doom of the Empire presses
hard upon it, fortune can bestow no greater blessing than
discord among our foes"; the other, the lengthy digression
in c. 37 on the 210 years of war between Germany and
Rome; "so long does the conquest of Germany take."   Nowhere else do we find a hint of any such purpose as Müllenhoff supposes.   From the fact that Tacitus expresses appre-
hension of the Germans in two passages and that Trajan at
the moment was occupied with the affairs of Germany, we
cannot fairly conclude that Tacitus wrote his monograph
solely, or even primarily, to awaken Rome to the German
peril (of which she was already well aware), or to stamp

[1] Cp. his studies of Britain in the *Agricola*, and of the Jews in
Hist. v. 1–12.

with his approval Trajan's cautious policy. All that we are entitled to say is that its publication was opportunely timed.

The view that the *Germania* was written as a 'mirror of morals' for the Romans is now antiquated, but deserves some consideration because of the facts which gave rise to it. The hypothesis itself is at once put out of court by the work's elaborate geography and ethnography, which would be irrelevant in a moral tract. Besides Tacitus by no means regards the Germans as patterns of morality; he sharply emphasises their intemperance, quarrelsomeness and sloth. Still the fact remains that he is continually drawing contrasts, explicit or implicit, between the luxury and immorality of Rome and the stern simplicity of Germany, where "no one laughs at vice and to corrupt and be corrupted is not called the spirit of the age" (19. 3). This tendency is not, however, peculiar to the *Germania*; it is almost equally visible in other Roman accounts of foreign countries. The truth is that writers trained in the rhetorical schools of the Empire, where ethical themes were constantly set as declamatory exercises, could not resist the opportunity presented by foreign customs for edifying moral comparisons, which at the same time added interest and point to their descriptions. Interest in primitive peoples was to some extent fostered by Stoicism with its doctrines of the brotherhood of man and of 'the life according to nature.' Such peoples were apt to be idealised, and the Germans in particular. Thus Seneca[1] admires their bravery, their devotion to arms and their

---

[1] *dial.* III. 11. 3. The passage is worth quoting for its resemblances to the *Germania: Germanis quid est animosius? quid ad incursum acrius? quid armorum cupidius, quibus innascuntur innutriunturque, quorum unica illis cura est in alia neglegentibus? quid induratius ad omnem patientiam, ut quibus magna ex parte non tegimenta corporum provisa sint, non suffugia adversus perpetuum caeli rigorem? hos tamen Hispani Gallique et Asiae Syriaeque molles bello viri, antequam legio visatur, caedunt ob nullam aliam rem opportunos quam iracundiam. agedum, illis corporibus illis animis delicias luxum opes ignorantibus da rationem, da disciplinam: ut nihil amplius dicam, necesse erit certe nobis mores Romanos repetere.*

endurance, "men who to a large extent have no covering for their bodies, no shelter against the unceasing rigour of their climate." The one fault he finds in them is their passionateness. "Only add discipline and reason," he exclaims, "to those bodies and minds which know not sensuality, luxury or wealth, and, to say the least, we shall have to resume the old Roman character." Scherer[1] well observes that "the unbroken might of this people was regarded by the Stoic as an ideal of moral strength, by the member of the aristocratic opposition as an ideal of freedom, by the diplomatist as an imminent danger." In ancient writers it is idle to look for that rigidly scientific interest in primitive races which distinguishes the modern anthropologist.

The sources of Tacitus' information upon Germany were literary and oral. There is nothing to show that he ever visited Germany and saw what he described. The concluding words of the general part of the *Germania*, "such is the account we have *received*," seem definitely to prove the contrary. First-hand evidence he could get through numerous channels, traders doing business with Germany, Roman officers stationed on the frontier or in charge of expeditionary forces, German prisoners at Rome or Germans in the Roman army. The remarkable story of the annihilation of a German tribe in c. 33 clearly came from a Roman eye-witness, though Tacitus need not have been the first to commit it to writing. Literary authorities existed in plenty. In c. 28. 1 Tacitus refers to Caesar as *summus auctorum*, and there can be little doubt that he carefully studied the relevant sections of the *Bellum Gallicum*. In a few places he seems to echo Caesar's words, in others silently, yet deliberately, to correct him[2]. One or two passages show

---

[1] Quoted by Schanz, p. 309.
[2] The question is elaborately discussed by Karl Eymer in *Neue Jahrbücher*, 1913, pp. 24–47. Eymer shows how differences between the accounts of Tacitus and Caesar can be explained partly by increased acquaintance with Germany, partly by social developments in the interval.

faint reminiscences of the section on Germany in Pomponius Mela's geography of the world, a work published apparently in Claudius' reign. Other writings, now lost, which Tacitus probably used, are Sallust's *Histories*, surviving fragments of which show that it contained some account of the Germans, the 104th book of Livy, which included a description of German geography and customs[1], Aufidius Bassus' history of Rome's wars with Germany (? published under Tiberius), and most important of all, the elder Pliny's work in 20 books on the same subject, particularly valuable because the author had himself seen service in Germany. Schwyzer does well to remind us of the great wall-map of the Roman Empire and neighbouring countries constructed in Rome by Augustus from the materials collected by M. Vipsanius Agrippa ; "it treated Germany to the Vistula as the Roman sphere of influence and represented it with Raetia and Noricum as the tenth region of the Empire."

There is doubtless truth in the remark that if Tacitus' sources for the *Germania* had been preserved rather than the *Germania* itself, archaeology would have been the gainer and literature the loser[2]. Yet Tacitus' account of Germany is remarkably comprehensive, in spite of a brevity and conciseness which no modern author of a descriptive work would dare to emulate. Its general accuracy too is thoroughly corroborated by the discoveries of archaeologists, by philological evidence and by later documentary records. Some indeed of his statements have given rise to acute controversy, particularly those in regard to the German system of land tenure and the *pagus* with its hundred picked fighting-men and hundred jurors. Some of the developments or supposed developments of institutions described by Tacitus unhappily do not throw much light upon the *Germania*, though the *Germania* may throw a good

---

[1] According to the Epitome *prima pars libri situm Germaniae moresque continet*, with which cp. the titles of the *Germania* as given in the MSS. See p. lii.

[2] See Schwyzer's edition, p. xii.

deal of light upon them. In excuse for the obscurities in Tacitus' account we may plead that he could not be expected to display the thirst for pure fact or the critical judgment of our present-day anthropologists, and that, being primarily a literary artist, he did not wish to spoil the unity and proportion of his work by explanations of inordinate length. We may perhaps regret that ancient authors were not acquainted with the use of footnotes. Archaeology has shown that the *Germania* is specially reliable in regard to dwellings, dress, weapons and tribal customs. On the purely geographical side it is weaker, though the weakness is not the fault of Tacitus but of his age. We venture to quote what Mr Tozer says on Roman knowledge of the topography of Germany :

"The acquaintance of the Romans with Germany derived from personal observation decreased rather than otherwise after the time of Augustus. The rule which was laid down by that emperor to the effect that the Roman arms should not advance beyond the Elbe was strictly adhered to by his successors; indeed, so little did they attempt to penetrate into the country at all, that Tacitus [*Germ.* 41. 2] speaks of that river as being known to his contemporaries only by hearsay. At the same time there arose a growing intercourse between the two peoples, and from this was derived the enlarged knowledge of the inhabitants of Germany which we find existing at a later period....Much of this was embodied in the *Germania* of Tacitus; but that treatise, interesting as it is from an ethnographical point of view, furnishes us with but little information about the physical features of the country, and even as to the situation of the various tribes. It is noticeable, as a proof of the ignorance which prevailed with regard to the north-eastern part of the country, that the name of so important a river as the Viadrus (Oder) does not occur in any writer before Ptolemy [c. 150 A.D.]; and though the Vistula was known at an earlier period, and was regarded as the boundary of Germany on its eastern side towards Sarmatia, yet this was probably due to the trade-route from the Baltic which passed through

Pannonia, rather than to any intelligence derived from Germany itself[1]."

§ 5. *Tacitus' literary style and the influences which moulded it.*

It has been well said that Tacitus was born to be a tragic poet. A note of tragedy pervades almost all that he wrote. His inborn pessimism, aggravated by Domitian's cruel persecution of the Senate, led him in his writings to dwell upon the wickedness of the Emperors and the corruption of Roman society, to the almost complete exclusion of the brighter elements in the Empire, the high efficiency of its government and the general well-being of its subjects. The prologue to the *Agricola* is perhaps the bitterest and most passionate expression of this attitude towards history to be found in his works. Not even the hopes aroused by Nerva's accession could make him forget his pessimism or check his gloomy vaticinations regarding the Empire's impending doom. His unscrupulous habit of innuendo is an outcome of this spirit of bitterness and readiness to believe the worst. He delights to suggest the truth of insinuations which he himself admits to rest upon no certain evidence. This tendency is found in his portraiture of Domitian in the *Agricola,* but reaches its height in the *Annals,* particularly in his treatment of Tiberius.

The writer to whom Tacitus owed most was undoubtedly Sallust. Akin to him in moral earnestness and pessimistic outlook upon life, he closely imitated the Sallustian literary manner. Sallust, says Professor Wight Duff[2], introduced into Latin prose "an unprecedented union of rapidity brevity and variety....His variety is far more than linguistic. It was not merely that he broke away from the Ciceronian balance of phrase and of grammatical form. He was a free

[1] *Hist. of Ancient Geography,* p. 289. For Roman information about Jutland, the Baltic and Scandinavia see notes on *Germ.* 37. 1, 44. 1–2. In 46. 2 there is some weak geography.
[2] *Literary History of Rome,* p. 422.

artist, quick to see new values in a juxtaposition of elements drawn from history, rhetoric, psychology, geography and ethics." Interest in all the subjects which go to make up this 'variety' was fostered by the rhetorical schools of the Empire. A romantic geography, such as we meet with in various passages of the *Agricola* and the *Germania*, figured largely in oratorical exercises upon the heroes of old, particularly Alexander, whose oriental exploits afforded free scope to the imagination[1]. Take for instance the following passage from the elder Seneca's First *Suasoria*, § 2 :

tempus est Alexandrum cum orbe et cum sole desinere. quod noveram vici: nunc concupisco quod nescio. quae tam ferae gentes fuerunt quae non Alexandrum posito genu adorarint? qui tam horridi montes quorum non iuga victor miles calcaverit? ultra Liberi patris tropaea consistimus, non quaerimus orbem sed amittimus. immensum et humanae intemplatum experientiae pelagus, totius orbis vinculum terrarumque custodia, inagitata remigio vastitas, litora modo saeviente fluctu inquieta, modo fugiente deserta: taetra caligo fluctus premit et nescio qui quod humanis natura subduxit oculis aeterna nox obruit.

These sounding phrases, turgid though their rhetoric may be, certainly succeed in creating an atmosphere of strangeness and mystery. Curtius produces similar effects in his history of Alexander. Thus Tacitus is only following precedent when he invests with an air of romance the northern expeditions of Agricola. The danger of wild beasts is another favourite rhetorical theme, and it is somewhat disappointing to think that the remark in *Agr.* 34. 2 is probably not based on information received from Agricola himself about the bears, wolves, boars and other beasts which then roamed the hills and forests of the north, but is merely an orator's commonplace[2].

The strong ethical motive in Tacitus, which reaches its climax in the *Germania*, deserves some discussion, as its

[1] See on *Agr.* 10. 6.
[2] Cp. Curtius III. 8. 10, IX. 3. 8.

purport has sometimes been misapprehended. It has been
held that in the *Germania* an ethical rather than a historical
purpose guides Tacitus' selection of facts, and that his
description for instance of the amber of the Baltic is introduced merely to permit a sarcastic allusion to Roman luxury.
This may be gravely doubted. It would be fairer to say
that, thanks to a rhetorical training, no writer of Tacitus'
age, even though his purpose be purely descriptive, can ever
resist an opportunity to make a moral point. Thus Curtius
cannot mention the pearls of India without adding

> *neque alia illis maior opulentiae causa est, utique post-*
> *quam vitiorum commercium vulgavere in exteras gentes:*
> *quippe aestimantur purgamenta exaestuantis freti pretio*
> *quod libido constituit* (VIII. 9. 19)[1].

In fact, throughout his account of India Curtius is
constantly harping upon the vices and luxury of its inhabitants[2]. Hardly a page of the elder Pliny's *Natural History*,
as scientific a work as the age can show, is without its
moralising. Thus Pliny embellishes his account of unguents
with a story of a proscribed person whose hiding-place was
revealed by the scent which he used; *quis enim non merito*
iudicet periisse tales? (XIII. 3. 25). He deplores the fact
that even worms which attack the bark of trees have become
instruments of luxury, *atque etiam farina saginati hi quo-*
que altiles fiunt (XVII. 24. 220). Or again, after briefly describing two wooden semi-circular theatres, placed back to
back, which by an ingenious mechanical contrivance could,
while the spectators kept their seats, be wheeled together so
as to form a single circular amphitheatre, he launches out
into more than a page of indignant protest:

> *en hic est ille terrarum victor et totius domitor orbis, qui*
> *gentes, regna diribet, iura exteris mittit, deorum quaedam*
> *immortalium generi humano portio, in machina pendens et*
> *ad periculum suum plaudens* and much more to the same

---

[1] Pearls give Tacitus a similar opportunity in *Agr.* 12. 7.

[2] VIII. 9. 23, 29 (*ne quid perditis moribus desit*), 31.

effect (XXXVI. 15. 118)[1]. In short we may say that the
words 'vice,' 'corruption' and 'luxury' run like some haunt-
ing refrain through practically all the literature of the
Tacitean period. Everywhere that tendency was at work
which found its consummation in the beast-books of the
Middle Ages, where natural history was treated simply as a
vehicle for moral or religious edification.

It cannot be said that the ethical colouring of the
Germania is always appropriate or free from exaggeration.
This is particularly noticeable in the section on the relations
between the sexes. Thus in *Germ.* 18. 1[2], in one of those
efforts to make an artistic transition which distinguish the
work, Tacitus after alluding to a slight freedom, as it
appeared to a Roman, in the costume of German ladies,
continues "*in spite of this* the marriage bond is strictly
observed among them." Again, as Mr Mackail[3] points out,
the fine epigram *nemo illic vitia ridet*, etc. (19. 3) "concludes
a passage in which Tacitus gravely suggests that the invention of writing is fatal to moral innocence." Though the
Agricola and the *Germania* contain some of Tacitus' most
brilliant and unforgettable epigrams, yet so far he has hardly
attained that unerring skill in their manufacture and disposition which he reveals in the *Annals*[4].

The speeches in the *Agricola* are noble examples of
generals' addresses after the traditional model. They can
have no claim to be considered historical. It is evident
from both the matter and the style of the Caledonian chief-
tain's address that it could only have been delivered by one
trained in the Roman schools of declamation. Calgacus,
who was apparently introduced by Tacitus simply to make
a speech, betrays a familiarity with Roman customs and

---

[1] My attention was called to this and the preceding passage by
Prof. Summers.
[2] See note *ad loc.*   [3] *Latin Literature*, p. 211.
[4] Even the smoothly flowing *dialogus* has a sprinkling of fine
epigrams in the characteristic Tacitean manner; cp. e.g. 18. 3 *vitio
autem malignitatis humanae vetera semper in laude, praesentia in
fastidio esse.*

Roman history[1] which would hardly have been looked for
in a barbarian dwelling at the world's end. His description
of the Romans as *raptores orbis*[2] has parallels in both
Sallust and Curtius, and in other of his remarks vague
reminiscences of Sallust are thought to be traceable.
Agricola's speech again is held to contain echoes of Sallust
and Livy. The composition of generals' addresses was undoubtedly a favourite exercise in the rhetorical schools, and a
stereotyped style had been evolved based on Sallust, Livy
and the 'fair copies' of distinguished professors.

The account of Agricola's final battle clearly contains
rhetorical elements. Thus the turning of the foe in 37. 2
is modelled upon Sallust, *Jug.* 101. 11[3]. But though Tacitus
is often said to sacrifice accuracy to style in his battle-pieces,
there is little reason to doubt that the main outlines of this
engagement are historical. The numbers of the foe, 30,000
(29. 4) and of the slain, 10,000 (37. 6), do not seem excessive.
It may be tentatively suggested that the mention of "Aulus
Atticus, commander of a cohort," among the dead is due
to a desire not so much to give immortality to this gallant
young officer as to follow what may possibly have become a
traditional manner. We are reminded of Caesar, who in
B.G. V. 15 after an account of a battle against the Britons
adds *eo die Q. Laberius Durus, tribunus militum, inter-
ficitur.*

The epilogue to the *Agricola* has the character of a
consolatio, a common Greek and Roman literary form, and
it is only natural that Tacitus' noble sentences should find
numerous parallels in surviving specimens of that style of
composition. The resemblances have been carefully worked
out by Gudeman. Reminiscences of Cicero's account of the

---

[1] *Agr.* 31. 3, 32. 4.
[2] 30. 6. Cp. Sall. *Hist. frag.* IV. 22 and Curt. VII. 8. 34. 19
(Gudeman). See also on *Agr.* 32. 2.
[3] *tum spectaculum horribile in campis patentibus, sequi, fugere,
occidi, capi...omnia qua visus erat constrata telis, armis, cadaveribus
et inter ea humus infecta sanguine.*

death of the orator Crassus in *de Oratore* III. 2. 8 are particularly noticeable.   But everywhere Tacitus stamps his borrowings with the impress of his own inimitable style. It is no question of plagiarism.   The Roman reader would experience the same pleasure in detecting echoes of earlier masterpieces of his country's literature that the Englishman finds in reminiscences of Shakespeare or the Bible.   Only in Roman literature, particularly under the Empire, literary reminiscences were employed to a greater extent and with more elaborate art than they are nowadays.   Virgil's borrowings from Ennius are perhaps the best Roman example of the custom.   And as Virgil borrowed from Ennius, so did subsequent writers, of prose as well as of poetry, borrow constantly from Virgil.

In speaking of contemporary oratory, Tacitus tells us that jurymen always liked to take home with them from the courts " something brilliant and worth remembering"; they would tell all their friends

sive sensus aliquis arguta et brevi sententia effulsit, sive locus exquisito et poetico cultu enituit. exigitur enim iam ab oratore etiam poeticus decor, non Accii aut Pacuvii veterno inquinatus, sed ex Horatii et Vergilii et Lucani sacrario prolatus (dial. 20. 4 f.).

These remarks upon oratory are equally applicable to history.   Even Cicero holds that history was *opus unum oratorium maxime (de legg.* I. 2. 5) and that Roman historians failed because they narrated without adornment *(non exornatores rerum sed tantummodo narratores fuerunt, de or.* II. 12. 54).   Later historians set themselves to remedy this defect by taking over from poetry its warmth of colouring and elevation of language.   In Livy we see the old boundaries between prose and poetry broken down, not only in his striking and varied phraseology but in his freer and less rigid syntax.   To realise the change produced by the introduction of *poeticus decor* into history we have only to compare the glowing prose of Livy with the succinct, business-like narrative of Caesar.   Virgil's influence upon this development was enormous. His works at once became classics and their diction was echoed everywhere. Livy contains numerous Virgilian reminiscences, and Tacitus scores of them. To mention a few of the most obvious instances, in the *Agricola* we have *cruda ac viridis senectus* (29. 4), *aliquando etiam victis ira virtusque* (37. 3), and in the *Germania* we have *originem gentis* (2. 3), *bellatorem equuum* (14. 4), *nuptiis ambiuntur* (18. 1), *silvam auguriis patrum et prisca formidine sacram* (39. 2)[1]. Lucan too, whom Tacitus tells us in the *dialogus* the orator was expected to quote, was drawn upon by the historian. He is the source of *incerta fugae vestigia* and *spargi bellum* in *Agr.* 38. 3 and of *exsanguis senectus* in *Germ.* 31. 5. The encroachment of poetry upon the domain of prose is no doubt ultimately responsible for such striking metaphors and personifications as the following: *Chattos suos saltus Hercynius prosequitur simul atque deponit* (*Germ.* 30. 1), *donec aetas separet ingenuos, virtus adgnoscat* (*Germ.* 20. 2), *sepulcrum caespes erigit* (*Germ.* 27. 2 ; also in Seneca), *prora paratam semper adpulsui frontem agit* (*Germ.* 44. 2), *Caledonia viros seposuerit* (*Agr.* 31. 5), *annus aperuit* (*Agr.* 22. 1 ; also in Cicero and Livy), *bellum aperuit* (*Germ.* 1. 1), some of which would be far less surprising in English than they are in Latin.

While Cicero was careful to express coordinate ideas by coordinate constructions, Tacitus, following Livy, deliberately avoided such uniformity in order to add point and vivacity to his style[2]. He is fond of strained collocations of concrete and abstract like *sinu indulgentiaque* (*Agr.* 4. 2), *mutuo metu et montibus* (*Germ.* 1. 1), *exemplum et rectores* (*Agr.* 28. 2), *nox et satietas* (*Agr.* 37. 5). He joins the nominative

---

[1] For a fuller list see Gudeman *Agr.* p. 27, Furneaux *Agr.* p. 19, *Germ.* p. 11.

[2] Cp. *Ann.* I. 64 *deliguntur legiones quinta dextro lateri, unetvicensima in laevum, primani ducendum ad agmen, vicensimanus adversum secuturos,* a far more elaborate instance than any to be found in the earlier works.

and the predicative dative, *vestitui pelles, cubile humus*
(*Germ.* 46. 3). He places simple cases side by side with
prepositions and cases, *virtute aut per artem* (*Agr.* 9. 5; a
particularly common variation), *citra fidem aut obtrectationi*
(*Agr.* 1. 3), *apud Chattos...Tencteris* (*Germ.* 32. 2). He
coordinates a substantive and a clause, *non in comparationem...sed quia* (*Agr.* 10. 1), *lingua coarguit...et
quod tributa patiuntur* (*Germ.* 43. 1), *victoriae...si pellerentur* (*Agr.* 35. 2), or an adjective or participle with the
case of a noun, *segnior et nullis...experimentis* (*Agr.*
16. 11)[1].

The love of brevity which Tacitus inherited from Sallust
is manifested in the *Agricola* and the *Germania* less syste-
matically than in the *Annals*. Indeed in these earlier writings
he seems to affect redundant expressions like *primo statim...
ortu* (*Agr.* 3. 1), *formidine territi, soliti plerumque* (*Agr.*
22. 1 and 3), and such rhetorical doublets as *vicit et supergressa est* (*Agr.* 1. 1), *sublime et erectum, dissensionibus ac
discordiis* (*Agr.* 4. 5, 32. 1, which chapters see *passim*),
pigrum et iners (*Germ.* 14. 5), *pax et quies* (*Germ.* 40. 4) are
so common as to form a marked stylistic feature[2]. The
intermittent conciseness of the earlier works is occasionally
a source of considerable obscurity. Abbreviated phrases
like *locum Graeca comitate et provinciali parsimonia mixtum* (*Agr.* 4. 3), *prima castrorum rudimenta...adprobavit*
(*Agr.* 5. 1, a combination of redundancy and conciseness),
virgines festinantur (*Germ.* 20. 3), *vallare noctem* (*Germ.*
30. 2), though daring, are effective and easily intelligible
in their contexts, but an exaggerated striving after brevity
and point sometimes results in harsh or nebulous expressions (cp. e.g. *Agr.* 6. 1, 6. 4, 7. 5, 10. 4, 11. 2, 19. 5, 24. 1,
30. 3, 38. 5). However, as Draeger says, there is no satisfaction in tracing out the small linguistic aberrations of so
great a genius, and we prefer to conclude with Mr Mackail's

---

[1] See Draeger, *Syntax und Stil des Tacitus* § 233, Gudeman *Agr.*
p. 24.

[2] See the long lists given by Gudeman and Furneaux.

admirable words: "by every artifice of style, by daring use of vivid words and elliptical expressions[1], by studied avoidance of the old balance of the sentence, he established a new historical manner, which whatever may be its failings...never drops dead or says a thing in a certain way because it is the way in which the ordinary rules of style would prescribe that it should be said."

§ 6. *Agricola and Britain.*

If the *Agricola* of Tacitus had not survived, we should have known of its hero only from two meagre references in Dio Cassius and an inscription on a piece of lead piping made "in the governorship of Julius Agricola[2]," and we could have formed no conception of his solid achievements in Britain. A member of a respectable provincial family, marked out by the example of his father and grandfathers for an official career, he was a characteristic product of the Flavian age, when the administrative posts of the empire tended to be filled by hardworking middle-class officials rather than by descendants of the old senatorial families. "Bourgeois in rank and bourgeois also in his virtues and his faults," says Prof. Haverfield[3], "he lacked the characteristic pride of the old senators, the stubbornest aristocrats known to history....Instead a shrewd obsequiousness helped him easily to fit his conduct to the times, to serve under Nero, to die in his bed under Domitian. *peritus obsequi eruditusque utilia honestis miscere*, so his son-in-law describes him, damning him with strange praise[4] and revealing by his unconscious candour the temper of an age and class."

When Agricola reached Britain in the middle of 78 A.D.,

---

[1] It has been noted that zeugma is far less common in the *Agr.* and *Germ.* than in the later works.

[2] See on *Agr.* 20. 2, 46. 4.

[3] *Edinburgh Review*, April, 1911, in a valuable article on Roman Scotland, to which I am much indebted.

[4] See however p. xxxvii.

Roman dominion extended over the east, south and west of England, the central plain, Yorkshire, and South Wales, where the Silures had been finally crushed by the preceding governor, Julius Frontinus (74–78 A.D.). Agricola's first business was to subjugate the Ordovices of North Wales, a task which he accomplished before the end of the summer. His work in Wales was thorough and lasting[1]. There is no record of any Welsh rising after 78 A.D., though the tribes of north Britain rose about once every twenty years. Wales was secured by a network of forts placed from 15 to 25 miles apart and commanding the principal valleys, avenues of communication and strategic points. At least 17 genuine Roman forts are known in Wales. Some of them, like the important post at Caersws, guarding the pass between the upper waters of the Severn and the Dovey estuary, are proved by excavation to have been occupied by 70–85 A.D., and may thus have been built by Agricola or his immediate predecessors. We know that as early as 50 A.D. Ostorius constructed forts in Wales (*Ann.* XII. 38). It seems indeed that all the Welsh forts, with the possible exception of Cardiff, existed by the beginning of the second century, and there is evidence that about 130 A.D. the country was quiet enough for some of the garrisons to be reduced. These military outposts, scattered over the country, rested upon the legionary fortresses of Isca Silurum (Caerleon-on-Usk), the headquarters of Legio II, and Deva (Chester), the head-quarters of Legio XX, and possibly upon Viroconium (near Shrewsbury), which seems to have been occupied by 80–90 A.D., if not earlier. As Professor Haverfield points out, the relation of Chester and Caerleon to the Welsh forts is the same as that of Mainz, Strasburg and Windisch, legionary centres in southern Germany, to the forts of the German *limes*, or, we may add, of Newstead to the forts of Agricola's Caledonian *limes*.

[1] For the following account of Roman Wales I am indebted to Prof. Haverfield's *Military Aspects of Roman Wales*, especially pp. 13, 50, 114, 115, 118.

In the north Agricola extended the Roman frontier to the Forth and Clyde, defending the isthmus by a line of forts[1] which was subsequently merged in the wall of Antoninus. Beyond this point he made little permanent impression upon the country, though we find relics of his presence as far north as Strathmore, where the large camp at Inchtuthill was probably constructed in his last campaign and may be near the scene of his great battle with the Caledonians[2]. Archaeology has thrown much light upon the route of Agricola's advance into Scotland, and there is every prospect that fresh discoveries will throw more. It now seems clear that his main line of march was not up the west coast, as has often been supposed, but that starting from Yorkshire he advanced through Durham and Northumberland by way of the ancient Dere Street, a line of road, guarded at intervals by forts, which runs through Corbridge (the ancient Corstopitum) across the Cheviots to Newstead under the Eildon Hills and thence to the Forth. The lowest stratum of remains at Corbridge yields relics of the Agricolan period. The great fort of Newstead[3], which has been so thoroughly explored by Mr Curle, was certainly occupied by Agricola and seems to have served as the base for his Caledonian operations. Cappuck, near Jedburgh, a strongly fortified station on Dere Street immediately south of Newstead, is believed to have been occupied at the same time. Other stations on this ancient line of road await exploration. The north of England was secured by a system of fortified posts similar to that which proved so effective in Wales.

[1] See on 23. 2. The system of frontier defence adopted by Agricola in Scotland was a year or two afterwards followed in Germany.

[2] But see on *Agr.* 29. 2.

[3] At Newstead are the remains of (1) an earth camp capable of holding a legion, (2) an earth fort of some 15 acres in area, which (3) was rebuilt with some change of plan and an increase of size, and (4) was rebuilt again about 140 A.D. under Antoninus Pius. Mr Curle holds that the first three stages belong to the Agricolan period. See Mr Curle's work *A Roman Frontier Post and its People*, and H. Dragendorff's review in *J.R.S.* I. 134 ff.

Agricola, says Tacitus, personally selected sites for camps and reconnoitred estuaries and forests, and in the opinion of experts was second to none in his skilful choice of strategic positions, none of his forts ever being stormed or evacuated. This does not seem too high praise. We can hardly judge from Tacitus' somewhat rhetorical and conventional descriptions of fighting whether Agricola was a great commander on the battlefield, but undoubtedly he possessed all the qualities necessary for a general advancing into a difficult and unexplored country, where everything depended upon careful reconnaisance, good engineering, a well organised commissariat and a strong line of communications between the operating force and its base. His realisation of the possibilities of combined offensive action by land and sea on the deeply indented coast of Scotland is a noteworthy feature of his military policy. He was the first and perhaps the only Roman to contemplate seriously the invasion of Ireland, which he imagined could be subdued by a single legion and a moderate complement of auxiliaries. As Julius Caesar thought that the conquest of Britain would facilitate the pacification of Gaul, so Agricola believed that the conquest of Ireland would overawe Britain. He believed too that Ireland would afford a convenient stepping-stone from Spain to Britain, because according to the common belief it lay midway between the two countries (*Agr.* 24). Ignorance of the true conditions of the problem rather than a visionary or over-sanguine temperament led Agricola to form a project which, perhaps happily for him, was never put into execution; for the highly improbable notion that he actually invaded Ireland seems now finally exploded.

There is little to comment upon in Tacitus' account of Agricola's government and administrative reforms. A just and conscientious ruler, convinced too that the best way to secure the loyalty of the natives was to study their comfort and material well-being, he sternly repressed the rapacity of his subordinates and did all he could to introduce Roman customs and Roman culture into the country[1]. So successful was this policy of Romanisation that Tacitus pays Agricola the poor compliment of saying that the Britons were gradually led astray into the "vicious allurements" of civilisation (*Agr.* 21. 3). Spotless integrity, caution, hard work and thoroughness are perhaps the outstanding features of Agricola's career. It was no discredit to him that he showed obsequiousness to the Emperors. Indeed he is rather to be praised for not allowing futile political prejudices to interfere with his usefulness as an official. It is a misfortune that the orthodox view of the Roman Empire is that of the uncompromising senatorial party, which could see nothing but evil in the imperial government and brought persecution upon itself simply because of its attitude of relentless opposition. Had the old Roman aristocracy been less obdurate, we might have had a very different picture of imperial history. Rome had good reason to be grateful for her middle-class officials of easy political views, whose invaluable military and administrative work is really far more admirable than the sullen obstinacy of the senatorial "Die-Hards."

In 85 A.D. Agricola was recalled and the fruits of his northern conquests were for the most part sacrificed[2]; *perdomita Britannia et statim missa* is Tacitus' comment (*Hist.* I. 2). The reason for his recall, Tacitus would lead us to believe, was the jealousy of Domitian, whose indifferent success in Germany compared unfavourably with Agricola's brilliant exploits. But Agricola had already served longer than was usually the case with provincial governors, and Mommsen thinks that the cessation of

[1] On this subject see Prof. Haverfield's fascinating little book, *The Romanisation of Roman Britain.*

[2] Newstead must have been evacuated by about 100 A.D., if not immediately after Agricola's recall. See Curle *op. cit.* p. 344. Hadrian's wall between Tyne and Solway, built about 120 A.D., proves that all the country north of it had been abandoned by that date. Some 20 years later a fresh northerly advance was made and the Forth and Clyde line reoccupied.

hostilities in Britain is sufficiently explained by the advance
of the Roman frontier across the Rhine in southern Germany
and the outbreak of war in Pannonia[1]. Besides, the Roman
government may have realised that further conquests in
Britain would be financially unprofitable and that the
Romanisation of the natives of Scotland and Ireland, who
were of a different race and spoke a different language from
the Britons, would present difficulties hardly worth facing[2].

§ 7. *History of the Text, Manuscripts, etc.*

In ancient times Tacitus was by no means so popular
an author as his greatness might lead us to expect.   References to his works are surprisingly few.   Indeed the Emperor
Claudius Tacitus found it necessary to give instructions for
the regular multiplication of copies of Tacitus and their
bestowal in public libraries, *ne lectorum incuria deperiret*[3].
The cloud under which he rested was perhaps partly due
to the hostility of the Church, which could not forgive his
offensive attitude towards Christianity.   In the Middle Ages
he was naturally still less read.   However Einhard (770–840)
knew the *Histories* and the *Germania*, and there is some
evidence that he wrote a work called *de adventu moribus et
superstitione Saxonum*, in which he incorporated extracts
from the latter[4].   In the so-called Annals of Fulda under
the year 852, the historian is mentioned by name as speaking
of the river Visurgis[5], and Rudolf of Fulda in his *Trans-
latio S. Alexandri*, telling how the bones of that saint were
brought from Rome to Saxony (851), borrows whole chapters

---

[1] Legio II Adiutrix seems to have been recalled from Britain to
reinforce the army on the Danube frontier about this time.

[2] Mommsen, *Provinces* I. 184.

[3] Vopiscus, *Tacitus* 10. 3.

[4] Manitius, *Gesch. der lat. Litt. des Mittelalters*, p. 645. Cp. the
title of the *Germania* as given in E.

[5] Cp. *Ann.* II. 9 and 12.

from the *Germania* without acknowledging their source[1]. Widukind of Corvey, author of *Res Gestae Saxonicae* (968), appears to have read Tacitus[2], and early in the twelfth century Guibert of Nogent's *modernum hoc saeculum corrumpitur et corrumpit* is a clear reminiscence of the *Germania*, 19. 3, *nec corrumpere nec corrumpi saeculum vocatur*.

The *Histories* too seem to have been known to one or two writers of this century, but it is not till the second half of the fourteenth century that Tacitus really re-emerges from darkness. Boccaccio (d. 1375) quotes from the *Histories* and the latter part of the *Annals*, and perhaps possessed the very manuscript, now known as Mediceus II, which in 1427 belonged to the collector and critic Niccolo Niccoli[3].

Poggio Bracciolini in a letter to Niccolo Niccoli, dated Nov. 1425, speaks of a monk at the German monastery of Hersfeld who had promised to procure him *aliqua opera Taciti nobis ignota*[4], but in a subsequent letter, dated Feb. 1429, laments that the monk had come to Rome without them. Not till 1455 did these works reach Italy, when they were brought home by Enoch of Ascoli, who had been sent by Pope Nicholas V[5] to search for classical manuscripts in France and Germany. In the same year Pier Candido Decembrio saw this 'Hersfeld' manuscript in Rome. It contained

    (a) *de origine et situ Germaniae*, written on 12 leaves in double columns,

    (b) *de vita Iulii Agricolae*, on 14 leaves in double columns,

---

[1] The borrowed passages are the whole of *Germ.* 9 and 10 and passages from 4 and 11. See Schanz, *op. cit.* p. 332, Manit. *op. cit.* p. 671.

[2] *op. cit.* p. 717.

[3] Cp. Sandys, *Harvard Lectures on the Revival of Learning,* p. 24.

[4] As early as 1422 Bartolomeo Capra, archbishop of Milan, had discovered the existence of these works in Germany. Annibaldi (see note below) p. 77, note 2.

[5] See Sandys, *op. cit.* pp. 137 f. for this enthusiastic humanist.

(*c*) the *dialogus*,

(*d*) Suetonius, *de grammaticis et rhetoribus*.

This MS. is the archetype of our text of the Minor Works of Tacitus, and in 1902 a fragment of it was discovered in the Library of Count G. Balleani at Jesi near Ancona. In this library is a parchment MS., known as E, containing the *Bellum Troianum* of Dictys, the *Agricola* and the *Germania*[1]. The *Agricola* section is written on 14 leaves with double columns, the first four and the last two[2] in a fifteenth century hand identical with that of most of the Dictys and the whole of the *Germania*. Leaves 5–12, from *munia*, 13. 1 to *ministeriis missum*, 40. 2, written in a fine ninth or tenth century hand, are clearly part of the MS. described by Decembrio, that is, of the Hersfeld MS. This is sufficiently proved by the paging and the double columns. The nucleus of the Jesi library is a collection made by two humanists, the brothers Stefano and Francesco Guarnieri in the second half of the fifteenth century. Stefano probably acquired the *Agricola* section of the Hersfeld MS. from Enoch or his heirs, and finding six leaves badly worn, made transcripts of them, line for line in the case of the

---

[1] For the Jesi MS. and its history see C. Annibaldi's *L' Agricola e la Germania di Cornelio Tacito nel ms. latino n. 8 della biblioteca del Conte G. Balleani in Jesi*, 1907, and Prof. Wünsch's convenient summary of Annibaldi's results in *Berl. phil. Woch.* Aug. 10, 1907, pp. 1025–30, to which I am largely indebted for this account.

[2] Leaves 69 and 76 of the Jesi MS. originally followed one on the other and contained the end of the *Agricola* from *ad Agricolam codicillos* (40. 2). The Renaissance copyist erased the *Agricola* from these leaves, though not without leaving traces of the original text and marginal notes, and substituted part of the *Germania* (*sua quoque fortia*, 14. 2, to *litterarum secreta*, 19. 1) on the first half of the doubled sheet, employing the other as a blank fly-leaf at the end of the MS. The erased writing on leaves 69 and 76 is a later and more closely written minuscule script than that of leaves 56 to 63 (leaves 5–12 of the *Agricola* portion and the oldest part of the MS.). It is possible that the Renaissance scribe erased the contents of these two leaves and rewrote them on the present leaves 64 and 65 (13 and 14 of the *Agricola* section) because of a bad stain visible on 76, or perhaps to avoid the occurrence of three different handwritings in one MS. (Annibaldi, *op. cit.* pp. 138–140).

first four leaves, and joined his transcripts to the eight undamaged leaves of the original MS. That the copy was made by Stefano appears from other known specimens of his handwriting. The obvious care with which the transcripts are executed makes their authority for the text almost equal to that of the old part.

The portion of E containing the *Germania*[1] is also in Stefano's handwriting, but it is a debated question whether he transcribed it directly from the Hersfeld MS. or from some intermediate copy. Its ten leaves are certainly not a line for line transcript of the Hersfeld *Germania*, which according to Decembrio's report was in twelve leaves, and it has a somewhat different title[2]. Unlike the Jesi *Agricola*, it appears to have no higher value for the text of the *Germania* than other copies made about the same time. The ultimate fate of the Hersfeld MS., apart from the surviving *Agricola* portion, is unknown. After Enoch's death in 1457 it is supposed to have become the property of Aeneas Sylvius Piccolomini, afterwards Pope Pius II, and then all trace of it is lost. The noteworthy fact that the *Agricola* does not appear in some of the oldest and best MSS. containing the *Germania*, the *dialogus* and the fragment of Suetonius is held by some to be due to Enoch's splitting up of the Hersfeld MS.[3]

In 1897 the existence of a MS. of the *Agricola* and the *Germania* in the library of Toledo cathedral became known. The archbishop at first objected to its readings being recorded, but a collation of the *Agricola* was obtained by Dr Leuze[4] in 1900–1 and of the *Germania* by Prof. F. F. Abbott[5] in 1903. The Toledo MS. (T), written in 1474

[1] See Annibaldi, *La Germania di Cornelio Tacito nel ms. latino n. 8 della biblioteca del Conte G. Balleani in Jesi*: edizione diplomatica-critica, 1910.

[2] See Wünsch, *op. cit.* p. 1029, Annibaldi, *op. cit.* pp. 19 ff.

[3] Wünsch following Wissowa, *op. cit.* p. 1029.

[4] *Die Agricola-Handschrift in Toledo*, in *Philologus*, Supplementband VIII. 1901, pp. 515 ff.

[5] *The Toledo MS. of the Germania of Tacitus*, University of Chicago Decennial Publications, 1903.

xlii *MANUSCRIPTS OF THE* AGRICOLA

by M. Angelo Grillo di Todi, chancellor of Foligno[1], proves
to be a direct transcript of the Jesi MS.

There are two other MSS. of the *Agricola*, both in the
library of the Vatican. The first (No. 3429), of paper,
known as A (or Γ), was transcribed by the distinguished
humanist, Julius Pomponius Laetus, towards the close of the
fifteenth century, to be bound up with his copy of the first
printed edition of Tacitus[2], which did not include the
Agricola. Pomponius wrote in a number of corrections and
variants, many of which appear to be conjectures of his own
or of other scholars. The second Vatican MS. (No. 4498),
of parchment, known as B (or Δ), is also assignable to the
latter part of the fifteenth century[3]. It contains all the
three Minor Works of Tacitus with the fragment of
Suetonius, like the Hersfeld MS., and other treatises as
well.

As Dr Leuze pointed out in his account of the Toledo
MS., the agreement of the three MSS. A, B and T in many
corrupt passages and the similar marginal notes of A and
T indicate a common origin. But A and B often agree
in readings which are different from those of T. The
agreement of A and B in such cases can only be explained
by supposing a common source (y), and their difference
from T by supposing that the common source was independent of T. Thus there are two families of derivative
MSS., one (and the best) represented by T, the other by A
and B, the offshoots of a lost y, which Pomponius must have
used in making his transcript. y and T are sprung from

[1] Foligno was a dependency of Perugia. Stefano Guarnieri was
chancellor of Perugia 1466–1488, and it is very probable that
the two chancellors were personally acquainted. See Annibaldi,
L' Agr. e la Germ. p. 142.

[2] By Vendelin de Spira, about 1470. Pomponius died in 1497,
so his copy must have been made between these dates.

[3] B seems to have been written by a purist in matters of
spelling; e.g. it frequently has *adf-*, *ads-* (e.g. *adflixit, adsumpserit*) where the other MSS. including E have *aff-*, *ass-*; it has
accusative plurals in *-is* instead of *-es*; and it avoids some of the
grosser misspellings of the other MSS.

a common parent, namely the Jesi MS. E. We have thus the following genealogical tree[1] of the MSS. of the *Agricola*:

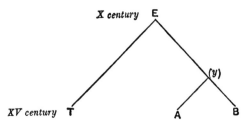

The discovery of the archetype of our MSS. of the *Agricola* has not produced any very material improvement in the text. It has confirmed a few conjectures, but nearly all the more serious corruptions are already present in E.

The first printed text of the *Agricola* was edited by Franciscus Puteolanus[2], who is commonly supposed to have used a MS. of the AB family, perhaps A itself, as Wex argued. Fossataro[3] thinks that he used a now vanished MS. superior to A and only a little inferior to T. Fulvio Orsini (Ursinus) in a volume of critical notes on various ancient historians, published in 1595, gives certain emendations of Puteolanus' text on the authority of a *vetus codex*. Six[4] of his readings do not occur in any of our extant MSS., but the only one which is not a perfectly easy conjecture is the nearly correct *in Temelium* for *in templo*, 7. 1. Orsini

---

[1] See Leuze, *op. cit.* p. 539 and Annibaldi, *op. cit.* p. 134. Leuze's results are accepted by Annibaldi, who has only to substitute E for Leuze's assumed archetype x.

[2] With the *panegyrici* of Pliny and others and a fragment of Petronius, probably at Milan in 1476. He printed it also in his two general editions of Tacitus, the later dated Venice, 1497. Puteolanus' reading *montem Grampium*, 29. 2, which seems to be a mere misprint for *montem Graupium*, has given the Grampians their name.

[3] *De vita et moribus Julii Agricolae;* recensione con un prospetto delle varianti e note critiche, 1911.

[4] Leuze's list of eight (*op. cit.* p. 541) must be reduced by two, as *incolentes* and *oppugnare*, 25. 3, both occur in E.

has been suspected of dishonestly inventing manuscript authority for his own conjectures upon Cicero, and his trustworthiness has been doubted in the present case. Schenkl thinks that Orsini really had a MS. before him, namely A, but that he has given wholly arbitrary conjectures as manuscript readings and has purposely misled his readers by printing mistakes like *in Temelium* 7. 2, *esse* 44. 5[1].

The editions of Beatus Rhenanus (Basel, 1519–1533) and of Justus Lipsius (Antwerp and Leyden, 1574, 1600) are important for the numerous improvements which they introduced into the text of the *Agricola* and the *Germania*.

The following are the most important of the numerous MSS. of the *Germania*:

B, Vaticanus 1862, which contains also the fragment of Suetonius and the *dialogus*[2].

b, Leidensis or Perizonianus, known to be a copy of a transcript made by the Neapolitan poet and critic, Jovianus Pontanus (1426–1503), from Enoch's codex. It was revised and corrected by a later hand, b[2]. Its contents are the same as those of B. This MS. belonged to Jacob Voorbroek (Perizonius), Professor of Greek at Leyden, and after his death in 1715 was acquired by the library there[3].

C, Vaticanus 1518, containing like B and b the Suetonius fragment and the *dialogus*, but with the addition of Porphyrio's commentary on Horace and other works.

c, Neapolitanus or Farnesianus, containing *Annals* XI–XVI, *Histories* I–V, the *dialogus*, the *Germania* and the Suetonius fragment.

E, Aesinus, the Jesi MS.,
 T, the Toledo MS., } for which see above.

[1] See Leuze, *op. cit.* p. 542.
[2] The MSS. here called BbCc are often designated ABCD respectively.
[3] A photographic facsimile of this MS. has been edited by G. Wissowa (Sitjthoff, Leyden).

These six MSS. form three distinct families, Bb, Cc, and
ET. No one of these families is very definitely superior to
the others. Of the two members of the first family B is a
more faithful reproduction of the archetype than b, as
Pontanus' transcript, of which b is a copy, seems to have
contained emendations of his own[1]. In the so-called E
family T, as we have seen above, is a direct copy of E. Of
T Professor F. F. Abbott says[2],—and his remarks are still
more applicable to the later discovery E—" The value of T
lies partly in the true readings which it has preserved at
points where Bb C and c are all in error—although no one of
these is new—but mainly in the fact that the testimony
of the E class settles the reading at the points where Bb
and Cc are at variance." Other less important members of
the E family are Vaticanus 2964 (Rd) and the Rimini MS.
(ρ)[3].

[1] See Peterson's edition of the *dialogus*, pp. lxx–lxxi.

[2] *op. cit.* pp. 41–42.

[3] For this MS. see *Philologus*, LVII. pp. 307–317.   Fossataro
includes the readings of ρ in his apparatus.

NOTES ON THE TEXT

AGRICOLA[1].

Title. Cornelii Taciti de vita Iulii Agricolae liber incipit E (so Decembrio, see p. xxxix): Cornelii Taciti de vita et moribus Iulii Agricolae liber explicit E in colophon and the other MSS. (cp. Corn. Nep. *Cato* 3. 5 huius de vita et moribus). The colophon of erased sheet 76 of E omitted de moribus. de vita Iulii Agricolae has thus the best manuscript authority. It is perhaps worth suggesting that the addition de moribus may be due to contamination with the title of the *Germania*. B has Cai Cornelii Taciti.

1 § 4. incusaturus tam saeva (without any stop) MSS., Wex, Halm, Gudeman.

3 § 1. animus et: animus set or sed ed. Bip., Halm, Gud. § 2. ut ita dixerim Rhenanus: et uti dixerim. § 3. servitutis ET Ursinus: senectutis AB.

4 § 4. ultra quam: ultraque quam Bährens, Furn., Gud. ac senatori bracketed by Gud.: ac senatorio Heraeus.

5 § 3. exercitatior: excitatior Büchner, Furn., Gud. intersepti: intercepti Puteolanus, Gud.

6 § 1. degressus ETA[1]: digressus A[2]B. § 3. auctus est ibi filia E[m]AB: nactus est ibi filiam ET. ac solacium ET: et solacium AB. transiit B: transit ETA. § 4. torpor

---

[1] For the following conspectus of readings I am mainly indebted to Annibaldi's transcript of E, to Leuze's collation of T, and to Fossataro's critical edition. It seemed worth while to record the readings of the newly discovered E and T with some fulness. E is specially interesting not merely for the actual improvements which it has introduced into the text, but also for the light it throws upon corruptions in the other MSS. Errors common to all the MSS. and emended by the early editors are not as a rule recorded.

accepted by Fossataro : certior EAB : certior or rectior
T : tenor Rhenanus.   medio rationis ETA : medio
luxuriae B : medio moderationis Gudeman.

7 § 1. Intimilium Mommsen : in templo ETAB : in Temelium Ursinus. matrem AB : nam matrem T : — matrem
E, nam having been erased. § 5. ubi decessor : sub
decessore Madvig, making legio subject of narrabatur.

8 § 1. Bolanus B : Volanus ETA (so too in 16. 6).
§ 2. Cerialem B : Caerialem ETA (in 17. 1 Cerealis B :
Caerealis ETA ; in 17. 3 Cerealis ETB : Caerealis A).

9 § 3. nullā ultra potestatis personaṃ (m expunged by
first hand) E : nullam...personam TAB. § 7. eligit
ET : elegit AB (possibly once in the margin of E. See
Annibaldi, p. 84, n. 4).

10 § 1. ita quae AB : itaque ET. § 4. unde et in universum fama est transgressis <u>unde et universis fama sed</u>
E, with alias written over the second unde. T gives the
same words with the omission of the second unde and
possibly forma for fama. unde et in (in om. by A)
universum fama est transgressis sed AB. Gudeman
after Leuze reads forma.

11 § 3. vicinam : vacuam Eᵐ. § 4. superstitionum : ac
superstitionum, Gudeman after Schömann, because a
verb thus inserted between two members of an asyndeton
is not found elsewhere in Tac. persuasiones Glück :
persuasione.

12 § 2. tribusve B : tribusque ETA. § 5. fecundum
EᵐTᵐAB : pecudumque ET.

13 § 1. munia ET : munera AB. § 4. ingenii mobilis B
§ 5. auctoritate operis EAB : auctor operis T, Put. :
text Wex.

14 § 2. ut vetere ETAB Fossataro : vetere...consuetudine
ut haberet Rhen. and most edd.

15 § 2. man' (=manus) E : manus Aᵐ (Pomp. Laetus) :
manum AB. § 5. felicibus omitted by AB.

16 § 1. Voadicca ETA : bouidicta EᵐTᵐ : Voaduca B.
ingeniis omitted by AB. § 2. proprius ET, Rhen. :
propius AB. ne quamquam Walch : nequaquam

ETAB : nequam E^mA^m. cuiusque Wex : eiusque
ETAB : quisque Nipp. § 5. indecorus E Put. : in-
decoris TAB. pacti exercitus licentiam dux salutem
E^m, T^m (an accidental omission from the text) A : facta
exercitus licentia ducis salute EA^m.

17 § 3. subiit E (inserted by second hand) T : omitted by
AB.

18 § 3. degredi ET, Acid. : digredi AB. § 4. a cuius ed.
Bip. : cuius ETAB. § 5. subitis ET, conjectured by
Gronovius : dubiis AB. patrius ET, Put. : p̄rius A :
prius B.

19 § 1. iniuriae ET, Put. : incuriae AB. § 2. primum B :
primam ETA. militesve ascire Wex : milites scire
with ne written above the sc E : milites nescire TAB.
§ 4. exactionem $E^mT^mA^mB$: auctionem $ETAB^m$.
aequalitate E, written ṃaequalitate with erasure of m,
hence in aequalitate AB : equalitate T. luere ET,
conjectured by Wex : ludere AB.

20 § 2. inf̊itamenta A : irritamenta TB and E (where the
first r is a correction of n) : invitamenta Acid. § 3. et
tanta : sunt tanta Bährens (s̃t might perhaps be misread
as et). pariter added by Fröhlich. Susius putting a
full stop at pars reads inlacessita transiit, which he joins
with the following.

21 § 1. adsumpta : absumpta Put. et castigando AB.
§ 3. balinea E, corr. in A : balnea E^mA.

22 § 1. ad Tanaum ETAB : ad Taum $E^mT^mA^m$. § 2. aut
fuga E^mB.

24 § 2. ni in melius, a marginal suggestion in the late
Prof. J. E. B. Mayor's copy of Kritz' edition : nec in
melius Stuart : in melius.

25 § 1. hostilis exercitus ETAB : hostili exercitu E^m.
timebantur ET : timebant AB. § 3. incolentes E, corr.
from -tis, hence incolentis TAB. magno paratu ET :
paratu magno AB. oppugnare E, first written oppugnasse, hence oppugnasse TAB. castella E^mT^mB :
castellum ET. et cedendum E^mT : excedendum E.
et excedendum is the common reading.

26 § 3. nonanis ET : Romanis corr. in E, AB. rediit Wex. ut tulisse, the original reading of E, altered to intulisse which TAB have.

27 § 2. condicio est TAB. E apparently has condicione. § 3. se victos ET, omitted in AB. & sacrificiis E : ac sacr. is the common reading.

28 § 2. inmixti E, altered to inmixtis, hence immixtis EᵐTAB. remigrante Put.: refugo, ante Urlichs (see also explan. note *ad loc.*). § 3. ad aquam atque ut illa raptis secum plerisque ETAB : text Halm (utilia is Selling's conject.). sorte : forte E (acc. to Annibaldi's transcript).

29 § 2. Graupium ETAB : Grampium Put.

30 § 1. colitis et omitted by AB. § 3. nec ulla ET : nec AB. § 5. atque omne ignotum pro magnifico est sed following patet in the MSS., placed after defendit by Brüys and most edd. ac saxa ET : et saxa AB. effugias ET : effugeris AB. § 6. terrae mare E, Stuart : terram et mare corr. in E, ABT : terrae iam et mare Halm. (The corrector of E did not see that terrae was subject of defuere.)

31 § 1. effugerunt ET : effugiant AB. § 2. ageratque ET : ager atque F. Jacob : aggerat AB. conterunt. (*sic*) E : conterunt TAB. § 5. arma inserted by Wex : bellaturi Koch.

32 § 3. trepidos Heumann : circum trepidos MSS., probably a dittography of *circum*spectantis below. vobis E : nobis TAB. § 4. tam deserent...quam ET : deserent... tamquam EᵐAB. nec quicquam corr. in E, T : ne quicquam EA. aegra municipia : taetra mancipia EᵐTᵐAᵐ.

33 § 1. fremitu cantuque ET : cantu fremituque AB. munimentis EᵐAᵐB : monitis ETA owing to a misunderstood compendium. § 2. vestra Nipp. : et. § 4. montesque Urlichs : montesve. acies Rhen. : animus (quando animus is queried in E): adimus Stuart. omniaque AB : omnia quae ET (cp. 10. 1 for the reverse mistake). § 5. evasisse silvas ET : silvas evasisse AB.

34 § 2. ruere ETAB : ruebant E^m. § 3. torpor Ritter : corpora. Rhen. has nov. res extremo metu corpora defixere, omitting et and aciem. Gudeman reads et extremus metus and omits aciem as a gloss on corpora. § 4. imputari ET Put. : -are AB.

35 § 2. bellandi : bellanti Rhen. § 3. agmen in aequo Bekker : agminae quo E : agmine quo AB. convexi MSS., Gantrelle : conexi Put. and recent edd. eques : et eques Rhen. § 4. ne in Fröhlich : ne simul in.

36 § 1. quattuor om. AB. in arto Fr. Medicis : in aperto. § 2. fodere (Gesner) et stratis (Ernesti) : foedare et tratis EAB : foedare et tractis T. § 3. fugere enim Wex : ut fugere Doederlein : fugere. equestres (corr. to -is) ea (ei E^m) enim ET : equestres ea (ei A²) enim AB : text Andresen : equestris eius Gudeman. aegre clivo instantes Schömann : aegra diu aut stante.

37 § 2. oblatis E Rhen. : ablatis AB. § 4. nam ET : ntem (obelised) A : item B : idem or identidem edd. gnari Dronke : ignari. equitem persultare Rhen. : equite persultari ETA : equites perlustrari B. § 5. versi ET (?), Put. : versis AB.

38 § 1. mixto ET : mixtoque AB. § 3. Horestorum Put. § 5. trucculensem ETA : trutulensem E^mA^m. latere prelecto TA^m : latere prelecta E : latere lecto E^mAB.

39 § 1. ut erat Domitiano moris E^mT^m : ut Domitiano moris erat A : ut erat Domitianus ETA^m : ut Domitianus erat B. § 3. principem ET : principis AB. cetera ET : et cetera AB. § 4. in praesens E^m.

40 § 2. eo praecepto ET : praecepto AB. Britanniam MSS. Halm suggested Britannia etiam. § 4. hausit Wex : auxit. ut plerique MSS. uti, restored by Stuart, has apparently no other warrant than Halm's text.

41 § 2. Moesia E, Lips. : Mesia T : Misia AB. tot E^m, original text of palimpsest sheet 69 of E, AB. totis E, margin of palimpsest sheet of E, T. § 3. vigorem ETA : vigorem et B. ceterorum Grotius : aliorum ed. Bip. : eorum. Halm, supposing a lacuna, reads eorum quibus exercitus committi solerent.

42 § 3. proconsulare (with i written over the e) E : proconsulari or -are (?) T : proconsulari AB : proconsuli consulari Mommsen R. *Staatsr.*² I. 284, Furn. § 5. illicita mirari moris est T, reversing the order. excedere : escendere Lips., Halm. in nullum reipublicae usum Tᵐ (T in text has ullum, see Leuze *op. cit.* p. 529), Muretus : in nullum re p̄ usum EᵐAᵐ : in ullum rei post usum EAB.

43 § 1. oblitus est MSS. § 2. intercepti Gudeman, following a correction in T. adfirmare ausim. Before these words Acidalius, Wex, Ritter and Ernesti respectively insert quod, ut, quodve, nec. § 3. constabat ET : constabant AB. animi vultu Bährens : nimii vultu Stuart : animo vultuque.

44 § 1. tertium Urs. : iterum Nipp. : ter MSS. quarto Petavius : quinto Nipp. : sexto. decumum ET : decumo AB. § 2. impetus ETA : metus EᵐTᵐAᵐ : metus et impetus B. § 4. speciosae non contigerant ETAB : text EᵐTᵐAᵐ. § 5. sicuti durare ETAB : text Dahl : sicuti magnae cuiusdam felicitatis esse (esset Wex) durare Urs., clearly only a supplement to make sense.

45 § 1. Mettius EᵐTᵐA² : mitius ETAB. etiam tum ET, Gronovius : iam tum A : tum B : nondum Gudeman. Maurici Rusticique visus ETAB Gudeman : text EᵐTᵐAᵐ. § 3. interfuere ET : -unt AB. § 6. comploratus ETAB : compositus EᵐAᵐ.

46 § 1. nosque et domum, Urlichs, Furn., Gud. § 2. et immortalibus Acid. : temporalibus et ET : temporalibus AB. similitudine Grotius : militum ETA. decoremus Urs. : decoramus EAB : -amus or -emus (?) T : colamus Muretus and most edd., apparently on the assumption that similitudine colamus could be more easily corrupted into the MS. reading militum decoramus. § 3. formamque T (Leuze p. 530), Muretus : famamque EAB. § 4. fama : in fama Halm. obruet : obruit Haupt and recent edd.

GERMANIA[1].

Title. de origine et moribus Germanorum E, cp. 27. 3 :
de vita moribus et origine Germanorum T (contaminated
with the title of the *Agricola*): de origine et situ Germanorum BC: de origine et situ Germaniae Hersfeld MS. acc.
to Decembrio's report : other variants in other MSS. The
differences seem due to the caprice of copyists and it is
impossible to be sure of the original title.

1 § 1. Danuvio, a spelling adopted from the Medicean MSS.
of *Ann.* and *Hist.* : Danubio.

2 § 3. Tuistonem C : Tuisconem ET. ei EB : et. conditoremque Andresen: conditorisque. hermiones EB¹C,
cp. Pliny *N. H.* IV. 28. 100 : herminones. § 4. Suevos
all MSS.

3 § 1. barditum : baritum EᵐTᵐρc². § 3. nominatumque
'ΑCΚΙΠΥΡΓΙΟΝ aram ETBCc : nominatumque aram
b : lacuna noted in margin of b.

4 § 1. opinionibus : opinioni Meiser. aliis deleted by
Lips. § 2. quamquam: tamquam BᵐCc Andresen,
Schwyzer.

5 § 3. perinde B¹ρ : proinde most MSS. followed by
Schwyzer. § 5. affectione Ccρ : affectatione.

7 § 4. aut exigere ETBb : et exigere.

8 § 3. Veledam : Velaedam most edd. following Med. MS.
of *Hist.* Albrunam Wackernagel : Auriniam or Albri-
niam.

9 § 1. et Marten ETBb : ac Martem Cc.

10 § 5. apud proceres ; sacerdotes enim Wölfflin : text
MSS.

---

[1] For further details see especially Annibaldi's conspectus of
readings in his edizione diplomatica-critica of the *Germania* section
of E (cp. p. xli, note 1 above).

11 § 1. pertractentur : praetractentur C²c. § 3. turbae : turba J. F. Gronovius.

13 § 2. dignationem ETCc : dignitatem Bb. ceteris : ceteri Lips. § 4. semper et ET : semper.

14 § 4. principis MSS., Schwyzer : a principis Acid. and most edd.

15 § 1. non before multum apparently omitted in ρ, deleted by Lips. § 3. magnifica Bährens, Schwyzer : magna. Cp. 34. 2 where the MSS. vary between magnificum and magnum.

16 § 3. lineamenta ETBC : liniamenta bc. § 4. hiemi : hiemis Reifferscheid and most edd. without good reason.

19 § 2. abscisis E : adcisis or accisis.

20 § 4. ad patrem : apud patrem b.

21 § 3. victus...comis bracketed by Bleter.

22 § 4. aut callida ET. res retractatur Meiser. Schwyzer reads mens postera die retractatur, omitting the stop.

25 § 1. descriptis : discriptis Reifferscheid and most edd. § 3. liberti...argumentum sunt misplaced after ignorantur at the end of c. 26 in Bb¹; b² adds them in the margin here with the note *in hoc loco potius.*

26 § 1. in vices EB : invices^m T : invicem b : vices C : vicis Waitz. praestant ETBC : praebent E^mT^mB²bc. § 2. et hortos Cb² : most MSS. give ut hortos, whence Nipperdey and Schwyzer read aut hortos.

28 § 2. Helvetii citeriora Möller, Schwyzer : Helvetii. § 3. Germanorum natione bracketed by Passow.

30 § 1. incohant : incohatur B.

33 § 2. urgentibus iam ETBb : in urgentibus C. It seems impossible to retain iam in view of iam praestare immediately following.

34 § 1. Dulgibini BCcE^m : Dulgibnii T^m : Dulgicubuni T. §2. magnificum Cc : magnum ET : magnu B (cp. 15. 3).

35 § 1. sinuatur ρ : sinatur CcE^mT^m.

36 § 1. nomina superiori Heinsius : text Put. : nomine superioris.

37 § 5. Gnaeoque Halm : Marcoque (or quoque). § 6. inde pulsi proximis Halm : inde pulsi in proximis b : pulsi inde proximis ET. Others have nam for inde.

38 § 1. Suebis, a spelling adopted on the authority of the Medicean MSS. of *Hist.* and *Ann.* The MSS. of *Germ.* spell Suevi throughout. § 3. retro agunt Schwyzer : retorquent Madvig, Halm : retro sequuntur. in ipso ρ : in ipso with solo above b : in solo with in ipso above or in margin BE : in ipso solo Cc. religatur BbE : ligant Cc. § 4. comptius Lachmann : compti ut.

39 § 1. se omitted by c, Halm, Furneaux. § 4. pagis habitant Ernesti, Schwyzer : pagi iis habitantur Brotier, Halm : pagis habitantur.

40 § 1. Suarines : Suardones b²EᵐTᵐ Halm. § 2. Nerthum b²c : Nertum ET : Neithum Bb.

41 § 2. passim et sine Cc : passim sine.

42 § 1. praecingitur Tagmann : peragitur. § 2. mansere BET : manserunt bCc.

43 § 2. iugumque bracketed by Acidalius. § 3. Lygiorum B²E² : other spellings in the MSS. are Le-, Li- and Leug-. Helisios E : elisios b, Halm : Helysios BCc. Nahanarvalos B¹C : naharvalos B²bTᵐEᵐ. Below the MSS. favour the shorter form.

44 § 1. Gotones, the spelling of Med. I in *Ann.* II. 62 : Gothones. § 2. ministrantur all MSS. : ministrant Lipsius and most edd.

45 § 1. ortus CcET : ortum Bb. equorum Colerus : eorum EᵐTᵐ : deorum. § 4. glesum MSS., generally altered to glaesum. § 5. profertur bET : Halm gives perfertur. § 9. transposed to the end of c. 44 by Schütz who alters Suionas into Sitonas in 45. 1.

46 § 1. Venetorum (-ethorum Bc¹) often wrongly altered to Venedorum. torpor : torpor ; ora Heraeus. § 2. usu ac MSS. restored by Schwyzer for the erroneous usu et.

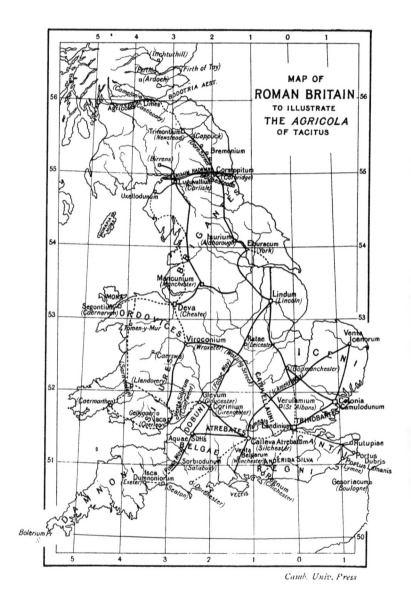

MAP OF
ROMAN BRITAIN
TO ILLUSTRATE
THE AGRICOLA
OF TACITUS

Camb. Univ. Press

CORNELII TACITI

DE VITA

IULII AGRICOLAE

LIBER

Clarorum virorum facta moresque posteris tradere, **1**

Biographical writing in Republican times. antiquitus usitatum, ne nostris quidem temporibus quamquam incuriosa suorum aetas omisit, quotiens magna aliqua ac nobilis virtus vicit ac supergressa est vitium parvis magnisque civitatibus commune, ignorantiam recti et invidiam. sed apud priores ut agere digna memoratu **2** pronum magisque in aperto erat, ita celeberrimus quisque ingenio ad prodendam virtutis memoriam sine gratia aut ambitione bonae tantum conscientiae pretio ducebatur. ac plerique suam ipsi vitam narrare fiduciam potius **3** morum quam adrogantiam arbitrati sunt, nec id Rutilio et Scauro citra fidem aut obtrectationi fuit : adeo virtutes isdem temporibus optime aestimantur, quibus facillime gignuntur. at nunc narraturo mihi vitam defuncti **4** hominis venia opus fuit, quam non petissem incusaturus. tam saeva et infesta virtutibus tempora.

Legimus, cum Aruleno Rustico Paetus Thrasea, **2**

Its dangers under Domitian. Herennio Senecioni Priscus Helvidius laudati essent, capitale fuisse, neque in ipsos modo auctores, sed in libros quoque.

eorum saevitum, delegato triumviris ministerio ut monumenta clarissimorum ingeniorum in comitio ac foro
2 urerentur. scilicet illo igne vocem populi Romani et
libertatem senatus et conscientiam generis humani aboleri
arbitrabantur, expulsis insuper sapientiae professoribus
atque omni bona arte in exilium acta, ne quid usquam
3 honestum occurreret. dedimus profecto grande patientiae
documentum; et sicut vetus aetas vidit quid ultimum in
libertate esset, ita nos quid in servitute, adempto per
inquisitiones etiam loquendi audiendique commercio.
4 memoriam quoque ipsam cum voce perdidissemus, si
tam in nostra potestate esset oblivisci quam tacere.

3   Nunc demum redit animus; et quamquam primo
statim beatissimi saeculi ortu Nerva Caesar

**Slow
revival of
literature.**

res olim dissociabiles miscuerit, principatum ac libertatem, augeatque cotidie
felicitatem temporum Nerva Traianus, nec spem modo
ac votum securitas publica, sed ipsius voti fiduciam ac
robur adsumpserit, natura tamen infirmitatis humanae
tardiora sunt remedia quam mala, et ut corpora nostra
lente augescunt, cito extinguuntur, sic ingenia studiaque
oppresseris facilius quam revocaveris: subit quippe
etiam ipsius inertiae dulcedo, et invisa primo desidia
2 postremo amatur. quid, si per quindecim annos, grande
mortalis aevi spatium, multi fortuitis casibus, promptissimus quisque saevitia principis interciderunt, pauci, ut
ita dixerim, non modo aliorum sed etiam nostri superstites sumus, exemptis e media vita tot annis, quibus
iuvenes ad senectutem, senes prope ad ipsos exactae
3 aetatis terminos per silentium venimus? non tamen
pigebit vel incondita ac rudi voce memoriam prioris
servitutis ac testimonium praesentium bonorum composuisse. hic interim liber honori Agricolae soceri mei

destinatus, professione pietatis aut laudatus erit aut excusatus.

Gnaeus Iulius Agricola, vetere et inlustri Foroiuli- 4

Agricola's birth, A.D. 40, family and education. ensium colonia ortus, utrumque avum procuratorem Caesarum habuit, quae equestris nobilitas est. pater illi Iulius Graecinus senatorii ordinis, studio eloquentiae sapientiaeque notus, iisque ipsis virtutibus iram Gai Caesaris meritus : namque M. Silanum accusare iussus et, quia abnuerat, interfectus est. mater Iulia Procilla fuit, rarae castitatis. in huius sinu indulgentiaque educatus per 2 omnem honestarum artium cultum pueritiam adulescentiamque transegit. arcebat eum ab inlecebris peccantium 3 praeter ipsius bonam integramque naturam, quod statim parvulus sedem ac magistram studiorum Massiliam habuit, locum Graeca comitate et provinciali parsimonia mixtum ac bene compositum. memoria teneo solitum 4 ipsum narrare se prima in iuventa studium philosophiae acrius, ultra quam concessum Romano ac senatori, hausisse, ni prudentia matris incensum ac flagrantem animum coercuisset. scilicet sublime et erectum in- 5 genium pulchritudinem ac speciem magnae excelsaeque gloriae vehementius quam caute adpetebat. mox mitigavit ratio et aetas, retinuitque, quod est difficillimum, ex sapientia modum.

Prima castrorum rudimenta in Britannia Suetonio 5

His first military service, A.D. 59. Paulino, diligenti ac moderato duci, adprobavit, electus quem contubernio aestimaret. nec Agricola licenter, more iuvenum, qui 2 militiam in lasciviam vertunt, neque segniter ad voluptates et commeatus titulum tribunatus et inscitiam rettulit : sed noscere provinciam, nosci exercitui, discere a peritis, sequi optimos, nihil adpetere in iactationem.

nihil ob formidinem recusare simulque et anxius et
3 intentus agere. non sane alias exercitatior magisque in
ambiguo Britannia fuit: trucidati veterani, incensae coloniae, intersepti exercitus; tum de salute, mox de victoria
4 certavere. quae cuncta etsi consiliis ductuque alterius
agebantur, ac summa rerum et reciperatae provinciae
gloria in ducem cessit, artem et usum et stimulos addi-
dere iuveni, intravitque animum militaris gloriae cupido,
ingrata temporibus, quibus sinistra erga eminentis interpre
tatio nec minus periculum ex magna fama quam ex mala.

6　　　　Hinc ad capessendos magistratus in urbem degressus

His
marriage,
magistracies,
etc.,
A.D. 62—68.

Domitiam Decidianam, splendidis natali-
bus ortam, sibi iunxit; idque matrimonium
ad maiora nitenti decus ac robur fuit.
vixeruntque mira concordia, per mutuam
caritatem et in vicem se anteponendo, nisi quod in bona
uxore tanto maior laus, quanto in mala plus culpae est.
2 sors quaesturae provinciam Asiam, pro consule Salvium
Titianum dedit, quorum neutro corruptus est, quamquam
et provincia dives ac parata peccantibus, et pro consule
in omnem aviditatem pronus quantalibet facilitate re-
3 dempturus esset mutuam dissimulationem mali. auctus
est ibi filia, in subsidium simul ac solacium ; nam filium
ante sublatum brevi amisit. mox inter quaesturam ac
tribunatum plebis atque ipsum etiam tribunatus annum
quiete et otio transiit, gnarus sub Nerone temporum,
4 quibus inertia pro sapientia fuit. idem praeturae torpor
et silentium ; nec enim iurisdictio obvenerat. ludos et
inania honoris medio rationis atque abundantiae duxit,
5 uti longe a luxuria ita famae propior. tum electus a
Galba ad dona templorum recognoscenda diligentissima
conquisitione fecit, ne cuius alterius sacrilegium res
publica quam Neronis sensisset.

Sequens annus gravi vulnere animum domumque 7
His mother's death. eius adflixit. nam classis Othoniana li- 2
center vaga dum Intimilium (Liguriae pars
est) hostiliter populatur, matrem Agricolae in praediis
suis interfecit, praediaque ipsa et magnam patrimonii
partem diripuit, quae causa caedis fuerat. igitur ad 3
sollemnia pietatis profectus Agricola, nuntio adfectati
a Vespasiano imperii deprehensus ac statim in partis
transgressus est. initia principatus ac statum urbis 4
Mucianus regebat, iuvene admodum Domitiano et ex
Legionary command in Britain, A.D. 70. paterna fortuna tantum licentiam usurpante.
is missum ad dilectus agendos Agricolam 5
integreque ac strenue versatum vicesimae
legioni tarde ad sacramentum transgressae praeposuit,
ubi decessor seditiose agere narrabatur: quippe legatis
quoque consularibus nimia ac formidolosa erat, nec
legatus praetorius ad cohibendum potens, incertum suo
an militum ingenio. ita successor simul et ultor electus 6
rarissima moderatione maluit videri invenisse bonos
quam fecisse.

Praeerat tunc Britanniae Vettius Bolanus, placidius 8
His conduct there. quam feroci provincia dignum est. tem-
peravit Agricola vim suam ardoremque
compescuit, ne incresceret, peritus obsequi eruditusque
utilia honestis miscere. brevi deinde Britannia con- 2
sularem Petilium Cerialem accepit. habuerunt virtutes
spatium exemplorum, sed primo Cerialis labores modo
et discrimina, mox et gloriam communicabat: saepe parti
exercitus in experimentum, aliquando maioribus copiis ex
eventu praefecit. nec Agricola umquam in suam famam 3
gestis exsultavit; ad auctorem ac ducem ut minister fortunam referebat. ita virtute in obsequendo, verecundia
in praedicando extra invidiam nec extra gloriam erat.

9   Revertentem ab legatione legionis divus Vespasianus

Governor of
Aquitania,
A.D. 74—76. inter patricios adscivit; ac deinde provinciae Aquitaniae praeposuit, splendidae inprimis dignitatis administratione ac spe

2 consulatus, cui destinarat. credunt plerique militaribus ingeniis subtilitatem deesse, quia castrensis iurisdictio secura et obtusior ac plura manu agens calliditatem fori

3 non exerceat. Agricola naturali prudentia, quamvis inter togatos, facile iusteque agebat. iam vero tempora curarum remissionumque divisa: ubi conventus ac iudicia poscerent, gravis intentus severus, et saepius misericors : ubi officio satis factum, nulla ultra potestatis persona.

4 tristitiam et adrogantiam et avaritiam exuerat. nec illi, quod est rarissimum, aut facilitas auctoritatem aut severitas amorem deminuit. integritatem atque abstinentiam in tanto viro referre iniuria virtutum fuerit.

5 ne famam quidem, cui saepe etiam boni indulgent, ostentanda virtute aut per artem quaesivit : procul ab aemulatione adversus collegas, procul a contentione adversus procuratores, et vincere inglorium et atteri

6 sordidum arbitrabatur. minus triennium in ea legatione detentus ac statim ad spem consulatus revocatus est, comitante opinione Britanniam ei provinciam dari, nullis in hoc suis sermonibus, sed quia par videbatur.

7 Consul,
A.D. 77.
Appointed to
Britain. haud semper errat fama; aliquando et eligit. consul egregiae tum spei filiam iuveni mihi despondit ac post consulatum collocavit, et statim Britanniae praepositus est, adiecto pontificatus sacerdotio.

10   Britanniae situm populosque multis scriptoribus

Geography
of Britain. memoratos non in comparationem curae ingeniive referam, sed quia tum primum perdomita est: ita quae priores, nondum comperta, eloquentia percoluere, rerum fide tradentur. Britannia, 2 insularum quas Romana notitia complectitur maxima, spatio ac caelo in orientem Germaniae, in occidentem Hispaniae obtenditur, Gallis in meridiem etiam inspicitur; septentrionalia eius, nullis contra terris, vasto atque aperto mari pulsantur. formam totius Britanniae 3 Livius veterum, Fabius Rusticus recentium eloquentissimi auctores oblongae scutulae vel bipenni adsimulavere. et est ea facies citra Caledoniam, unde et in universum 4 fama, sed transgressis inmensum et enorme spatium procurrentium extremo iam litore terrarum velut in cuneum tenuatur. hanc oram novissimi maris tunc 5 primum Romana classis circumvecta insulam esse Britanniam adfirmavit, ac simul incognitas ad id tempus insulas, quas Orcadas vocant, invenit domuitque. dis- 6 pecta est et Thyle, quia hactenus iussum: et hiems adpetebat. sed mare pigrum et grave remigantibus perhibent ne ventis quidem perinde attolli, credo quod rariores terrae montesque, causa ac materia tempestatum, et profunda moles continui maris tardius impellitur. naturam Oceani atque aestus neque quaerere huius 7 operis est, ac multi rettulere: unum addiderim, nusquam latius dominari mare, multum fluminum huc atque illuc ferre, nec litore tenus adcrescere aut resorberi, sed influere penitus atque ambire, et iugis etiam ac montibus inseri velut in suo.

    Ceterum Britanniam qui mortales initio coluerint, 11

Its inhabitants and their characteristics. indigenae an advecti, ut inter barbaros parum compertum. habitus corporum varii atque ex eo argumenta. namque rutilae 2 Caledoniam habitantium comae, magni artus Germanicam originem adseverant; Silurum colorati vultus, torti plerumque crines et posita contra Hispania Hiberos

veteres traiecisse easque sedes occupasse fidem faciunt ;
proximi Gallis et similes sunt, seu durante originis vi, seu
procurrentibus in diversa terris positio caeli corporibus
3 habitum dedit. in universum tamen aestimanti Gallos
4 vicinam insulam occupasse credibile est. eorum sacra
deprehendas, superstitionum persuasiones ; sermo haud
multum diversus, in deposcendis periculis eadem audacia
5 et, ubi advenere, in detrectandis eadem formido. plus
tamen ferociae Britanni praeferunt, ut quos nondum
longa pax emollierit. nam Gallos quoque in bellis
floruisse accepimus ; mox segnitia cum otio intravit,
amissa virtute pariter ac libertate. quod Britannorum
olim victis evenit : ceteri manent quales Galli fuerunt.

12   In pedite robur ; quaedam nationes et curru proe-
British
warfare and
politics. liantur. honestior auriga, clientes pro-
pugnant. olim regibus parebant, nunc
per principes factionibus et studiis tra-
2 huntur. nec aliud adversus validissimas gentis pro
nobis utilius quam quod in commune non consulunt.
rarus duabus tribusve civitatibus ad propulsandum
commune periculum conventus : ita singuli pugnant,
3 universi vincuntur. caelum crebris imbribus ac nebulis
Climate,
products, etc. foedum ; asperitas frigorum abest. dierum
spatia ultra nostri orbis mensuram ; nox
clara et extrema Britanniae parte brevis, ut finem atque
4 initium lucis exiguo discrimine internoscas. quod si
nubes non officiant, aspici per noctem solis fulgorem,
nec occidere et exsurgere, sed transire adfirmant.
scilicet extrema et plana terrarum humili umbra non
erigunt tenebras, infraque caelum et sidera nox cadit.
5 solum praeter oleam vitemque et cetera calidioribus terris
oriri sueta patiens frugum, fecundum : tarde mitescunt,
cito proveniunt ; eademque utriusque rei causa, multus

umor terrarum caelique. fert Britannia aurum et argen- 6
tum et alia metalla, pretium victoriae. gignit et Oceanus
margarita, sed subfusca ac liventia. quidam artem abesse 7
legentibus arbitrantur; nam in rubro mari viva ac spi-
rantia saxis avelli, in Britannia, prout expulsa sint,
colligi: ego facilius crediderim naturam margaritis deesse
quam nobis avaritiam.

 Ipsi Britanni dilectum ac tributa et iniuncta imperii 13
      munia impigre obeunt, si iniuriae absint:
Roman
relations with has aegre tolerant, iam domiti ut pareant,
Britain, B.C.
55—A.D. 43. nondum ut serviant. igitur primus omnium 2
Romanorum divus Iulius cum exercitu Britanniam in-
gressus, quamquam prospera pugna terruerit incolas ac
litore potitus sit, potest videri ostendisse posteris, non
tradidisse. mox bella civilia et in rem publicam versa 3
principum arma, ac longa oblivio Britanniae etiam in
pace: consilium id divus Augustus vocabat, Tiberius
praeceptum. agitasse Gaium Caesarem de intranda 4
Britannia satis constat, ni velox ingenio mobili paenitentiae, et ingentes adversus Germaniam conatus frustra
fuissent. divus Claudius auctor iterati operis, transvectis 5
legionibus auxiliisque et adsumpto in partem rerum
Vespasiano, quod initium venturae mox fortunae fuit:
domitae gentes, capti reges et monstratus fatis Vespasianus.

 Consularium primus Aulus Plautius praepositus ac 14
      subinde Ostorius Scapula, uterque bello
Governors
of Britain. egregius: redactaque paulatim in formam
provinciae proxima pars Britanniae; addita insuper
veteranorum colonia. quaedam civitates Cogidumno 2
regi donatae (is ad nostram usque memoriam fidissimus
mansit), ut, vetere ac iam pridem recepta populi Romani
consuetudine, haberet instrumenta servitutis et reges.

3 mox Didius Gallus parta a prioribus continuit, paucis
admodum castellis in ulteriora promotis, per quae fama
aucti officii quaereretur. Didium Veranius excepit, isque
4 intra annum extinctus est. Suetonius hinc Paulinus
biennio prosperas res habuit, subactis nationibus firma-
tisque praesidiis ; quorum fiducia Monam insulam ut
vires rebellibus ministrantem adgressus terga occasioni
patefecit.

15   Namque absentia legati remoto metu Britanni agitare

Grievances
of the
Britons.

inter se mala servitutis, conferre iniurias
et interpretando accendere: nihil profici
patientia nisi ut graviora tamquam ex facili
2 tolerantibus imperentur. singulos sibi olim reges fuisse,
nunc binos imponi, e quibus legatus in sanguinem, procurator in bona saeviret. aeque discordiam praepositorum,
aeque concordiam subiectis exitiosam. alterius manus,
centuriones, alterius servos vim et contumelias miscere.
3 nihil iam cupiditati, nihil libidini exceptum. in proelio
fortiorem esse qui spoliet: nunc ab ignavis plerumque et
inbellibus eripi domos, abstrahi liberos, iniungi dilectus,
4 tamquam mori tantum pro patria nescientibus. quantulum enim transisse militum, si sese Britanni numerent?
sic Germanias excussisse iugum : et flumine, non
5 Oceano defendi. sibi patriam coniuges parentes, illis
avaritiam et luxuriam causas belli esse. recessuros, ut
divus Iulius recessisset, modo virtutem maiorum suorum
aemularentur. neve proelii unius aut alterius eventu
pavescerent: plus impetus felicibus, maiorem constantiam
6 penes miseros esse. iam Britannorum etiam deos mis-
ereri, qui Romanum ducem absentem, qui relegatum
in alia insula exercitum detinerent ; iam ipsos, quod
difficillimum fuerit, deliberare. porro in eius modi
consiliis periculosius esse deprehendi quam audere.

His atque talibus in vicem instincti, Boudicca generis **16**
Boudicca, regii femina duce (neque enim sexum in
Rebellion
under
Boudicca, imperiis discernunt) sumpsere universi bel-
A.D. 61. lum ; ac sparsos per castella milites con-
sectati, expugnatis praesidiis ipsam coloniam invasere
ut sedem servitutis, nec ullum in barbaris ingeniis
saevitiae genus omisit ira et victoria. quod nisi Paulinus **2**
cognito provinciae motu propere subvenisset, amissa
Britannia foret; quam unius proelii fortuna veteri
patientiae restituit, tenentibus arma plerisque, quos conscientia defectionis et proprius ex legato timor agitabat,
ne quamquam egregius cetera adroganter in deditos et
ut suae cuiusque iniuriae ultor durius consuleret. missus **3**
igitur Petronius Turpilianus tamquam exorabilior et
Further delictis hostium novus eoque paenitentiae
governors, mitior, compositis prioribus nihil ultra
A.D. 61—78. ausus Trebellio Maximo provinciam tradi-
dit. Trebellius segnior et nullis castrorum experimentis, **4**
comitate quadam curandi provinciam tenuit. didicere
ıam barbari quoque ignoscere vitiis blandientibus, et
interventus civilium armorum praebuit iustam segnitiae
excusationem : sed discordia laboratum, cum adsuetus
expeditionibus miles otio lasciviret. Trebellius, fuga ac **5**
latebris vitata exercitus ira indecorus atque humilis,
precario mox praefuit, ac velut pacti exercitus licentiam
dux salutem; et seditio sine sanguine stetit. nec Vettius **6**
Bolanus, manentibus adhuc civilibus bellis, agitavit
Britanniam disciplina : eadem inertia erga hostis, similis
petulantia castrorum, nisi quod innocens Bolanus et
nullis delictis invisus caritatem paraverat loco auctoritatis.

Sed ubi cum cetero orbe Vespasianus et Britanniam **17**
reciperavit, magni duces, egregii exercitus, minuta hostium
spes. et terrorem statim intulit Petilius Cerialis, Bri- **2**

gantum civitatem, quae numerosissima provinciae totius
perhibetur, adgressus. multa proelia, et aliquando non
incruenta; magnamque Brigantum partem aut victoria
3 amplexus est aut bello. et Cerialis quidem alterius
successoris curam famamque obruisset: subiit sustinuitque molem Iulius Frontinus, vir magnus, quantum
licebat, validamque et pugnacem Silurum gentem armis
subegit, super virtutem hostium locorum quoque diffi-
cultates eluctatus.

18   Hunc Britanniae statum, has bellorum vices media
iam aestate transgressus Agricola invenit,
Agricola's
first campaign cum et milites velut omissa expeditione
A.D. 78.   ad securitatem et hostes ad occasionem
2 verterentur. Ordovicum civitas haud multo ante ad-
ventum eius alam in finibus suis agentem prope universam
3 obtriverat, eoque initio erecta provincia. et quibus
bellum volentibus erat, probare exemplum ac recentis
legati animum opperiri, cum Agricola, quamquam transvecta aestas, sparsi per provinciam numeri, praesumpta
apud militem illius anni quies, tarda et contraria bellum
incohaturo, et plerisque custodiri suspecta potius videbatur, ire obviam discrimini statuit; contractisque
legionum vexillis et modica auxiliorum manu, quia in
aequum degredi Ordovices non audebant, ipse ante
agmen, quo ceteris par animus simili periculo esset,
4 erexit aciem. caesaque prope universa gente, non
ignarus instandum famae ac, prout prima cessissent,
terrorem ceteris fore, Monam insulam, ⟨a⟩ cuius posses-
Reduction   sione revocatum Paulinum rebellione totius
of Mona.   Britanniae supra memoravi, redigere in
5 potestatem animo intendit. sed ut in subitis consiliis
naves deerant: ratio et constantia ducis transvexit.
depositis omnibus sarcinis lectissimos auxiliarium, quibus

nota vada et patrius nandi usus, quo simul seque et
arma et equos regunt, ita repente inmisit, ut obstupefacti
hostes, qui classem, qui navis, qui mare exspectabant,
nihil arduum aut invictum crediderint sic ad bellum
venientibus. ita petita pace ac dedita insula clarus ac 6
magnus haberi Agricola, quippe cui ingredienti provinciam, quod tempus alii per ostentationem et officiorum
ambitum transigunt, labor et periculum placuisset. nec 7
Agricola prosperitate rerum in vanitatem usus, expedi-
tionem aut victoriam vocabat victos continuisse ; ne
laureatis quidem gesta prosecutus est, sed ipsa dissimula-
tione famae famam auxit, aestimantibus quanta futuri
spe tam magna tacuisset.

    Ceterum animorum provinciae prudens, simulque 19
Principles of doctus per aliena experimenta parum pro-
government fici armis, si iniuriae sequerentur, causas
and reforms. bellorum statuit excidere. a se suisque 2
orsus primum domum suam coercuit, quod plerisque
haud minus arduum est quam provinciam regere. nihil
per libertos servosque publicae rei, non studiis privatis
nec ex commendatione aut precibus centurionem militesve ascire, sed optimum quemque fidissimum putare.
omnia scire, non omnia exsequi. parvis peccatis veniam, 3
magnis severitatem commodare ; nec poena semper, sed
saepius paenitentia contentus esse ; officiis et adminis-
trationibus potius non peccaturos praeponere, quam
damnare cum peccassent. frumenti et tributorum ex- 4
actionem aequalitate munerum mollire, circumcisis quae
in quaestum reperta ipso tributo gravius tolerabantur.
namque per ludibrium adsidere clausis horreis et emere
ultro frumenta ac luere pretio cogebantur. divortia 5
itinerum et longinquitas regionum indicebatur, ut civitates proximis hibernis in remota et avia deferrent,

donec quod omnibus in promptu erat paucis lucrosum
fieret.

20   Haec primo statim anno comprimendo egregiam
famam paci circumdedit, quae vel incuria vel intolerantia
2 priorum haud minus quam bellum timebatur. sed ubi
aestas advenit, contracto exercitu multus
in agmine, laudare modestiam, disiectos
coercere; loca castris ipse capere, aestuaria
ac silvas ipse praetemptare; et nihil interim apud hostis
quietum pati, quo minus subitis excursibus popularetur;
atque ubi satis terruerat, parcendo rursus incitamenta
3 pacis ostentare. quibus rebus multae civitates, quae in
illum diem ex aequo egerant, datis obsidibus iram
posuere, et praesidiis castellisque circumdatae, et tanta
ratione curaque, ut nulla ante Britanniae nova pars
pariter inlacessita transierit.

Second campaign, A.D. 79.

21   Sequens hiems saluberrimis consiliis adsumpta.
namque ut homines dispersi ac rudes eoque
in bella faciles quieti et otio per voluptates
adsuescerent, hortari privatim, adiuvare
publice, ut templa fora domos exstruerent, laudando
promptos, castigando segnis: ita honoris aemulatio pro
2 necessitate erat. iam vero principum filios liberalibus
artibus erudire, et ingenia Britannorum studiis Gallorum
anteferre, ut qui modo linguam Romanam abnuebant,
3 eloquentiam concupiscerent. inde etiam habitus nostri
honor et frequens toga. paulatimque discessum ad de-
lenimenta vitiorum, porticus et balinea et conviviorum
elegantiam. idque apud inperitos humanitas vocabatur,
cum pars servitutis esset.

Process of Romanisation.

22   Tertius expeditionum annus novas gentis aperuit,
vastatis usque ad Tanaum (aestuario nomen
est) nationibus. qua formidine territi hostes

Third campaign, A.D. 80.

quamquam conflictatum saevis tempestatibus exercitum
lacessere non ausi; ponendisque insuper castellis spatium fuit. adnotabant periti non alium ducem op- 2
portunitates locorum sapientius legisse; nullum ab
Agricola positum castellum aut vi hostium expugnatum
aut pactione ac fuga desertum; crebrae eruptiones; nam
adversus moras obsidionis annuis copiis firmabantur.
ita intrepida ibi hiems, et sibi quisque praesidio, inritis 3
hostibus eoque desperantibus, quia soliti plerumque
damna aestatis hibernis eventibus pensare tum aestate
atque hieme iuxta pellebantur. nec Agricola umquam 4
per alios gesta avidus intercepit: seu centurio seu praefectus incorruptum facti testem habebat. apud quosdam
acerbior in conviciis narrabatur: ut erat comis bonis, ita
adversus malos iniucundus. ceterum ex iracundia nihil 5
supererat secretum, ut silentium eius non timeres:
honestius putabat offendere quam odisse.

Quarta aestas obtinendis quae percucurrerat insumpta; 23

Fourth
campaign,
A.D. 81.

ac si virtus exercituum et Romani nominis
gloria pateretur, inventus in ipsa Britannia
terminus. namque Clota et Bodotria di- 2
versi maris aestibus per inmensum revectae, angusto
terrarum spatio dirimuntur: quod tum praesidiis firma-
batur atque omnis propior sinus tenebatur, summotis
velut in aliam insulam hostibus.

Quinto expeditionum anno nave prima transgressus 24

Fifth
campaign,
A.D. 82.

ignotas ad id tempus gentis crebris simul
ac prosperis proeliis domuit; eamque
partem Britanniae quae Hiberniam aspicit
copiis instruxit, in spem magis quam ob formidinem,
si quidem Hibernia medio inter Britanniam atque
Hispaniam sita et Gallico quoque mari opportuna
valentissimam imperii partem magnis in vicem usibus

2 miscuerit. spatium eius, si Britanniae comparetur,

Ireland. angustius, nostri maris insulas superat.

solum caelumque et ingenia cultusque hominum haud multum a Britannia differunt ⟨ni⟩ in melius.
aditus portusque per commercia et negotiatores cogniti.

3 Agricola expulsum seditione domestica unum ex regulis
gentis exceperat ac specie amicitiae in occasionem retine-
bat. saepe ex eo audivi legione una et modicis auxiliis
debellari obtinerique Hiberniam posse; idque etiam
adversus Britanniam profuturum, si Romana ubique
arma et velut e conspectu libertas tolleretur.

25 Ceterum aestate, qua sextum officii annum incohabat,

Sixth amplexus civitates trans Bodotriam sitas,

campaign, quia motus universarum ultra gentium et

A.D. 83. infesta hostilis exercitus itinera timebantur,

portus classe exploravit; quae ab Agricola primum
adsumpta in partem virium sequebatur egregia specie,
cum simul terra, simul mari bellum impelleretur, ac
saepe isdem castris pedes equesque et nauticus miles
mixti copiis et laetitia sua quisque facta, suos casus
attollerent, ac modo silvarum ac montium profunda,
modo tempestatum ac fluctuum adversa, hinc terra et
hostis, hinc victus Oceanus militari iactantia compara-
2 rentur. Britannos quoque, ut ex captivis audiebatur,
visa classis obstupefaciebat, tamquam aperto maris sui
3 secreto ultimum victis perfugium clauderetur. ad manus
et arma conversi Caledoniam incolentes populi, magno
paratu, maiore fama, uti mos est de ignotis, obpugnare
ultro castella adorti, metum ut provocantes addiderant;
regrediendumque citra Bodotriam et cedendum potius
quam pellerentur ignavi specie prudentium admonebant,
cum interim cognoscit hostis pluribus agminibus in-
4 rupturos. ac ne superante numero et peritia locorum

circumiretur, diviso et ipse in tris partes exercitu incessit.

Quod ubi cognitum hosti, mutato repente consilio 26
universi nonam legionem ut maxime invalidam nocte adgressi, inter somnum ac trepidationem caesis vigilibus inrupere.

Camp of the IXth legion attacked.

iamque in ipsis castris pugnabatur, cum Agricola iter 2 hostium ab exploratoribus edoctus et vestigiis insecutus, velocissimos equitum peditumque adsultare tergis pugnantium iubet, mox ab universis adici clamorem; et propinqua luce fulsere signa. ita ancipiti malo territi 3 Britanni; et nonanis redit animus, ac securi pro salute de gloria certabant. ultro quin etiam erupere, et fuit atrox in ipsis portarum angustiis proelium, donec pulsi hostes, utroque exercitu certante, his, ut tulisse opem, illis, ne eguisse auxilio viderentur. quod nisi paludes et 4 silvae fugientis texissent, debellatum illa victoria foret.

Cuius conscientia ac fama ferox exercitus nihil virtuti 27
suae invium et penetrandam Caledoniam inveniendumque tandem Britanniae terminum continuo proeliorum cursu fremebant. atque illi 2 modo cauti ac sapientes prompti post eventum ac magniloqui erant. iniquissima haec bellorum condicio est: prospera omnes sibi vindicant, adversa uni imputantur. at Britanni non virtute se victos, sed occasione et arte 3 ducis rati, nihil ex adrogantia remittere, quo minus iuventutem armarent, coniuges ac liberos in loca tuta transferrent, coetibus et sacrificiis conspirationem civitatum sancirent. atque ita inritatis utrimque animis discessum.

Feelings on both sides.

Eadem aestate cohors Usiporum per Germanias 28
conscripta et in Britanniam transmissa magnum ac memorabile facinus ausa est. occiso centurione ac militibus, qui ad 2

Adventures of a body of Usipi.

tradendam disciplinam inmixti manipulis exemplum et
rectores habebantur, tris liburnicas adactis per vim
gubernatoribus ascendere; et uno remigante, suspectis
duobus eoque interfectis, nondum vulgato rumore ut
3 miraculum praevehebantur. mox ad aquandum atque
utilia raptum egressi et cum plerisque Britannorum sua
defensantium proelio congressi ac saepe victores, aliquando pulsi, eo ad extremum inopiae venere, ut
infirmissimos suorum, mox sorte ductos vescerentur.
4 atque ita circumvecti Britanniam, amissis per inscitiam
regendi navibus, pro praedonibus habiti, primum a
5 Suebis, mox a Frisiis intercepti sunt. ac fuere quos
per commercia venumdatos et in nostram usque ripam
mutatione ementium adductos indicium tanti casus in-
lustravit.

29   Initio aestatis Agricola domestico vulnere ictus, anno

Agricola's   ante natum filium amisit. quem casum
bereavement.   neque ut plerique fortium virorum ambitiose, neque per lamenta rursus ac maerorem muliebriter
2 tulit: et in luctu bellum inter remedia erat. igitur
praemissa classe, quae pluribus locis praedata magnum
et incertum terrorem faceret, expedito exercitu, cui ex

Seventh   Britannis fortissimos et longa pace explo-
campaign,   ratos addiderat, ad montem Graupium
A.D. 84.
3 Advance to   pervenit, quem iam hostis insederat. nam
Mons   Britanni nihil fracti pugnae prioris eventu,
Graupius.
                et ultionem aut servitium exspectantes,
tandemque docti commune periculum concordia propulsandum, legationibus et foederibus omnium civitatum
4 vires exciverant. iamque super triginta milia armatorum
aspiciebantur, et adhuc adfluebat omnis iuventus et
quibus cruda ac viridis senectus, clari bello et sua
quisque decora gestantes, cum inter pluris duces virtute

et genere praestans nomine Calgacus apud contractam multitudinem proelium poscentem in hunc modum locutus fertur :

'Quotiens causas belli et necessitatem nostram intueor, **30**
Speech of Calgacus. magnus mihi animus est hodiernum diem consensumque vestrum initium libertatis toti Britanniae fore : nam et universi colitis et servitutis expertes, et nullae ultra terrae ac ne mare quidem securum inminente nobis classe Romana. ita proelium **2** atque arma, quae fortibus honesta, eadem etiam ignavis tutissima sunt. priores pugnae, quibus adversus Romanos **3** varia fortuna certatum est, spem ac subsidium in nostris manibus habebant, quia nobilissimi totius Britanniae eoque in ipsis penetralibus siti nec ulla servientium litora aspicientes, oculos quoque a contactu dominationis invio- latos habebamus. nos terrarum ac libertatis extremos **4** recessus ipse ac sinus famae in hunc diem defendit; atque omne ignotum pro magnifico est. sed nunc ter- **5** minus Britanniae patet, nulla iam ultra gens, nihil nisi fluctus ac saxa, et infestiores Romani, quorum superbiam frustra per obsequium ac modestiam effugias. raptores **6** orbis, postquam cuncta vastantibus defuere terrae, mare scrutantur : si locuples hostis est, avari, si pauper, ambi- tiosi, quos non Oriens, non Occidens satiaverit : soli omnium opes atque inopiam pari adfectu concupiscunt. auferre trucidare rapere falsis nominibus imperium, atque **7** ubi solitudinem faciunt, pacem appellant.

' Liberos cuique ac propinquos suos natura carissimos **31** esse voluit : hi per dilectus alibi servituri auferuntur : coniuges sororesque etiam si hostilem libidinem effuge- runt, nomine amicorum atque hospitum polluuntur. bona fortunaeque in tributum, ager atque annus in **2** frumentum, corpora ipsa ac manus silvis ac paludibus

emuniendis inter verbera ac contumelias conteruntur. nata servituti mancipia semel veneunt, atque ultro a dominis aluntur: Britannia servitutem suam cotidie emit,
3 cotidie pascit. ac sicut in familia recentissimus quisque servorum etiam conservis ludibrio est, sic in hoc orbis terrarum vetere famulatu novi nos et viles in excidium petimur ; neque enim arva nobis aut metalla aut portus
4 sunt, quibus exercendis reservemur. virtus porro ac ferocia subiectorum ingrata imperantibus; et longinquitas ac secretum ipsum quo tutius, eo suspectius. ita sublata spe veniae tandem sumite animum, tam quibus salus
5 quam quibus gloria carissima est. Brigantes femina duce exurere coloniam, expugnare castra, ac nisi felicitas in socordiam vertisset, exuere iugum potuere: nos integri et indomiti et in libertatem, non in paenitentiam ⟨arma⟩ laturi, primo statim congressu ostendamus, quos sibi Caledonia viros seposuerit.

32 'An eandem Romanis in bello virtutem quam in pace lasciviam adesse creditis? nostris illi dissensionibus ac discordiis clari vitia hostium in gloriam exercitus sui vertunt ; quem contractum ex diversissimis gentibus ut secundae res tenent, ita adversae dissolvent: nisi si Gallos et Germanos et (pudet dictu) Britannorum plerosque, licet dominationi alienae sanguinem commodent, diutius tamen hostis quam servos, fide et adfectu teneri
2 putatis. metus ac terror sunt infirma vincla caritatis; quae ubi removeris, qui timere desierint, odisse incipient. omnia victoriae incitamenta pro nobis sunt: nullae Romanos coniuges accendunt, nulli parentes fugam exprobraturi
3 sunt; aut nulla plerisque patria aut alia est. paucos numero, trepidos ignorantia, caelum ipsum ac mare et silvas, ignota omnia circumspectantis, clausos quodam modo ac vinctos di vobis tradiderunt. ne terreat vanus

aspectus et auri fulgor atque argenti, quod neque tegit
neque vulnerat. in ipsa hostium acie inveniemus nostras 4
manus. adgnoscent Britanni suam causam, recorda-
buntur Galli priorem libertatem: tam deserent illos
ceteri Germani, quam nuper Usipi reliquerunt. nec
quicquam ultra formidinis: vacua castella, senum coloniae,
inter male parentis et iniuste imperantis aegra municipia
et discordantia. hic dux, hic exercitus: ibi tributa et 5
metalla et ceterae servientium poenae, quas in aeternum
perferre aut statim ulcisci in hoc campo est. proinde
ituri in aciem et maiores vestros et posteros cogitate.'

Excepere orationem alacres, ut barbaris moris, fre- 33
mitu cantuque et clamoribus dissonis. iamque agmina
et armorum fulgores audentissimi cuiusque procursu :
simul instruebatur acies, cum Agricola quamquam laetum
et vix munimentis coercitum militem accendendum adhuc
Speech of ratus, ita disseruit: 'septimus annus est, 2
Agricola. commilitones, ex quo virtute vestra, auspiciis imperii Romani, fide atque opera nostra Britanniam vicistis. tot expeditionibus, tot proeliis, seu
fortitudine adversus hostis seu patientia ac labore paene
adversus ipsam rerum naturam opus fuit, neque me
militum neque vos ducis paenituit. ergo egressi, ego 3
veterum legatorum, vos priorum exercituum terminos,
finem Britanniae non fama nec rumore, sed castris et
armis tenemus: inventa Britannia et subacta.' equidem 4
saepe in agmine, cum vos paludes montesque et flumina
fatigarent, fortissimi cuiusque voces audiebam: "quando
dabitur hostis, quando acies?" veniunt, e latebris suis
extrusi, et vota virtusque in aperto, omniaque prona
victoribus atque eadem victis adversa. nam ut superasse 5
tantum itineris, evasisse silvas, transisse aestuaria pul-
chrum ac decorum in frontem, ita fugientibus periculo-

sissima quae hodie prosperrima sunt ; neque enim nobis
aut locorum eadem notitia aut commeatuum eadem
6 abundantia, sed manus et arma, et in his omnia. quod
ad me attinet, iam pridem mihi decretum est neque
exercitus neque ducis terga tuta esse. proinde et honesta
mors turpi vita potior, et incolumitas ac decus eodem
loco sita sunt; nec inglorium fuerit in ipso terrarum ac
naturae fine cecidisse.

34   'Si novae gentes atque ignota acies constitisset,
aliorum exercituum exemplis vos hortarer : nunc vestra
decora recensete, vestros oculos interrogate. hi sunt,
quos proximo anno unam legionem furto noctis adgressos
clamore debellastis ; hi ceterorum Britannorum fugacis-
2 simi ideoque tam diu superstites. quo modo silvas
saltusque penetrantibus fortissimum quodque animal
contra ruere, pavida et inertia ipso agminis sono pellebantur, sic acerrimi Britannorum iam pridem ceciderunt,
3 reliquus est numerus ignavorum et metuentium. quos
quod tandem invenistis, non restiterunt, sed deprehensi
sunt ; novissimae res et extremo metu torpor defixere
aciem in his vestigiis, in quibus pulchram et spectabilem
4 victoriam ederetis. transigite cum expeditionibus, im-
ponite quinquaginta annis magnum diem, adprobate rei
publicae numquam exercitui imputari potuisse aut moras
belli aut causas rebellandi.'

35   Et adloquente adhuc Agricola militum ardor eminebat,
et finem orationis ingens alacritas consecuta
est, statimque ad arma discursum. in-
stinctos ruentisque ita disposuit, ut peditum
auxilia, quae octo milium erant, mediam aciem firmarent,
equitum tria milia cornibus adfunderentur. legiones
pro vallo stetere, ingens victoriae decus citra Romanum
3 sanguinem bellandi, et auxilium, si pellerentur. Britan-

Disposition
2 of the
opposing
forces.

norum acies in speciem simul ac terrorem editioribus
locis constiterat ita, ut primum agmen in aequo, ceteri
per adclive iugum convexi velut insurgerent ; media
campi covinnarius eques strepitu ac discursu complebat.
tum Agricola superante hostium multitudine veritus, ne 4
in frontem simul et latera suorum pugnaretur, diductis
ordinibus, quamquam porrectior acies futura erat et
arcessendas plerique legiones admonebant, promptior in
spem et firmus adversis, dimisso equo pedes ante vexilla
constitit.

Ac primo congressu eminus certabatur ; simulque 36
constantia, simul arte Britanni ingentibus
gladiis et brevibus caetris missilia nostrorum vitare vel excutere, atque ipsi magnam
vim telorum superfundere, donec Agricola quattuor
Batavorum cohortis ac Tungrorum duas cohortatus est,
ut rem ad mucrones ac manus adducerent ; quod et
ipsis vetustate militiae exercitatum et hostibus inhabile,
parva scuta et enormis gladios gerentibus ; nam Britannorum gladii sine mucrone complexum armorum et in
arto pugnam non tolerabant. igitur ut Batavi miscere 2
ictus, ferire umbonibus, ora fodere, et stratis qui in
aequo adstiterant, erigere in collis aciem coepere, ceterae
cohortes aemulatione et impetu conisae proximos quosque
caedere : ac plerique semineces aut integri festinatione
victoriae relinquebantur. interim equitum turmae, fugere 3
enim covinnarii, peditum se proelio miscuere. et quamquam recentem terrorem intulerant, densis tamen hostium
agminibus et inaequalibus locis haerebant ; minimeque
equestris ei pugnae facies erat, cum aegre clivo instantes
simul equorum corporibus impellerentur ; ac saepe vagi
currus, exterriti sine rectoribus equi, ut quemque formido
tulerat, transversos aut obvios incursabant.

Battle of
Mons
Graupius

37 Et Britanni, qui adhuc pugnae expertes summa
collium insederant et paucitatem nostrorum vacui spernebant, degredi paulatim et circumire terga vincentium
coeperant, ni id ipsum veritus Agricola quattuor equitum
alas, ad subita belli retentas, venientibus opposuisset,
quantoque ferocius adcucurrerant, tanto acrius pulsos in
2 fugam disiecisset. ita consilium Britannorum in ipsos
versum, transvectaeque praecepto ducis a fronte pugnantium alae aversam hostium aciem invasere. tum vero
patentibus locis grande et atrox spectaculum : sequi,
vulnerare, capere, atque eosdem oblatis aliis trucidare.
3 iam hostium, prout cuique ingenium erat, catervae
armatorum paucioribus terga praestare, quidam inermes
ultro ruere ac se morti offerre. passim arma et corpora
et laceri artus et cruenta humus ; et aliquando etiam
victis ira virtusque, postquam silvis adpropinquaverunt.
4 nam primos sequentium incautos collecti et locorum
gnari circumveniebant. quod ni frequens ubique Agricola
validas et expeditas cohortis indaginis modo, et sicubi
artiora erant, partem equitum dimissis equis, simul
rariores silvas equitem persultare iussisset, acceptum
5 aliquod vulnus per nimiam fiduciam foret. ceterum ubi
compositos firmis ordinibus sequi rursus videre, in fugam
versi, non agminibus, ut prius, nec alius alium respectantes, rari et vitabundi in vicem longinqua atque avia
6 petiere. finis sequendi nox et satietas fuit. caesa
hostium ad decem milia : nostrorum trecenti sexaginta
cecidere, in quis Aulus Atticus praefectus cohortis,
iuvenili ardore et ferocia equi hostibus inlatus.

38 Et nox quidem gaudio praedaque laeta victoribus :
After the battle. Britanni palantes mixto virorum mulie-
rumque ploratu trahere vulneratos, vocare
integros, deserere domos ac per iram ultro incendere,

eligere latebras et statim relinquere; miscere in vicem
consilia aliqua, dein separare; aliquando frangi aspectu
pignorum suorum, saepius concitari. satisque constabat 2
saevisse quosdam in coniuges ac liberos, tamquam
misererentur. proximus dies faciem victoriae latius
aperuit: vastum ubique silentium, secreti colles, fumantia
procul tecta, nemo exploratoribus obvius. quibus in 3
omnem partem dimissis, ubi incerta fugae vestigia neque
usquam conglobari hostis compertum (et exacta iam
aestate spargi bellum nequibat), in finis Borestorum
exercitum deducit. ibi acceptis obsidibus, praefecto 4
Circumnavi- classis circumvehi Britanniam praecipit.
gation of datae ad id vires, et praecesserat terror.
Britain. ipse peditem atque equites lento itinere,
quo novarum gentium animi ipsa transitus mora terre-
rentur, in hibernis locavit. et simul classis secunda 5
tempestate ac fama Trucculensem portum tenuit, unde
proximo Britanniae latere praelecto omni redierat.

Hunc rerum cursum, quamquam nulla verborum 39
Domitian's iactantia epistulis Agricolae auctum, ut
jealousy. erat Domitiano moris, fronte laetus, pectore
anxius excipit. inerat conscientia derisui fuisse nuper 2
falsum e Germania triumphum, emptis per commercia,
quorum habitus et crines in captivorum speciem formarentur: at nunc veram magnamque victoriam tot
milibus hostium caesis ingenti fama celebrari. id sibi 3
maxime formidolosum, privati hominis nomen supra
principem adtolli: frustra studia fori et civilium artium
decus in silentium acta, si militarem gloriam alius
occuparet; cetera utcumque facilius dissimulari, ducis
boni imperatoriam virtutem esse. talibus curis exercitus, 4
quodque saevae cogitationis indicium erat, secreto suo
satiatus, optimum in praesentia statuit reponere odium,

donec impetus famae et favor exercitus langucesceret: nam
etiam tum Agricola Britanniam obtinebat.

40 Igitur triumphalia ornamenta et inlustris statuae
     Agricola   honorem et quidquid pro triumpho datur,
recalled.   multo verborum honore cumulata, decerni
in senatu iubet addique insuper opinionem, Suriam provinciam Agricolae destinari, vacuam tum morte Atilii
2 Rufi consularis et maioribus reservatam. credidere
plerique libertum ex secretioribus ministeriis missum
ad Agricolam codicillos, quibus ei Suria dabatur, tulisse,
cum eo praecepto ut, si in Britannia foret, traderentur;
eumque libertum in ipso freto Oceani obvium Agricolae,
ne appellato quidem eo ad Domitianum remeasse, sive
verum istud. sive ex ingenio principis fictum ac com-
3 positum est. tradiderat interim Agricola successori suo
provinciam quietam tutamque. ac ne notabilis celebritate
et frequentia occurrentium introitus esset, vitato amicorum officio noctu in urbem, noctu in Palatium, ita ut
praeceptum erat, venit; exceptusque brevi osculo et
4 nullo sermone turbae servientium inmixtus est. ceterum
uti militare nomen, grave inter otiosos, aliis virtutibus
temperaret, tranquillitatem atque otium penitus hausit,
cultu modicus, sermone facilis, uno aut altero amicorum
comitatus, adeo ut plerique, quibus magnos viros per
ambitionem aestimare mos est, viso aspectoque Agricola
quaererent famam, pauci interpretarentur.

41 Crebro per eos dies apud Domitianum absens ac-
     His   cusatus, absens absolutus est. causa peri-
dangerous   culi non crimen ullum aut querela laesi
position.   cuiusquam, sed infensus virtutibus princeps
et gloria viri ac pessimum inimicorum genus, laudantes.
2 et ea insecuta sunt rei publicae tempora, quae sileri
Agricolam non sinerent: tot exercitus in Moesia Dacia-

que et Germania et Pannonia temeritate aut per ignaviam
ducum amissi, tot militares viri cum tot cohortibus
expugnati et capti; nec iam de limite imperii et ripa, sed
de hibernis legionum et possessione dubitatum. ita cum 3
damna damnis continuarentur atque omnis annus funeri-
bus et cladibus insigniretur, poscebatur ore vulgi dux
Agricola, comparantibus cunctis vigorem constantiam
et expertum bellis animum cum inertia et formidine
ceterorum. quibus sermonibus satis constat Domitiani 4
quoque auris verberatas, dum optimus quisque libertorum
amore et fide, pessimi malignitate et livore pronum
deterioribus principem exstimulabant. sic Agricola simul
suis virtutibus, simul vitiis aliorum in ipsam gloriam
praeceps agebatur.

Aderat iam annus, quo proconsulatum Africae et 42
Asiae sortiretur, et occiso Civica nuper

He declines a proconsulship. nec Agricolae consilium deerat nec Domitiano exemplum. accessere quidam cogi-
tationum principis periti, qui iturusne esset in provinciam
ultro Agricolam interrogarent. ac primo occultius 2
quietem et otium laudare, mox operam suam in adprobanda excusatione offerre, postremo non iam obscuri
suadentes simul terrentesque pertraxere ad Domitianum.
qui paratus simulatione, in adrogantiam compositus, et 3
audiit preces excusantis et, cum adnuisset, agi sibi gratias
passus est, nec erubuit beneficii invidia. salarium tamen
proconsulare solitum offerri et quibusdam a se ipso
concessum Agricolae non dedit, sive offensus non peti-
tum, sive ex conscientia, ne quod vetuerat videretur
emisse. proprium humani ingenii est odisse quem 4
laeseris: Domitiani vero natura praeceps in iram, et quo
obscurior, eo inrevocabilior, moderatione tamen pruden-
tiaque Agricolae leniebatur, quia non contumacia neque

inani iactatione libertatis famam fatumque provocabat.
5 sciant, quibus moris est inlicita mirari, posse etiam sub
malis principibus magnos viros esse, obsequiumque ac
modestiam, si industria ac vigor adsint, eo laudis excedere, quo plerique per abrupta, sed in nullum rei publicae
usum, ambitiosa morte inclaruerunt.

43   Finis vitae eius nobis luctuosus, amicis tristis, ex-

His last illness.   traneis etiam ignotisque non sine cura fuit.
vulgus quoque et hic aliud agens populus
et ventitavere ad domum et per fora et circulos locuti
sunt; nec quisquam audita morte Agricolae aut laetatus
2 est aut statim oblitus. augebat miserationem constans
rumor veneno interceptum : nobis nihil comperti adfirmare ausim. ceterum per omnem valetudinem eius
crebrius quam ex more principatus per nuntios visentis
et libertorum primi et medicorum intimi venere, sive cura
3 illud sive inquisitio erat. supremo quidem die momenta
ipsa deficientis per dispositos cursores nuntiata constabat,
nullo credente sic adcelerari quae tristis audiret. speciem tamen doloris animi vultu prae se tulit, securus
iam odii et qui facilius dissimularet gaudium quam metum.
4 satis constabat lecto testamento Agricolae, quo coheredem optimae uxori et piissimae filiae Domitianum scrip-
sit, laetatum eum velut honore iudicioque. tam caeca
et corrupta mens adsiduis adulationibus erat, ut nesciret
a bono patre non scribi heredem nisi malum principem.

44   Natus erat Agricola Gaio Caesare tertium consule

**His death,
23 Aug. A.D.
93, and happy** idibus Iuniis : excessit quarto et quinqua-
gesimo anno, decumum kalendas Septem-
2 **fortune.** bris Collega Priscoque consulibus. quod
si habitum quoque eius posteri noscere velint, decentior
quam sublimior fuit : nihil impetus in vultu : gratia oris
supererat. bonum virum facile crederes, magnum libenter.

et ipse quidem, quamquam medio in spatio integrae 3
aetatis ereptus, quantum ad gloriam, longissimum aevum
peregit. quippe et vera bona, quae in virtutibus sita
sunt, impleverat, et consulari ac triumphalibus ornamen-
tis praedito quid aliud adstruere fortuna poterat? opibus 4
nimiis non gaudebat, speciosae contigerant. filia atque
uxore superstitibus potest videri etiam beatus incolumi
dignitate, florente fama, salvis adfinitatibus et amicitiis
futura effugisse. nam sicut ei ⟨non licuit⟩ durare in 5
hanc beatissimi saeculi lucem ac principem Traianum
videre, quod augurio votisque apud nostras auris ominabatur, ita festinatae mortis grande solacium tulit evasisse
postremum illud tempus, quo Domitianus non iam per
intervalla ac spiramenta temporum, sed continuo et velut
uno ictu rem publicam exhausit.

Non vidit Agricola obsessam curiam et clausum armis 45
senatum et eadem strage tot consularium
The horrors
which he   caedes, tot nobilissimarum feminarum ex-
escaped.   ilia et fugas. una adhuc victoria Carus
Mettius censebatur, et intra Albanam arcem sententia
Messalini strepebat, et Massa Baebius etiam tum reus
erat: mox nostrae duxere Helvidium in carcerem manus;
nos Mauricum Rusticumque divisimus, nos innocenti
sanguine Senecio perfudit. Nero tamen subtraxit oculos 2
suos iussitque scelera, non spectavit: praecipua sub
Domitiano miseriarum pars erat videre et aspici, cum
suspiria nostra subscriberentur, cum denotandis tot
hominum palloribus sufficeret saevus ille vultus et rubor,
quo se contra pudorem muniebat.

Tu vero felix, Agricola, non vitae tantum claritate, 3
sed etiam opportunitate mortis. ut perhibent qui interfuere novissimis sermonibus tuis, constans et libens fatum
excepisti, tamquam pro virili portione innocentiam

4 principi donares.   sed mihi filiaeque eius praeter acerbi-

Tacitus'
sorrow. tatem parentis erepti auget maestitiam, quod adsidere valetudini, fovere deficien-

5 tem, satiari vultu complexuque non contigit. excepis-
semus certe mandata vocesque, quas penitus animo
figeremus.   noster hic dolor, nostrum vulnus, nobis tam
longae absentiae condicione ante quadriennium amissus

6 est.   omnia sine dubio, optime parentum, adsidente
amantissima uxore superfuere honori tuo: paucioribus
tamen lacrimis comploratus es, et novissima in luce
desideravere aliquid oculi tui.

46   Si quis piorum manibus locus, si, ut sapientibus

Epilogue. placet, non cum corpore extinguuntur magnae animae, placide quiescas, nosque,

domum tuam, ab infirmo desiderio et muliebribus
lamentis ad contemplationem virtutum tuarum voces,

2 quas neque lugeri neque plangi fas est.   admiratione te
potius et inmortalibus laudibus et, si natura suppeditet,
similitudine decoremus: is verus honos, ea coniunctis-

3 simi cuiusque pietas.   id filiae quoque uxorique praeceperim, sic patris, sic mariti memoriam venerari, ut omnia
facta dictaque eius secum revolvant, formamque ac
figuram animi magis quam corporis complectantur, non
quia intercedendum putem imaginibus quae marmore
aut aere finguntur, sed, ut vultus hominum, ita simulacra
vultus inbecilla ac mortalia sunt, forma mentis aeterna,
quam tenere et exprimere non per alienam materiam

4 et artem, sed tuis ipse moribus possis.   quidquid ex
Agricola amavimus, quidquid mirati sumus, manet mansu-
rumque est in animis hominum, in aeternitate temporum,
fama rerum; nam multos veterum velut inglorios et
ignobilis oblivio obruet: Agricola posteritati narratus et
traditus superstes erit.

CORNELII TACITI

DE ORIGINE ET MORIBUS

GERMANORUM

Germania omnis a Gallis Raetisque et Pannoniis 1
Boundaries Rheno et Danuvio fluminibus, a Sarmatis
of Germany. Dacisque mutuo metu aut montibus sepa-
ratur: cetera Oceanus ambit, latos sinus et insularum
inmensa spatia complectens, nuper cognitis quibusdam
gentibus ac regibus, quos bellum aperuit. Rhenus, Raeti- 2
carum Alpium inaccesso ac praecipiti vertice ortus, modico
flexu in occidentem versus septentrionali Oceano misce-
tur. Danuvius molli et clementer edito montis Abnobae 3
iugo effusus pluris populos adit donec in Ponticum mare
sex meatibus erumpat: septimum os paludibus hauritur.

Ipsos Germanos indigenas crediderim, minimeque 2
Inhabitants aliarum gentium adventibus et hospitiis
probably mixtos, quia nec terra olim sed classibus
indigenous. advehebantur qui mutare sedes quaere-
bant, et inmensus ultra utque sic dixerim adversus
Oceanus raris ab orbe nostro navibus aditur. quis porro, 2
praeter periculum horridi et ignoti maris, Asia aut Africa
aut Italia relicta Germaniam peteret, informem terris,
asperam caelo, tristem cultu aspectuque, nisi si patria
sit?

3   Celebrant carminibus antiquis, quod unum apud

Native   illos memoriae et annalium genus est,

traditions.   Tuistonem deum terra editum. ei filium

Mannum, originem gentis conditoremque, Manno tris

filios adsignant, e quorum nominibus proximi Oceano

Ingaevones, medii Hermiones, ceteri Istaevones vocen-

4 tur. quidam, ut in licentia vetustatis, pluris deo ortos

plurisque gentis appellationes, Marsos Gambrivios Suebos

Vandilios adfirmant, eaque vera et antiqua nomina.

5   *The name*   ceterum Germaniae vocabulum recens et

Germani.   nuper additum, quoniam qui primi Rhe-

num transgressi Gallos expulerint ac nunc Tungri, tunc

Germani vocati sint: ita nationis nomen, non gentis,

evaluisse paulatim, ut omnes primum a victore ob metum,

mox etiam a se ipsis invento nomine Germani vocarentur.

3   Fuisse apud eos et Herculem memorant, primumque

Hercules.   omnium virorum fortium ituri in proelia

          canunt. sunt illis haec quoque carmina,

quorum relatu, quem barditum vocant, accendunt animos

The 'bar-   futuraeque pugnae fortunam ipso cantu

ditus.'   augurantur; terrent enim trepidantve, prout

sonuit acies, nec tam vocis ille quam virtutis concentus

2 videtur. adfectatur praecipue asperitas soni et fractum

murmur, obiectis ad os scutis, quo plenior et gravior

3 vox repercussu intumescat. ceterum et Ulixen quidam

opinantur longo illo et fabuloso errore in hunc Oceanum

Ulixes.   delatum adiisse Germaniae terras, Asci

         burgiumque, quod in ripa Rheni situm

hodieque incolitur, ab illo constitutum nominatumque

'ΑϹΚΙΠΥΡΓΙΟΝ; aram quin etiam Ulixi consecratam,

adiecto Laertae patris nomine, eodem loco olim repertam,

monumentaque et tumulos quosdam Graecis litteris in-

scriptos in confinio Germaniae Raetiaeque adhuc extare.

quae neque confirmare argumentis neque refellere in ₄
animo est: ex ingenio suo quisque demat vel addat
fidem.

Ipse eorum opinionibus accedo, qui Germaniae popu- **4**
Uniform los nullis aliis aliarum nationum conubiis
physical
features of the infectos propriam et sinceram et tantum
people. sui similem gentem extitisse arbitrantur.
unde habitus quoque corporum, quamquam in tanto ₂
hominum numero, idem omnibus; truces et caerulei
oculi, rutilae comae, magna corpora et tantum ad impetum valida: laboris atque operum non eadem patientia, ₃
minimeque sitim aestumque tolerare, frigora atque ine-
diam caelo solove adsueverunt.

Terra etsi aliquanto specie differt, in universum tamen **5**
Character aut silvis horrida aut paludibus foeda,
and products of umidior qua Gallias, ventosior qua Nori-
the country. cum ac Pannoniam aspicit; satis ferax,
frugiferarum arborum inpatiens, pecorum fecunda, sed
plerumque inprocera. ne armentis quidem suus honor ₂
aut gloria frontis: numero gaudent, eaeque solae et
gratissimae opes sunt. argentum et aurum propitiine ₃
an irati di negaverint dubito. nec tamen adfirmaverim
nullam Germaniae venam argentum aurumve gignere:
quis enim scrutatus est? possessione et usu haud perinde adficiuntur. est videre apud illos argentea vasa, ₄
legatis et principibus eorum muneri data, non in alia
vilitate quam quae humo finguntur; quamquam proximi
Use of Roman ob usum commerciorum aurum et argen-
money. tum in pretio habent formasque quasdam
nostrae pecuniae adgnoscunt atque eligunt: interiores
simplicius et antiquius permutatione mercium utuntur.
pecuniam probant veterem et diu notam, serratos biga- ₅
tosque. argentum quoque magis quam aurum sequuntur,

S. 3

nulla adfectione animi, sed quia numerus argenteorum facilior usui est promiscua ac vilia mercantibus.

6 Ne ferrum quidem superest, sicut ex genere telorum

Arms and military organisation. colligitur. rari gladiis aut maioribus lanceis utuntur: hastas vel ipsorum vocabulo frameas gerunt angusto et brevi ferro, sed ita acri et ad usum habili, ut eodem telo, prout ratio 2 poscit, vel comminus vel eminus pugnent. et eques quidem scuto frameaque contentus est, pedites et missilia spargunt, pluraque singuli, atque in inmensum vibrant, nudi aut sagulo leves. nulla cultus iactatio; 3 scuta tantum lectissimis coloribus distinguunt. paucis loricae, vix uni alterive cassis aut galea. equi non forma, non velocitate conspicui. sed nec variare gyros in morem nostrum docentur: in rectum aut uno flexu dextros 4 agunt, ita coniuncto orbe ut nemo posterior sit. in universum aestimanti plus penes peditem roboris; eoque mixti proeliantur, apta et congruente ad equestrem pugnam velocitate peditum, quos ex omni iuventute delectos 5 ante aciem locant. definitur et numerus: centeni ex singulis pagis sunt, idque ipsum inter suos vocantur, et quod primo numerus fuit, iam nomen et honor est. 6 acies per cuneos componitur. cedere loco, dummodo rursus instes, consilii quam formidinis arbitrantur. corpora suorum etiam in dubiis proeliis referunt. scutum reliquisse praecipuum flagitium, nec aut sacris adesse aut concilium inire ignominioso fas; multique superstites bellorum infamiam laqueo finierunt.

7 Reges ex nobilitate, duces ex virtute sumunt. nec

Kings and 'leaders.' regibus infinita aut libera potestas, et duces exemplo potius quam imperio, si prompti, si conspicui, si ante aciem agant, admiratione 2 praesunt. ceterum neque animadvertere neque vincire, ne verberare quidem nisi sacerdotibus permissum, non

Priests. quasi in poenam nec ducis iussu, sed velut deo imperante, quem adesse bellantibus credunt. effigiesque et signa quaedam detracta lucis 3 in proelium ferunt; quodque praecipuum fortitudinis incitamentum est, non casus nec fortuita conglobatio turmam aut cuneum facit, sed familiae et propinquitates; et in proximo pignora, unde feminarum ululatus audiri, unde vagitus infantium. hi cuique sanctissimi 4

Influence of women in war; testes, hi maximi laudatores: ad matres, ad coniuges vulnera ferunt; nec illae numerare aut exigere plagas pavent, cibosque et hortamina pugnantibus gestant. memoriae proditur 8 quasdam acies inclinatas iam et labantis a feminis restitutas constantia precum et obiectu pectorum et monstrata comminus captivitate, quam longe inpatientius feminarum suarum nomine timent, adeo ut efficacius obligentur animi civitatum quibus inter obsides puellae quoque nobiles imperantur. inesse quin etiam sanctum 2

their prophetic powers. aliquid et providum putant, nec aut consilia earum aspernantur aut responsa neglegunt. vidimus sub divo Vespasiano Veledam diu apud plerosque numinis loco habitam; sed et olim Albrunam et compluris alias venerati sunt, non adulatione nec tamquam facerent deas.

Deorum maxime Mercurium colunt, cui certis diebus 9

Gods and mode of worship. humanis quoque hostiis litare fas habent. Herculem et Martem concessis animalibus placant. pars Sueborum et Isidi sacrificat: unde causa et origo peregrino sacro parum comperi nisi quod signum ipsum in modum liburnae figuratum docet advectam religionem. ceterum nec cohibere parietibus deos neque in ullam humani oris speciem adsimu-

lare ex magnitudine caelestium arbitrantur: lucos ac
nemora consecrant deorumque nominibus appellant secretum illud, quod sola reverentia vident.

10 Auspicia sortesque ut qui maxime observant: sortium
Divination consuetudo simplex. virgam frugiferae ar-
by lot. bori decisam in surculos amputant eosque
notis quibusdam discretos super candidam vestem temere
2 ac fortuito spargunt. mox, si publice consultetur, sacerdos civitatis, sin privatim, ipse pater familiae, precatus
deos caelumque suspiciens ter singulos tollit, sublatos
3 secundum impressam ante notam interpretatur. si prohibuerunt, nulla de eadem re in eundem diem consultatio;
sin permissum, auspiciorum adhuc fides exigitur. et illud
quidem etiam hic notum, avium voces volatusque interro-
Methods of gare: proprium gentis equorum quoque
4 augury. praesagia ac monitus experiri. publice
aluntur isdem nemoribus ac lucis, candidi et nullo mortali
opere contacti; quos pressos sacro curru sacerdos ac rex
vel princeps civitatis comitantur hinnitusque ac fremitus
5 observant. nec ulli auspicio maior fides, non solum
apud plebem, sed apud proceres, apud sacerdotes; se
enim ministros deorum, illos conscios putant. est et alia
observatio auspiciorum, qua gravium bellorum eventus
6 explorant. eius gentis cum qua bellum est captivum
quoquo modo interceptum cum electo popularium suorum, patriis quemque armis, committunt: victoria huius
vel illius pro praeiudicio accipitur.

11 De minoribus rebus principes consultant, de maiori-
The bus omnes, ita tamen ut ea quoque, quorum
'concilium. penes plebem arbitrium est, apud principes
2 pertractentur. coeunt, nisi quid fortuitum et subitum
incidit, certis diebus, cum aut incohatur luna aut impletur;
nam agendis rebus hoc auspicatissimum initium credunt.

nec dierum numerum, ut nos, sed noctium computant.
sic constituunt, sic condicunt: nox ducere diem videtur.
illud ex libertate vitium, quod non simul nec ut iussi 3
conveniunt, sed et alter et tertius dies cunctatione co-
euntium absumitur. ut turbae placuit, considunt armati. 4
silentium per sacerdotes, quibus tum et coercendi ius
est, imperatur. mox rex vel princeps, prout aetas cuique, 5
prout nobilitas, prout decus bellorum, prout facundia est,
audiuntur, auctoritate suadendi magis quam iubendi
potestate. si displicuit sententia, fremitu aspernantur; 6
sin placuit, frameas concutiunt: honoratissimum adsensus
genus est armis laudare.

    Licet apud concilium accusare quoque et discrimen 12
capitis intendere. distinctio poenarum ex
delicto. proditores et transfugas arboribus
suspendunt, ignavos et inbellis et corpore
infamis caeno ac palude, iniecta insuper crate, mergunt.
diversitas supplicii illuc respicit, tamquam scelera ostendi 2
oporteat, dum puniuntur, flagitia abscondi. sed et levioribus delictis pro modo poena: equorum pecorumque
numero convicti multantur. pars multae regi vel civitati,
pars ipsi qui vindicatur, vel propinquis eius exsolvitur.
eliguntur in isdem conciliis et principes, qui iura per 3
pagos vicosque reddunt; centeni singulis ex plebe
comites consilium simul et auctoritas adsunt.

Its judicial and elective functions.

    Nihil autem neque publicae neque privatae rei nisi 13
armati agunt. sed arma sumere non ante
cuiquam moris quam civitas suffecturum
probaverit. tum in ipso concilio vel principum aliquis vel pater vel propinqui scuto frameaque
iuvenem ornant: haec apud illos toga, hic primus iuventae honos; ante hoc domus pars videntur, mox rei
publicae. insignis nobilitas aut magna patrum merita 2

Investiture of youths with arms.

principis dignationem etiam adulescentulis adsignant:
ceteris robustioribus ac iam pridem probatis adgregantur.
3 nec rubor inter comites adspici. gradus quin etiam ipse
comitatus habet, iudicio eius quem sec-
tantur; magnaque et comitum aemulatio,
quibus primus apud principem suum locus, et principum,
4 cui plurimi et acerrimi comites. haec dignitas, hae vires,
magno semper et electorum iuvenum globo circumdari,
in pace decus, in bello praesidium. nec solum in sua
gente cuique, sed apud finitimas quoque civitates id
nomen, ea gloria est, si numero ac virtute comitatus
emineat; expetuntur enim legationibus et muneribus
ornantur et ipsa plerumque fama bella profligant.

The 'comitatus.'

14   Cum ventum in aciem, turpe principi virtute vinci,
turpe comitatui virtutem principis non
adaequare. iam vero infame in omnem
vitam ac probrosum superstitem principi
suo ex acie recessisse: illum defendere, tueri, sua quoque fortia facta gloriae eius adsignare praecipuum sacramentum est: principes pro victoria pugnant, comites
3 pro principe. si civitas in qua orti sunt longa pace et
otio torpeat, plerique nobilium adulescentium petunt
ultro eas nationes, quae tum bellum aliquod gerunt,
quia et ingrata genti quies et facilius inter ancipitia
clarescunt magnumque comitatum non nisi vi belloque
4 tueare: exigunt enim principis sui liberalitate illum
bellatorem equum, illam cruentam victricemque fra-
meam; nam epulae et quamquam incompti, largi tamen
apparatus pro stipendio cedunt. materia munificentiae
5 per bella et raptus. nec arare terram aut exspectare
annum tam facile persuaseris quam vocare hostem et
vulnera mereri. pigrum quin immo et iners videtur
sudore adquirere quod possis sanguine parare.

Relations 2 between 'princeps' and 'comitatus.'

Quotiens bella non ineunt, non multum venatibus, 15
plus per otium transigunt, dediti somno
ciboque. fortissimus quisque ac bellico-
sissimus nihil agens, delegata domus et penatium et
agrorum cura feminis senibusque et infirmissimo cuique
ex familia, ipsi hebent, mira diversitate naturae, cum
idem homines sic ament inertiam et oderint quietem.
mos est civitatibus ultro ac viritim conferre principibus 2
vel armentorum vel frugum, quod pro
honore acceptum etiam necessitatibus sub-
venit. gaudent praecipue finitimarum gentium donis, 3
quae non modo a singulis, sed et publice mittuntur, electi
equi, magnifica arma, phalerae torquesque; iam et pecuniam accipere docuimus.

Idleness in peace.

Presents to chiefs.

Nullas Germanorum populis urbes habitari satis notum 16
est, ne pati quidem inter se iunctas sedes.
colunt discreti ac diversi, ut fons, ut
campus, ut nemus placuit. vicos locant non in nostrum 2
morem conexis et cohaerentibus aedificiis: suam quisque
domum spatio circumdat, sive adversus casus ignis
remedium sive inscitia aedificandi. ne caementorum 3
quidem apud illos aut tegularum usus: materia ad omnia
utuntur informi et citra speciem aut delectationem.
quaedam loca diligentius inlinunt terra ita pura ac splen-
dente, ut picturam ac lineamenta colorum imitetur. solent 4
et subterraneos specus aperire eosque multo insuper fimo
onerant, suffugium hiemi et receptaculum frugibus, quia
rigorem frigorum eius modi locis molliunt, et si quando
hostis advenit, aperta populatur, abdita autem et defossa
aut ignorantur aut eo ipso fallunt quod quaerenda sunt.

Dwellings.

Tegimen omnibus sagum fibula aut, si desit, spina 17
consertum: cetera intecti totos dies iuxta
focum atque ignem agunt. locupletissimi

Clothing.

veste distinguuntur, non fluitante, sic ut Sarmatae ac
2 Parthi, sed stricta et singulos artus exprimente. gerunt et
ferarum pellis, proximi ripae neglegenter, ulteriores exqui-
sitius, ut quibus nullus per commercia cultus. eligunt
feras et detracta velamina spargunt maculis pellibusque
beluarum, quas exterior Oceanus atque ignotum mare
3 gignit. nec alius feminis quam viris habitus, nisi quod
feminae saepius lineis amictibus velantur eosque purpura
variant, partemque vestitus superioris in manicas non
extendunt, nudae bracchia ac lacertos; sed et proxima
18 pars pectoris patet. quamquam severa illic matrimonia,
nec ullam morum partem magis laudaveris.
Marriage. nam prope soli barbarorum singulis uxoribus
contenti sunt, exceptis admodum paucis, qui non libidine
sed ob nobilitatem plurimis nuptiis ambiuntur.

2   Dotem non uxor marito, sed uxori maritus offert.
Bridal intersunt parentes et propinqui ac munera
ceremonies. probant, munera non ad delicias muliebres
quaesita nec quibus nova nupta comatur, sed boves et
3 frenatum equum et scutum cum framea gladioque. in
haec munera uxor accipitur, atque in vicem ipsa armorum
aliquid viro adfert: hoc maximum vinculum, haec arcana
4 sacra, hos coniugalis deos arbitrantur. ne se mulier
extra virtutum cogitationes extraque bellorum casus putet,
ipsis incipientis matrimonii auspiciis admonetur venire
se laborum periculorumque sociam, idem in pace, idem
in proelio passuram ausuramque: hoc iuncti boves, hoc
5 paratus equus, hoc data arma denuntiant. sic vivendum,
sic pereundum: accipere se quae liberis inviolata ac
digna reddat, quae nurus accipiant rursusque ad nepotes
referantur.

19   Ergo saepta pudicitia agunt, nullis spectaculorum
inlecebris, nullis conviviorum irritationibus corruptae.

litterarum secreta viri pariter ac feminae ignorant. pau- 2
cissima in tam numerosa gente adul-
High standard of morality. teria, quorum poena praesens et maritis
permissa: abscisis crinibus nudatam coram
propinquis expellit domo maritus ac per omnem vicum
verbere agit; publicatae enim pudicitiae nulla venia: non
forma, non aetate, non opibus maritum invenerit. nemo 3
enim illic vitia ridet, nec corrumpere et corrumpi saeculum vocatur. melius quidem adhuc eae civitates, in
quibus tantum virgines nubunt et cum spe votoque
uxoris semel transigitur. sic unum accipiunt maritum 4
quo modo unum corpus unamque vitam, ne ulla cogi-
tatio ultra, ne longior cupiditas, ne tamquam maritum
sed tamquam matrimonium ament. numerum liberorum 5
finire aut quemquam ex adgnatis necare flagitium habetur,
plusque ibi boni mores valent quam alibi bonae leges.

In omni domo nudi ac sordidi in hos artus, in haec **20**
corpora, quae miramur, excrescunt. sua
Bringing up of children. quemque mater uberibus alit, nec ancillis
aut nutricibus delegantur. dominum ac servum nullis 2
educationis deliciis dignoscas: inter eadem pecora, in
eadem humo degunt, donec aetas separet ingenuos,
virtus adgnoscat. sera iuvenum venus, eoque inexhausta 3
pubertas. nec virgines festinantur; eadem iuventa, similis proceritas: pares validaeque miscentur, ac robora
parentum liberi referunt.

Sororum filiis idem apud avunculum qui ad patrem 4
honor. quidam sanctiorem artioremque
Rules of succession. hunc nexum sanguinis arbitrantur et in
accipiendis obsidibus magis exigunt, tamquam et animum firmius et domum latius teneant. heredes tamen 5
successoresque sui cuique liberi, et nullum testamentum.
si liberi non sunt, proximus gradus in possessione fratres,

patrui, avunculi. quanto plus propinquorum, quanto
maior adfinium numerus, tanto gratiosior senectus; nec
ulla orbitatis pretia.

21	Suscipere tam inimicitias seu patris seu propinqui

Blood feud. quam amicitias necesse est; nec implaca-
biles durant: luitur enim etiam homicidium
certo armentorum ac pecorum numero recipitque satis-
factionem universa domus, utiliter in publicum, quia
periculosiores sunt inimicitiae iuxta libertatem.

2	Convictibus et hospitiis non alia gens effusius indulget

Hospitality. quemcumque mortalium arcere tecto nefas
habetur; pro fortuna quisque apparatis
epulis excipit. cum defecere, qui modo hospes fuerat,
monstrator hospitii et comes; proximam domum non
3 invitati adeunt. nec interest: pari humanitate accipiuntur. notum ignotumque quantum ad ius hospitis
nemo discernit. abeunti, si quid poposcerit, concedere
moris; et poscendi in vicem eadem facilitas. gaudent
muneribus, sed nec data imputant nec acceptis obligantur. [victus inter hospites comis.]

22	Statim e somno, quem plerumque in diem extrahunt,

Domestic lavantur, saepius calida, ut apud quos
habits. plurimum hiems occupat. lauti cibum
capiunt: separatae singulis sedes et sua cuique mensa.
tum ad negotia nec minus saepe ad convivia procedunt
2 armati. diem noctemque continuare potando nulli pro-
brum. crebrae, ut inter vinolentos, rixae raro conviciis,

Drunkenness saepius caede et vulneribus transiguntur.
3 **and its uses.** sed et de reconciliandis in vicem inimicis
et iungendis adfinitatibus et adsciscendis principibus, de
pace denique ac bello plerumque in conviviis consultant,
tamquam nullo magis tempore aut ad simplices cogita-
4 tiones pateat animus aut ad magnas incalescat. gens

non astuta nec callida aperit adhuc secreta pectoris
licentia ioci; ergo detecta et nuda omnium mens. postera
die retractatur, et salva utriusque temporis ratio est:
deliberant, dum fingere nesciunt, constituunt, dum errare
non possunt.

Potui umor ex hordeo aut frumento, in quandam 23
similitudinem vini corruptus: proximi ripae
Drink and diet. et vinum mercantur. cibi simplices, agrestia poma, recens fera aut lac concretum: sine apparatu,
sine blandimentis expellunt famem. adversus sitim 2
non eadem temperantia. si indulseris ebrietati sugge-
rendo quantum concupiscunt, haud minus facile vitiis
quam armis vincentur.

Genus spectaculorum unum atque in omni coetu 24
idem. nudi iuvenes, quibus id ludicrum
Sword dance. est, inter gladios se atque infestas frameas
saltu iaciunt. exercitatio artem paravit, ars decorem, 2
non in quaestum tamen aut mercedem: quamvis audacis
lasciviae pretium est voluptas spectantium. aleam, quod 3
mirere, sobrii inter seria exercent, tanta lucrandi per-
dendive temeritate, ut, cum omnia defecerunt, extremo
ac novissimo iactu de libertate ac de
Gambling. corpore contendant. victus voluntariam 4
servitutem adit: quamvis iuvenior, quamvis robustior,
adligari se ac venire patitur. ea est in re prava pervicacia; ipsi fidem vocant. servos condicionis huius per
commercia tradunt, ut se quoque pudore victoriae
exsolvant.

Ceteris servis non in nostrum morem descriptis per 25
familiam ministeriis utuntur: suam quis-
Slaves. que sedem, suos penates regit. frumenti
modum dominus aut pecoris aut vestis ut colono iniungit,
et servus hactenus paret: cetera domus officia uxor ac

2 liberi exsequuntur. verberare servum ac vinculis et opere coercere rarum: occidere solent, non disciplina et severitate, sed impetu et ira, ut inimicum, nisi quod 3 inpune est. liberti non multum supra servos sunt, raro

Freedmen. aliquod momentum in domo, numquam in civitate, exceptis dumtaxat iis gentibus quae regnantur. ibi enim et super ingenuos et super nobiles ascendunt: apud ceteros inpares libertini libertatis argumentum sunt.

26 Faenus agitare et in usuras extendere ignotum;

Usury unknown. ideoque magis servatur quam si vetitum esset.

Agri pro numero cultorum ab universis in vices

Occupation and tillage of land. occupantur, quos mox inter se secundum dignationem partiuntur; facilitatem par-
2 tiendi camporum spatia praestant. arva per annos mutant, et superest ager. nec enim cum ubertate et amplitudine soli labore contendunt, ut pomaria conserant et prata separent et hortos rigent: sola 3 terrae seges imperatur. unde annum quoque ipsum non in totidem digerunt species: hiems et ver et aestas intellectum ac vocabula habent, autumni perinde nomen ac bona ignorantur.

27 Funerum nulla ambitio: id solum observatur ut

Funeral corpora clarorum virorum certis lignis 2 **customs.** crementur. struem rogi nec vestibus nec odoribus cumulant: sua cuique arma, quorundam igni et equus adicitur. sepulcrum caespes erigit: monumentorum arduum et operosum honorem ut gravem defunctis aspernantur. lamenta ac lacrimas cito, dolorem et tristitiam tarde ponunt. feminis lugere honestum est, viris meminisse.

Haec in commune de omnium Germanorum origine 3
ac moribus accepimus: nunc singularum
gentium instituta ritusque, quatenus differant, quae nationes e Germania in Gallias
commigraverint, expediam.

Transition to account of particular tribes.

Validiores olim Gallorum res fuisse summus aucto- 28
rum divus Iulius tradit; eoque credibile
est etiam Gallos in Germaniam trans-
gressos: quantulum enim amnis obstabat
quo minus, ut quaeque gens evaluerat, occuparet per-
mutaretque sedes promiscuas adhuc et nulla regnorum
potentia divisas? igitur inter Hercyniam silvam Rhe- 2
numque et Moenum amnes Helvetii, ulteriora Boii,
Gallica utraque gens, tenuere. manet adhuc Boiohaemi
nomen significatque loci veterem memoriam quamvis
mutatis cultoribus.

Gallic immigrants into Germany.

Sed utrum Aravisci in Pannoniam ab Osis Germa- 3
norum natione an Osi ab Araviscis in
Germaniam commigraverint, cum eodem
adhuc sermone institutis moribus utantur,
incertum est, quia pari olim inopia ac libertate eadem
utriusque ripae bona malaque erant.

Peoples of doubtful origin.

Treveri et Nervii circa adfectationem Germanicae 4
originis ultro ambitiosi sunt, tamquam
per hanc gloriam sanguinis a similitudine
et inertia Gallorum separentur. ipsam
Rheni ripam haud dubie Germanorum populi colunt,
Vangiones, Triboci, Nemetes. ne Ubii quidem, quam- 5
quam Romana colonia esse meruerint ac libentius
Agrippinenses conditoris sui nomine vocentur, origine
erubescunt, transgressi olim et experimento fidei super
ipsam Rheni ripam collocati, ut arcerent, non ut custo-
direntur.

Supposed and real Germans in Gaul.

29 Omnium harum gentium virtute praecipui Batavi non

Batavi. multum ex ripa, sed insulam Řheni amnis
colunt, Chattorum quondam populus et
seditione domestica in eas sedes transgressus, in quibus
2 pars Romani imperii fierent. manet honos et antiquae
societatis insigne; nam nec tributis contemnuntur nec
publicanus atterit; exempti oneribus et collationibus et
tantum in usum proeliorum sepositi, velut tela atque
3 arma, bellis reservantur. est in eodem obsequio et

Mattiaci. Mattiacorum gens; protulit enim magnitudo populi Romani ultra Rhenum ultraque veteres terminos imperii reverentiam. ita sede
finibusque in sua ripa, mente animoque nobiscum agunt,
cetera similes Batavis, nisi quod ipso adhuc terrae suae
solo et caelo acrius animantur.

4 Non numeraverim inter Germaniae populos, quam-

People of the quam trans Rhenum Danuviumque con-
'Tithe Lands.' sederint, eos qui decumates agros exercent:
levissimus quisque Gallorum et inopia audax dubiae
possessionis solum occupavere; mox limite acto pro-
motisque praesidiis sinus imperii et pars provinciae
habentur.

30 Ultra hos Chatti initium sedis ab Hercynio saltu

Chatti; incohant, non ita effusis ac palustribus
situation and locis ut ceterae civitates in quas Germania
customs. patescit: durant siquidem colles, paulatim rarescunt, et Chattos suos saltus Hercynius prose-
2 quitur simul atque deponit. duriora genti corpora, stricti
artus, minax vultus et maior animi vigor. multum, ut
inter Germanos, rationis ac sollertiae: praeponere electos,
audire praepositos, nosse ordines, intellegere occasiones,
differre impetus, disponere diem, vallare noctem, fortunam inter dubia, virtutem inter certa numerare, quodque

rarissimum nec nisi Romanae disciplinae concessum, plus reponere in duce quam in exercitu. omne robur 3 in pedite, quem super arma ferramentis quoque et copiis onerant: alios ad proelium ire videas, Chattos ad bellum. rari excursus et fortuita pugna. equestrium sane virium id proprium, cito parare victoriam, cito cedere: velocitas iuxta formidinem, cunctatio propior constantiae est.

Et aliis Germanorum populis usurpatum raro et 31 privata cuiusque audentia apud Chattos in consensum vertit, ut primum adoleverint, crinem barbamque submittere, nec nisi hoste caeso exuere votivum obligatumque virtuti oris habitum. super 2 sanguinem et spolia revelant frontem, seque tum demum pretia nascendi rettulisse dignosque patria ac parentibus ferunt: ignavis et inbellibus manet squalor. fortissimus 3 quisque ferreum insuper anulum (ignominiosum id genti) velut vinculum gestat, donec se caede hostis absolvat. plurimis Chattorum hic placet habitus, iamque canent 4 insignes et hostibus simul suisque monstrati. omnium penes hos initia pugnarum; haec prima semper acies, visu nova: nam ne in pace quidem cultu mitiore mansuescunt. nulli domus aut ager aut aliqua cura: prout 5 ad quemque venere, aluntur, prodigi alieni, contemptores sui, donec exsanguis senectus tam durae virtuti inpares faciat

Their military vows.

Proximi Chattis certum iam alveo Rhenum quique 32 terminus esse sufficiat Usipi ac Tencteri colunt. Tencteri super solitum bellorum 2 decus equestris disciplinae arte praecellunt; nec maior apud Chattos peditum laus quam Tencteris equitum. sic instituere maiores: posteri imitantur. hi lusus in- 3 fantium, haec iuvenum aemulatio: perseverant senes. inter familiam et penates et iura successionum equi 4

Usipi and Tencteri.

traduntur: excipit filius, non ut cetera, maximus natu sed prout ferox bello et melior.

33 Iuxta Tencteros Bructeri olim occurrebant: nunc

Chamavi, Angrivarii, Bructeri.

Chamavos et Angrivarios inmigrasse narratur, pulsis Bructeris ac penitus excisis vicinarum consensu nationum, seu superbiae odio seu praedae dulcedine seu favore quodam erga nos deorum; nam ne spectaculo quidem proelii invidere.

2 super sexaginta milia non armis telisque Romanis, sed, quod magnificentius est, oblectationi oculisque ceciderunt. maneat, quaeso, duretque gentibus, si non amor nostri, at certe odium sui, quando urgentibus imperii fatis nihil iam praestare fortuna maius potest quam hostium discordiam.

34 Angrivarios et Chamavos a tergo Dulgibini et Chasu-

Dulgibini, Chasuarii, Frisii.

arii cludunt aliaeque gentes haud perinde memoratae, a fronte Frisii excipiunt. maioribus minoribusque Frisiis vocabulum est ex modo virium. utraeque nationes usque ad Oceanum Rheno praetexuntur ambiuntque inmensos insuper

2 lacus et Romanis classibus navigatos. ipsum quin etiam Oceanum illa temptavimus: et superesse adhuc Herculis

Pillars of Hercules.

columnas fama vulgavit, sive adiit Hercules, seu quidquid ubique magnificum est, in

3 claritatem eius referre consensimus. nec defuit audentia Druso Germanico, sed obstitit Oceanus in se simul atque in Herculem inquiri. mox nemo temptavit, sanctiusque ac reverentius visum de actis deorum credere quam scire.

35 Hactenus in occidentem Germaniam novimus; in sep-

Chauci, noblest of the Germans.

tentrionem ingenti flexu recedit. ac primo statim Chaucorum gens, quamquam incipiat a Frisiis ac partem litoris occupet, omnium quas exposui gentium lateribus obtenditur, donec in Chattos usque sinuetur. tam inmensum ter- 2 rarum spatium non tenent tantum Chauci sed et implent, populus inter Germanos nobilissimus quique magnitudinem suam malit iustitia tueri. sine cupiditate, sine 3 inpotentia, quieti secretique nulla provocant bella, nullis raptibus aut latrociniis populantur. id praecipuum 4 virtutis ac virium argumentum est, quod, ut superiores agant, non per iniurias adsequuntur; prompta tamen omnibus arma ac, si res poscat, exercitus, plurimum virorum equorumque; et quiescentibus eadem fama.

In latere Chaucorum Chattorumque Cherusci nimiam 36

Cherusci. ac marcentem diu pacem inlacessiti nutrierunt: idque iucundius quam tutius fuit, quia inter inpotentes et validos falso quiescas; ubi manu agitur, modestia ac probitas nomina superioris sunt. ita 2 qui olim boni aequique Cherusci, nunc inertes ac stulti vocantur; Chattis victoribus fortuna in sapientiam cessit.

Fosi tracti ruina Cheruscorum et Fosi, con- 3 termina gens. adversarum rerum ex aequo socii sunt, cum in secundis minores fuissent.

Eundem Germaniae sinum proximi Oceano Cimbri 37

Cimbri. tenent, parva nunc civitas, sed gloria ingens. veterisque famae lata vestigia manent, utraque ripa castra ac spatia, quorum ambitu nunc quoque metiaris molem manusque gentis et tam magni exitus fidem. sescentesimum et quadragesimum 2

Digression on Germany's long resistance to Rome. annum urbs nostra agebat, cum primum Cimbrorum audita sunt arma, Caecilio Metello ac Papirio Carbone consulibus. ex quo si ad alterum imperatoris Traiani consulatum computemus, ducenti ferme et decem anni colliguntur: tam diu Germania vincitur. medio tam longi aevi 3

S. 4

spatio multa in vicem damna.   non Samnis, non Poeni,
non Hispaniae Galliaeve, ne Parthi quidem saepius admonuere : quippe regno Arsacis acrior est Germanorum
4 libertas.   quid enim aliud nobis quam caedem Crassi,
amisso et ipse Pacoro, infra Ventidium deiectus Oriens
5 obiecerit?   at Germani Carbone et Cassio et Scauro
Aurelio et Servilio Caepione Gnaeoque Mallio fusis vel
captis quinque simul consularis exercitus populo Romano, Varum trisque cum eo legiones etiam Caesari
abstulerunt; nec inpune C. Marius in Italia, divus Iulius
in Gallia, Drusus ac Nero et Germanicus in suis eos
sedibus perculerunt: mox ingentes C. Caesaris minae
6 in ludibrium versae.   inde otium, donec occasione dis-
cordiae nostrae et civilium armorum expugnatis legionum
hibernis etiam Gallias adfectavere; ac rursus inde
pulsi proximis temporibus triumphati magis quam victi
sunt.

38   Nunc de Suebis dicendum est, quorum non una, ut

Suebic   Chattorum Tencterorumve, gens; maiorem
tribes,   enim Germaniae partem obtinent, propriis
cc. 38—45.   adhuc nationibus nominibusque discreti,

quamquam in commune Suebi vocentur.

2   Insigne gentis obliquare crinem nodoque substringere :

Their cha-   sic Suebi a ceteris Germanis, sic Suebo-
racteristics.   rum ingenui a servis separantur; in aliis
gentibus seu cognatione aliqua Sueborum seu, quod
saepe accidit, imitatione, rarum et intra iuventae spa-
3 tium: apud Suebos usque ad canitiem horrentem
capillum retro agunt, ac saepe in ipso vertice religatur;
4 principes et ornatiorem habent.   ea cura formae, sed
innoxia; neque enim ut ament amenturve, in altitudinem quandam et terrorem adituri bella comptius hostium
oculis ornantur.

Vetustissimos se nobilissimosque Sueborum Semno- **39**
nes memorant; fides antiquitatis religione
Semnones;
their ancient firmatur. stato tempore in silvam auguriis 2
worship. patrum et prisca formidine sacram omnes
eiusdem sanguinis populi legationibus coeunt caesoque
publice homine celebrant barbari ritus horrenda primordia. est et alia luco reverentia: nemo nisi vinculo 3
ligatus ingreditur, ut minor et potestatem numinis prae
se ferens. si forte prolapsus est, attolli et insurgere
haud licitum: per humum evolvuntur. eoque omnis 4
superstitio respicit, tamquam inde initia gentis, ibi regnator omnium deus, cetera subiecta atque parentia.
adicit auctoritatem fortuna Semnonum: centum pagis
habitant, magnoque corpore efficitur ut se Sueborum
caput credant.

Contra Langobardos paucitas nobilitat: plurimis ac **40**
valentissimis nationibus cincti non per
Langobardi. obsequium sed proeliis ac periclitando
tuti sunt.

Reudigni deinde et Aviones et Anglii et Varini et
Eudoses et Suarines et Nuithones flumini-
Seven tribes
which worship bus aut silvis muniuntur. nec quicquam 2
Nerthus. notabile in singulis, nisi quod in commune Nerthum, id est Terram matrem, colunt eamque
intervenire rebus hominum, invehi populis arbitrantur.
est in insula Oceani castum nemus, dicatumque in eo
vehiculum, veste contectum; attingere uni sacerdoti
concessum. is adesse penetrali deam intellegit vectam- 3
que bubus feminis multa cum veneratione prosequitur.
laeti tunc dies, festa loca, quaecumque adventu hospitio-
que dignatur. non bella ineunt, non arma sumunt; 4
clausum omne ferrum; pax et quies tunc tantum nota,
tunc tantum amata, donec idem sacerdos satiatam con

5 versatione mortalium deam templo reddat. mox vehiculum et vestes et, si credere velis, numen ipsum secreto
lacu abluitur. servi ministrant, quos statim idem lacus
haurit. arcanus hinc terror sanctaque ignorantia, quid
sit illud quod tantum perituri vident.

41   Et haec quidem pars Sueborum in secretiora Ger-

Hermun-
duri, friendly
to Rome.

maniae porrigitur: propior, ut, quo modo
paulo ante Rhenum, sic nunc Danuvium
sequar, Hermundurorum civitas, fida Romanis; eoque solis Germanorum non in ripa commer-
cium, sed penitus atque in splendidissima Raetiae
2 provinciae colonia. passim et sine custode trànseunt;
et cum ceteris gentibus arma modo castraque nostra
ostendamus, his domos villasque patefecimus non concupiscentibus. in Hermunduris Albis oritur, flumen
inclutum et notum olim; nunc tantum auditur.

42   Iuxta Hermunduros Naristi ac deinde Marcomani et

Naristi,
Marcomani,
Quadi.

Quadi agunt. praecipua Marcomanorum
gloria viresque, atque ipsa etiam sedes
pulsis olim Boiis virtute parta. nec Naristi Quadive degenerant. eaque Germaniae velut frons
2 est, quatenus Danuvio praecingitur. Marcomanis Qua-
disque usque ad nostram memoriam reges mansere ex
gente ipsorum, nobile Marobodui et Tudri genus (iam et
externos patiuntur), sed vis et potentia regibus ex auctoritate Romana. raro armis nostris, saepius pecunia iu-
vantur, nec minus valent.

43   Retro Marsigni, Cotini, Osi, Buri terga Marcoma-

Four hill-
tribes, two of
them not
German.

norum Quadorumque cludunt. e quibus
Marsigni et Buri sermone cultuque Suebos
referunt: Cotinos Gallica, Osos Pannonica
lingua coarguit non esse Germanos, et quod tributa
2 patiuntur. partem tributorum Sarmatae, partem Quadi

ut alienigenis imponunt: Cotini, quo magis pudeat,
et ferrum effodiunt. omnesque hi populi pauca cam-
pestrium, ceterum saltus et vertices montium [iugumque]
insederunt. dirimit enim scinditque Suebiam continuum 3
montium iugum, ultra quod plurimae gentes agunt, ex
Divisions of quibus latissime patet Lygiorum nomen
the Lygii. in pluris civitates diffusum. valentissimas
nominasse sufficiet, Harios, Helveconas, Manimos, Helisios, Nahanarvalos. apud Nahanarvalos antiquae religionis 4
lucus ostenditur. praesidet sacerdos muliebri ornatu,
Worship of sed deos interpretatione Romana Castorem
Alcis. Pollucemque memorant. ea vis numini,
nomen Alcis. nulla simulacra, nullum peregrinae super- 5
stitionis vestigium; ut fratres tamen, ut iuvenes venerantur. ceterum Harii super vires, quibus 6
Harii. enumeratos paulo ante populos antece-
dunt, truces insitae feritati arte ac tempore lenocinantur:
nigra scuta, tincta corpora; atras ad proelia noctes legunt
ipsaque formidine atque umbra feralis exercitus terrorem
inferunt, nullo hostium sustinente novum ac velut infernum adspectum; nam primi in omnibus proeliis oculi
vincuntur.

   Trans Lygios Gotones regnantur, paulo iam adductius 44
Gotones, quam ceterae Germanorum gentes, non-
Rugii, dum tamen supra libertatem. protinus
Lemovii. deinde ab Oceano Rugii et Lemovii;
omniumque harum gentium insigne rotunda scuta, breves
gladii et erga reges obsequium.

   Suionum hinc civitates, ipso in Oceano, praeter viros 2
Suiones; armaque classibus valent. forma navium
their ships, eo differt quod utrimque prora paratam
semper adpulsui frontem agit. nec velis ministrantur
nec remos in ordinem lateribus adiungunt: solutum,

ut in quibusdam fluminum, et mutabile, ut res poscit,
3 hinc vel illinc remigium. est apud illos et opibus honos,
their   eoque unus imperitat, nullis iam excep-
4 government.   tionibus, non precario iure parendi. nec
arma, ut apud ceteros Germanos, in promiscuo, sed clausa
sub custode, et quidem servo, quia subitos hostium in-
cursus prohibet Oceanus, otiosae porro armatorum manus
facile lasciviunt: enimvero neque nobilem neque in-
genuum, ne libertinum quidem armis praeponere regia
utilitas est.

45   Trans Suionas aliud mare, pigrum ac prope inmotum,
The limit of   quo cingi cludique terrarum orbem hinc
the world.   fides, quod extremus cadentis iam solis
fulgor in ortus edurat adeo clarus ut sidera hebetet;
sonum insuper emergentis audiri formasque equorum et
radios capitis adspici persuasio adicit. illuc usque et
fama vera tantum natura.

2   Ergo iam dextro Suebici maris litore Aestiorum gentes
Aestii.   adluuntur, quibus ritus habitusque Sueborum, lingua Britannicae propior. ma-
3 trem deum venerantur. insigne superstitionis formas
aprorum gestant: id pro armis omniumque tutela securum deae cultorem etiam inter hostis praestat. rarus
4 ferri, frequens fustium usus. frumenta ceterosque fructus
patientius quam pro solita Germanorum inertia laborant.
sed et mare scrutantur, ac soli omnium sucinum, quod
Amber.   ipsi glesum vocant, inter vada atque in
5   ipso litore legunt. nec quae natura quaeve
ratio gignat, ut barbaris, quaesitum compertumve; diu
quin etiam inter cetera eiectamenta maris iacebat, donec
luxuria nostra dedit nomen. ipsis in nullo usu: rude
legitur, informe profertur, pretiumque mirantes acci-
6 piunt. sucum tamen arborum esse intellegas, quia terrena

quaedam atque etiam volucria animalia plerumque inter-
lucent, quae implicata umore mox durescente materia
cluduntur. fecundiora igitur nemora lucosque sicut 7
orientis secretis, ubi tura balsamaque sudantur, ita occi-
dentis insulis terrisque inesse crediderim, quae vicini
solis radiis expressa atque liquentia in proximum mare
labuntur ac vi tempestatum in adversa litora exundant.
si naturam sucini admoto igni temptes, in modum tae- 8
dae accenditur alitque flammam pinguem et olentem;
mox ut in picem resinamve lentescit.

Suionibus Sitonum gentes continuantur. cetera simi- 9

Sitones. les uno differunt, quod femina dominatur:
in tantum non modo a libertate sed etiam
a servitute degenerant.

Hic Suebiae finis. Peucinorum Venetorumque et 46

Peoples of Fennorum nationes Germanis an Sarma-
doubtful race. tis adscribam dubito, quamquam Peucini,
1 Peucini. quos quidam Bastarnas vocant, sermone
cultu sede ac domiciliis ut Germani agunt. sordes
omnium ac torpor procerum; conubiis mixtis nonnihil

2. Veneti. in Sarmatarum habitum foedantur. Veneti 2
multum ex moribus traxerunt; nam quid-
quid inter Peucinos Fennosque silvarum ac montium
erigitur latrociniis pererrant. hi tamen inter Germanos
potius referuntur, quia et domos figunt et scuta gestant
et pedum usu ac pernicitate gaudent: quae omnia diversa
Sarmatis sunt in plaustro equoque viventibus. Fennis 3
mira feritas, foeda paupertas: non arma, non equi,

3. Fenni. non penates; victui herba, vestitui pelles,
cubile humus: solae in sagittis spes, quas
inopia ferri ossibus asperant. idemque venatus viros pariter ac feminas alit; passim enim comitantur partemque
praedae petunt. nec aliud infantibus ferarum imbrium- 4

que suffugium quam ut in aliquo ramorum nexu contegantur: huc redeunt iuvenes, hoc senum receptaculum.
5 sed beatius arbitrantur quam ingemere agris, inlaborare domibus, suas alienasque fortunas spe metuque versare: securi adversus homines, securi adversus deos. rem difficillimam adsecuti sunt, ut illis ne voto quidem opus esset.

6   Cetera iam fabulosa: Hellusios et Oxionas ora ho-
    Fabulous   minum vultusque, corpora atque artus
    tribes.   ferarum gerere: quod ego ut incompertum
in medium relinquam.

NOTES ON THE AGRICOLA

CHAPTER I

1. antiquitus usitatum, 'a practice of the past,' in apposition with the phrase *clarorum...tradere*, itself the object of *omisit*. For the sake of brevity Tacitus not infrequently uses a neuter adjective or perfect participle passive appositionally, where one might have expected a relative clause. Cp. *usurpatum, Germ.* 31. 1.

ne nostris quidem temporibus...aetas, equivalent to *ne nostra quidem aetas*, but the words *nostris temporibus* afford a better contrast to *antiquitus. aetas,* 'the age,' personified.

quamquam incuriosa suorum, 'although neglectful of her own.' Cp. *vetera extollimus, recentium incuriosi, Ann.* II. 88, a passage which suggests that *suorum* here is neuter. Note *quamquam* used without a finite verb, like *quamvis* in classical prose.

supergressa est, 'has risen superior to,' a post-Augustan word.

ignorantiam recti et invidiam, 'insensibility to righteousness and envy.' *rectum, honestum* and *virtus* are practically synonyms. Excellence, Tacitus means, must be conspicuous enough to overcome the misunderstanding and prejudice which it inevitably excites, if it is ever to find a biographer.

2. pronum magisque in aperto, cp. 33. 4. *pronus,* 'downwards' (opposite to *arduus* 'uphill'), hence 'easy,' as in Sallust, *Jug.* 80 and 114. *in aperto* involves the metaphor of an open space, free of obstacles. Sall. *Jug.* 5 uses the phrase in the sense of 'evident,' imitating the Greek ἐν φανερῷ. This class of expression becomes very common after the Augustan age, cp. *in ambiguo, in medio, in aequo.* (See Peterson on *dial.* 18.)

ingenio, to be taken with *celeberrimus. celeber* in the sense of 'famous' is mainly post-Augustan.

sine gratia aut ambitione, with *prodendam. gratia* means 'favour,' 'partiality,' towards the subject of the biography, *ambitione* 'self-seeking' or 'self-advertisement' on the part of the author.

bonae tantum conscientiae pretio, 'simply by the reward of
a good conscience.' *conscientia,* 'consciousness,' then in particular
'consciousness of right and wrong,' so 'conscience.' *mala conscientia* occurs in Sall. *Jug.* 62, but *bona conscientia* is not found till
Celsus (ap. Quintil. II. 15. 32). Cicero uses *recta conscientia, ad
Att.* XIII. 20. 4. For *pretium,* 'reward,' cp. 12. 6, *Germ.* 24. 2.
Cornelius Nepos' Life of Atticus is the most important specimen of
Roman biography by a contemporary which survives from the first
century B.C. It gives a very clear portrait of the man but is somewhat too eulogistic.

3. ac plerique, 'and indeed many,' cp. 36. 2. *ac* in this
confirmatory sense is common in Tacitus, cp. 28. 5 *ac fuere.*

suam ipsi. *suam ipsos* (subject to *narrare*) or *suam ipsorum*
might have been expected. The nom. is due to the attraction of
plerique. Cp. Livy IV. 44 *causa ipse pro se dicta quindecim milibus
aeris damnatur,* where *ab ipso* would be quite unidiomatic. The
phrase *suam...narrare* is the object of *arbitrati sunt.*

fiduciam...morum, '(showed) confidence in their own
character.'

Rutilio. Publius Rutilius Rufus, soldier, lawyer, historian and
Stoic philosopher, was consul in 105 B.C. In 98 B.C., as *legatus* to
his friend Mucius Scaevola, then governor of Asia, he assisted him
in repressing the rapacity of the tax-farmers, and in revenge for
this some six years later was himself prosecuted for extortion and
convicted by a jury of capitalist *equites.* He retired to Smyrna, one
of the scenes of his alleged crimes, and refusing Sulla's offer of
restoration, devoted himself to literature. Cicero admired him
immensely (*de orat.* I. 53. 229), Velleius (II. 13. 2) called him the
best man of all time, and Seneca more than once alludes to him as a
model of patient endurance.

Scauro. M. Aemilius Scaurus, a rival of Rutilius and a promi-
nent aristocrat, was consul in 115 B.C. and again in 107, and
princeps senatus for 25 years. Cicero speaks of him with high
praise, but Sallust (*Jug.* 15) describes him as secretly vicious, and
he appears to have accepted bribes from Jugurtha. Like Rutilius
he played an important part in the Jugurthine war. He wrote his
autobiography in three books, which Cicero (*Brut.* 29. 112)
characterises as 'useful but read by nobody.' Still they are quoted
by several authors.

citra fidem, 'short of credit,' 'a reason for being discredited.'
Cp. 35. 2 *citra Romanum sanguinem, Germ.* 16. 3 *citra speciem,*
'short of beauty,' *dial.* 27. 2 *citra damnum,* 41. 5 *citra obtrecta-*

tionem. The use is common in Silver Latin but, curiously enough, does not occur in the *Histories* or the *Annals*.

adeo, 'to such an extent' or 'so true is it that.'

4. nunc, 'in these days,' as opposed to the happier past.

narraturo...incusaturus, 'when about to record the life of one who has passed away, I have had to request an indulgence which I should not have asked for, had I been going to arraign it.' There is emphasis on *defuncti*. A dead man might be supposed to be beyond the reach of misunderstanding and envy and the biographer therefore in less need of indulgence. But, says Tacitus, though Agricola is dead, the necessity of asking indulgence still remains, because the present age hates to hear panegyrics and welcomes attacks upon virtue; *obtrectatio et livor pronis auribus accipiuntur*, *Hist.* I. I.

opus fuit, perfect, because all the preceding passage 'has been' in the nature of an apology.

incusaturus, contrasted with *narraturo*, for a biography to a Roman would imply panegyric.

tam saeva, supply *sunt*. The sentence explains *nunc* above. Men are still hostile to virtue. Even though a brighter age is dawning, *tardiora sunt remedia quam mala*, 3. I. *tam* is rarely used like *adeo* to introduce an explanatory statement. Its presence here may be due to the occurrence of *adeo* a few lines back.

Many editors, including Gudeman, put no stop after *incusaturus*, which they construe with the following words, 'were I about to inveigh against times so cruel and hostile to instances of merit.' But a better contrast seems to be obtained by connecting *incusaturus* with *vitam defuncti hominis* (cp. Goodhart, *Class. Rev.* II. p. 226), and, as Furneaux points out, Tacitus *does* inveigh against Domitian's times in the next chapter and elsewhere in the book.

CHAPTER II

1. legimus, present tense. Wex holds that Tacitus refers to written records in order to exclude any doubt as to the terms of the indictment, incredible though they may seem. Reports of the trials would be found in the *acta senatus* or minutes of the Senate, which in part at least were, subject to the emperor's permission, published in the *acta diurna* or *acta populi*, the daily gazette of Rome. The items of news appear to have been posted on a placard in the forum, whence manuscript copies were made by slaves. See below for contributory reasons for the condemnation of the accused.

Gantrelle, offended by *legimus*, reads *exegimus*, 'we have lived through,' taking it with the preceding sentence *tam saeva...tempora.* This necessitates the alteration of *fuisse* to *fuit.*

Aruleno Rustico, dative of agent. Arulenus Rusticus, when tribune in 66 A.D., proposed to veto Thrasea's trial but was prevented by Thrasea himself (*Ann.* XVI. 26). He was a great friend of the younger Pliny (*Ep.* I. 14). Domitian put him to death in 93 A.D. 'because he was a philosopher and because he called Thrasea a saint' (Dio Cassius LXVII. 13). After his death Regulus, one of his accusers, published a book in which he named him 'the ape of the Stoics' (Pliny, *Ep.* I. 5).

Paetus Thrasea, the chief of the Stoic irreconcilables under Nero. He lost no opportunity of expressing his disgust with the imperial rule, till finally in 66 A.D. Nero *virtutem ipsam exscindere concupivit interfecto Thrasea Paeto* (*Ann.* XVI. 21). He was condemned in the Senate without being allowed to answer the charge against him. The news reached him while he was entertaining a party of philosophic friends in his garden. He opened his veins with the words *libamus Iovi Liberatori* (*Ann.* XVI. 35).

Herennio Senecioni. Herennius Senecio had been associated with his friend Pliny in the prosecution of Baebius Massa (see on 45. 1). He was tried at the same time as Rusticus (93 A.D.), his accuser being Mettius Carus (45. 1). Dio Cassius, LXVII. 13, says he was executed 'because in the course of a long life he had never sought any office after the quaestorship and because he had written the life of Priscus Helvidius.' Not to ask the emperor for office was a sign of disaffection.

Priscus Helvidius, son-in-law of Paetus Thrasea. He was banished on Thrasea's death, but returned under Galba, when he started, but ultimately dropped, the impeachment of Thrasea's accuser, Marcellus Eprius (*Hist.* IV. 6; see also IV. 43, *dial.* 6. 4). He was banished again for refusing to show proper respect to Vespasian and ultimately put to death in 73 A.D. (Suet. *Vespas.* 15). "He was unable to distinguish between the tyranny of a Nero and the good government of a Vespasian" (Bury). Tacitus greatly admired his Stoic principles (*Hist.* IV. 5). Juvenal, v. 36, speaks of wine,

> *quale coronati Thrasea Helvidiusque bibebant*
> *Brutorum et Cassi natalibus.*

saevitum, sc. *esse.*

triumviris, sc. *capitalibus.* The *triumviri* or *tresviri capitales,* a section of the *vigintiviri* (cp. Introd. p. x) had the superintendence of prisons and were responsible for the carrying out of

sentences. In another instance (*Ann.* IV. 35) the aediles were
charged with the duty of burning condemned books. It has been
supposed that the assignment of the office to the inferior *triumviri*
was intended as an additional ignominy.

in comitio ac foro, a recognised formula (cp. Pliny, *H.N.* XV.
20. 77), which by its redundancy seems to emphasise the publicity
of the act. The *comitium*, a square space at the northern end of
the forum close to the senate house, had been the meeting-place
of the old *comitia curiata* and was used for trials and the infliction
of punishments.

One copy at least of Senecio's panegyric escaped the flames,
that of Helvidius' wife, Fannia, who *tulit in exilium exilii causam*
(Pliny, *Ep.* VII. 19).

2. conscientiam generis humani, 'the world's knowledge of
the facts.' Cp. Cic. *de fin.* II. 9. 28 *hominum conscientia remota.*

arbitrabantur, sc. Domitian and his satellites.

expulsis...acta. The participles (aoristic) do not denote occur-
rences prior to the time of the main clause, but merely add
further facts. Cp. on 5. 1. The expulsion took place in 93 A.D.,
the year in which Senecio and Arulenus were put to death (Pliny,
Ep. III. 11).

omni bona arte, 'every noble accomplishment.' *ars*, particularly in the plural, is used of intellectual and moral qualities or
pursuits in all periods of Latin.

ne quid usquam honestum occurreret, epigram rather than
history. However noble the motives of the Stoics may have been,
their obstinate hostility to the imperial government, sometimes
culminating in a contemptuous refusal to take any part in public
affairs, made it impossible for even a good ruler like Vespasian to
refrain from repressive measures.

3. patientiae, 'subjection.' Cp. Sall. *Jug.* 31. 1.

ultimum, 'the extreme.' The allusion is to the later Republic,
when liberty degenerated into anarchy.

nos quid, sc. *vidimus quid ultimum esset.*

inquisitiones, 'espionage,' carried on by professional informers.
The system of *delatio*, inaugurated by Tiberius, was revived in all
its terrors by Nero and Domitian in the latter part of their reigns,
though at first they refused to countenance it.

commercio, lit. 'the interchange': tr. 'the power of speaking
and listening to one another.' Wex quotes Livy, XXXII. 32, *ex pro-
pinquo dicamus audiamusque invicem.* Cp. Thuc. IV. 22 λέγοντες
καὶ ἀκούοντες περὶ ἑκάστου ξυμβήσονται, a common Greek formula.

CHAPTER III

1. et, 'and yet,' a meaning not uncommon in Tacitus, cp. 9. 3.
quamquam, taking the subjunctive, although introducing a
fact. The construction is regular in Tacitus, though very rare in
Cicero.

primo statim, etc., 'at the very earliest dawn of a most happy
era.' See 44. 5 for similar phraseology. Nerva's reign did indeed
inaugurate the happiest period of the Roman Empire.

Nerva Caesar. M. Cocceius Nerva, an elderly lawyer, was
elected emperor by the Senate after Domitian's murder (Sept. 18th,
96 A.D.). The absence of *divus* with the emperor's name in this
passage has been taken as a proof that the *Agricola* was composed
before his death (Jan. 27th, 98). But this hypothesis is ruled out by
44. 5, which mentions Trajan as *princeps* (see note below) and so
cannot have been written while Nerva was still alive. Gudeman
thinks that the omission here may be due to the fact that as yet
there had been no formal consecration of the deceased emperor,
which may have been carried out on Trajan's return to Rome in 99.
divus is by no means always inserted with the name of a dead
emperor.

dissociabiles, 'incompatible,' a rare adjective, here equivalent
in meaning to *insociabilis*. In Hor. *Odes* I. 3. 22, *Oceano dissocia-*
bili, it has the active sense of 'dividing.'

principatum ac libertatem. Nerva was a mild ruler and constantly consulted the Senate on matters of administration. Hence
despotism seemed at an end. In these remarks Tacitus is only
voicing the general sentiment of the time. Cp. the famous inscription found on the Capitol *Libertati ab imp. Nerva Caesare Aug....*
restitutae and the legends *Libertas publica* and *Felicitas publica* on
coins. Writing about this time Martial says, XI. 5. 14, *si Cato*
reddatur, Caesarianus erit.

Nerva Traianus. M. Ulpius Traianus, a Spaniard, who had
seen much military service and was then legate of Upper Germany,
was adopted by Nerva and on Oct. 27th, 97 A.D., made junior
partner in the imperial power, *non solum successor imperii sed*
particeps etiam sociusque, Pliny, *Paneg.* 9. Three months later
Nerva died and Trajan became emperor (*princeps*, cp. 44. 5).

securitas publica, a personified abstraction often named on
coins; 'and although the national security has not only framed
hopes and prayers but has won the assurance, nay the substance,
of her prayers' fulfilment.' *ipsius voti*, lit. 'of her actual prayer,

emphasises the completeness of the realisation. With *votum ac spem* supply *conceperit* out of *adsumpserit*. For *robur*, 'reality,' 'substance,' cp. Cic. *pro Mur.* 28. 58 *firmamentum ac robur* ('substance,' 'gist') *totius accusationis;* Seneca, *de ira* I. 20. 7 *terribilia enim esse possunt; magnitudinem quidem, cuius firmamentum roburque bonitas est, non habebunt.*

tardiora, 'work less quickly.'

ingenia studiaque, 'genius and its pursuits' (C. and B.), with special reference to literature.

oppresseris, 'potential' subjunctive (not future-perfect indicative; forms of the 1st person like *videro, fecero,* used colloquially in the comedians and sometimes in Cicero with practically the same meaning as *videbo, faciam,* occur but rarely in later authors). The usage is particularly common in Tacitus; cp. 10. 7 *addiderim,* 12. 7 *crediderim,* 46. 3 *praeceperim,* Germ. 2. 1 *crediderim,* 5. 3 *nec... adfirmaverim,* 14. 5 *nec persuaseris,* 18. 1 *laudaveris,* 19. 2 *non invenerit, dial.* 18. 1 *vocaverimus.* For doubtful cases see 24. 1 and 33. 6.

subit, 'steals upon us,' a word of poetical associations.

2. quid, si, 'what (must be the case) if...?,' a rhetorical question equivalent to an additional and more forcible argument; 'nay more.'

quindecim annos, Domitian's reign, 81—96 A.D.

promptissimus, 'most active, energetic.'

ut ita dixerim, a formula apparently found only twice elsewhere and here due to Rhenanus (see note on text). For the perf. subjunct. cp. the common Silver expression *ut sic dixerim,* which tends to oust *ut ita dicam.* Cp. on 9. 4.

The phrase apologises for *nostri superstites,* 'surviving our own selves,' with which Draeger compares Seneca, *ep.* 30. 5 *videtur mihi vivere tamquam superstes sibi.*

iuvenes. Up to the age of 46 a Roman was *iunior,* beyond that age *senior.*

3. vel incondita...voce. For the affectation of modesty cp. Libanius, *or.* XI. κοινὸν τῶν ἐγκωμιαζόντων ἔθος λείπεσθαι φάσκειν τὴν αὑτῶν ἀσθένειαν τοῦ μεγέθους τῶν ἔργων οἷς προσάγουσι τὸν λόγον. Tacitus, it must be remembered, was making his first essay in historical composition.

memoriam, etc. Tacitus means that he is writing a work on Domitian's reign of terror and the blessings of Nerva's rule. In the *Histories,* as published between 104 and 109 A.D., he deals with the period from Galba to Domitian (69—96 A.D.), telling us

(*Hist.* I. 1) that 'he has reserved for his old age' a history of Nerva and Trajan. This scheme was never executed.

composuisse, 'to have composed.' He is thinking of the time of completion. Cp. I. 4 and *dial.* 31. 5 *dedisse operam dialecticae proficiet*.

professione, etc., 'as an expression of dutiful affection will stand approved or at least excused.' *professione* is a causal ablative.

CHAPTER IV

1. Foroiuliensium. Forum Julii, now Fréjus, on the coast of Gaul, S.W. of the modern Nice, was founded by Julius Caesar and became an important naval station.

procuratorem, etc., 'a procurator of the imperial house.' The procurators were the emperor's financial officers at home and abroad. They were sometimes made governors of the lesser imperial provinces, while in the greater their position corresponded to that of the quaestors in the senatorial provinces. "The title 'procurator Caesarum,' which occurs in a few passages and inscriptions, does not differ materially in meaning from the more usual 'proc. Augustorum'...and seems therefore to denote a man in the financial service of the imperial house" (H. Mattingly, *The Imperial Civil Service of Rome*, p. 98, where see note). Commentators on the present passage hold that *Caesarum* refers to service under different emperors, Augustus and Tiberius, but possibly the plural genitive had become stereotyped in the phrase.

quae equestris nobilitas est, 'a position which is the patent of equestrian nobility' or 'which is the crowning dignity of the equestrian order.' One of the most notable political innovations of the Empire was the formation of a regular *cursus honorum* for the *equites*, who were encouraged to undertake posts not unlike those provided by our own Civil Service—(some of these posts, it is true, were at first filled by freedmen, especially under Claudius, but after Vitellius they were almost entirely confined to *equites*). At the summit of this new *cursus honorum* were the procuratorships, especially those which were not merely financial inspectorships, but in themselves involved administration over lesser imperial provinces (see previous note). These posts were to the equestrian order what the curule offices were to the senatorial order, i.e. they conferred *nobilitas* on their holders, who became known as *equites illustres* or *splendidi*, in contrast to the equites *modici* or *municipales*. (Cp. Mommsen, *Röm. Staatsrecht* III. I. 563.)

Graecinus. Seneca, *de benef.* II. 21, says *si exemplo magni animi opus est, utamur Graecini Iulii, viri egregii, quem C. Caesar occidit ob hoc unum quod melior vir esset quam esse quemquam tyranno expediret.*

senatorii ordinis. Genitives and ablatives of description without the addition of a general name, e.g. *vir, homo,* are common in Tacitus ; cp. § 2 below. They sometimes occur even in Caesar, cp. *B.G.* I. 18 *Dumnorigem, summa audacia.*

eloquentiae perhaps in the broader sense of 'literature,' cp. *dial.* 10. 4 (Gudeman). He wrote a book on vines.

sapientiae, 'philosophy,' cp. **2. 2.** *philosophia* is rare in Tacitus, but see **4. 4.**

M. Silanum, father-in-law of Gaius (better known as Caligula, emperor 37—41 A.D.). In 38 Silanus was compelled by the emperor to commit suicide. Graecinus' death cannot have taken place till 39, as Agricola was not born till 40 (see on 44. 1). Wex argues that the tense of *abnuerat* suggests an interval between Graecinus' refusal and death.

2. sinu indulgentiaque, virtually a hendiadys, 'under her tender care.' Cp. Tacit. *dial.* 28 *filius...non in cella* ('garret') *emptae nutricis, sed gremio ac sinu matris educabatur,* which shows that the practice of putting out to nurse was common. See also *dial.* 29. 1 and cp. *Germ.* 20. 1.

honestarum artium. The *artes liberales* of the day were practically those of the mediaeval universities,—grammar, logic, rhetoric (the mediaeval *trivium*), music, arithmetic, geometry, astronomy (the *quadrivium*). Most of these are mentioned in *dial.* 30 in an account of Cicero's education.

3. peccantium, substantival, cp. 40. 3, 41. 1 ; 'from the temptations of unprincipled men.'

integram, 'stainless.' The *quod*-clause is subject to *arcebat.*

sedem ac magistram, 'the scene and guide' (C. and B.). Massilia, now Marseilles, a Greek colony founded by the Phocaeans in 600 B.C., is eulogised for its learning by Cicero (*pro Flacco,* 26. 63), while Strabo (IV. p. 181), writing about 20 A.D., speaks of it as a place of education more favoured by Romans than Athens itself, and as remarkable for the frugality and temperance of its inhabitants. According to Val. Max. II. 6. 7 the town was so careful of public morals that it prohibited the performance of mimes. Tacitus, *Ann.* III. 55 and Pliny, *Ep.* I. 14. 4, allude to provincial thriftiness, which sometimes degenerated into meanness and 'rusticity.' In the case of Massilia these exaggerations were prevented by its 'Greek refinement.'

locum...mixtum ac bene compositum, 'a place where...were mingled and happily blended.'

4. ultra quam, etc., explanatory of *acrius*. The long-standing prejudice against philosophy in Rome (cp. Cicero, *de off.* II. I. 2) reached its height under Nero, who in 66 A.D. started a persecution of philosophers. The cosmopolitan ideas of the Stoics, which made them despise the state 'in which the fortune of their birth had enlisted them' (Seneca, *de otio* 4. 1), their republican prejudices, and their sullen refusal to accept the imperial system, led to their withdrawal from public affairs and sometimes to actual disloyalty. Hence the danger of too much philosophy to 'a Roman and a future senator.' Nero's mother *a philosophia eum avertit, monens imperaturo contrariam esse,* Suet. *Nero,* 52. In *Hist.* IV. 5 Tacitus refers to philosophy as an excuse for quietism, *ingenium inlustre altioribus studiis iuvenis admodum dedit* (sc. *Helvidius Priscus*), non ut plerique, ut nomine magnifico segne otium velaret, *sed,* etc. The average Athenian felt very much as the Roman about philosophy. Cp. Plato, *Gorg.* 484 c, φιλοσοφία γάρ τοί ἐστιν, ὦ Σώκρατες, χαρίεν, ἄν τις αὐτοῦ μετρίως ἅψηται ἐν τῇ ἡλικίᾳ· ἐὰν δὲ περαιτέρω τοῦ δέοντος ἐνδιατρίψῃ, διαφθορὰ τῶν ἀνθρώπων.

hausisse, a vivid rhetorical substitute for *hausturum fuisse,* implying that he 'had absorbed and would have continued to absorb,' cp. 13. 4 *agitasse, ni...fuissent.* The *oratio recta* form would have been *hauriebat, ni,* etc., with which cp. 37. 1 *coeperant ni...opposuisset,* and Tacitus *passim.*

5. pulchritudinem ac speciem, 'beautiful ideal' (F.). *species* has philosophical associations, as representing the Greek εἶδος or ἰδέα. Cp. Cic. *orator* 5 *species eloquentiae, quam cernebat animo, re ipsa non videbat.*

magnae excelsaeque gloriae. For the 'glory' of a philosopher see *Hist.* II. 91 *aliis id ipsum placebat, quod neminem ex praepotentibus, sed Thraseam ad exemplar verae gloriae legisset.* Cp. *altioribus studiis* and *nomine magnifico* in the passage quoted on § 4. The Stoics believed that *bonus* (i.e. the philosopher) *tempore tantum a deo differt,* Seneca, *dial.* I. I. 5. Notice the heaping up of synonyms in this passage, so unlike Tacitus' later manner.

vehementius quam caute, irregular for *quam cautius,* cp. *Hist.* I. 83 *acrius quam considerate.* No other exact parallel is quoted, but Tacitus not infrequently blends positive with comparative, cp. I. 2, 6. 4, *Germ.* 32. 4, *Hist.* II. 99 *quantum hebes...tanto promptior.*

ratio atque aetas, 'the discretion of maturer years.' With *mitigavit* supply *eum* (cp. on 9. 1), 'tempered his ardour.' Cp. Cic. *pro Mur.* 31. 65 *te ipsum* (sc. *Catonem)...nunc et animi quodam impetu concitatum et vi naturae et ingenii elatum et recentibus praeceptorum studiis flagrantem iam usus flectet, dies leniet, aetas mitigabit.*

retinuitque, etc., 'and he retained from philosophy the quality of moderation, a most difficult achievement,'—especially under the Empire, when philosophy generally led to political fanaticism. Note the change of subject with *retinuit*. *modus* = τὸ μέσον, μεσότης, μηδὲν ἄγαν of the Greeks. Cp. Hor. *Sat.* I. I. 106 *est modus in rebus*, Lucan, II. 380, *haec duri immota Catonis | secta fuit servare modum finemque tenere.*

CHAPTER V

1. prima castrorum rudimenta, 'his military apprenticeship.'

Suetonio Paulino, governor of Britain 59—61 A.D. See cc. 14—16. In 42 A.D. he had reduced Mauretania. Tacitus, *Hist.* II. 25, speaks of him as *cunctator natura et cui cauta potius consilia cum ratione quam prospera ex casu placerent*, a passage which illustrates *moderato*, 'cautious,' here.

adprobavit, 'served to the satisfaction of.' *adprobo* here = 'cause to be approved,' as in 42. 2 and *Ann.* XV. 59 *dum posteris mortem adprobaret.*

electus, etc., 'and was selected as one whom he (Suetonius) thought worthy to share his quarters,' the subjunctive being generic or causal and the ablative denoting value (lit. 'estimated at' or 'as worth *contubernium*'); cp. *una victoria censebatur* 45. 1. The participle is aoristic, describing an act simultaneous with, not prior to, *adprobavit*. (Others interpret 'selected as one whom he might test by allowing him to share his quarters,' in which case the subjunct. is final and the abl. instrumental.) Young men of rank were often attached to the general's staff and lived in his quarters, *in contubernio ducis.* Cp. Frontinus IV. I. 12 *P. Rutilius consul cum secundum leges in contubernio suo filium posset habere, in legione militem fecit.*

2. nec, connecting with the preceding and negativing the following clause. 'Nor did Agricola in a frivolous spirit, like young men who turn the profession of war into a pastime, or through laziness make use of his titular tribunate and his inexperience for the purpose of enjoying himself and getting leave of absence.' *licenter*, explained by *more...vertunt*, seems to be balanced by *ad voluptates, segniter* by *ad commeatus.* ' Referring his title of tribunate to pleasure' (as to an end, cp. Cic. *Lael.* 9. 32 *qui...ad voluptatem omnia referunt*) is equivalent to 'using his titular tribunate for pleasure' or 'making pleasure the object of it.' A titular or honorary tribunate, the invention of Claudius, is described by Suetonius, *Claud.* 25, as *imaginariae militiae genus, quod vocatur supra numerum, quo absentes et titulo tenus fungerentur.* Inexperienced young men were naturally given only the title, not the duties, of a responsible office. The title was important to the aspirant after political honours, as the military tribunate qualified for the *cursus honorum.* See Introd. p. x.

noscere...nosci, etc., historic infinitives.

nihil adpetere in iactationem, 'he never courted any office for self-advertisement.' For *in* cp. 8. 2, etc.

simulque et anxius et intentus agere, 'and at the same time acted with both circumspection and energy.' This use of *anxius =* 'cautious, careful' is slightly strained, but cp. Val. Max. 8. 7. 7 *haec sunt attenti et anxii et nunquam cessantis studii praemia.*

3. exercitatior, 'more troubled,' a sense of *exercitatus* which seems commoner than is generally supposed ; cp. Cic. *Rep.* 6. 26 *curis agitatus et exercitatus animus,* Hor. *Epodes* 9. 31 *Syrtes Noto exercitatas,* Petr. 83 *senex exercitati vultus* ('with a worried face') *ibid.* 18 *forensibus ministeriis exercitati.* These instances show Büchner's *excitatior* to be unnecessary.

incensae coloniae. See 16. 1, *Ann.* XIV. 31—33. Three important towns, Camulodunum (Colchester), Londinium and Verulamium (St Albans), were destroyed in the revolt of Boudicca 61 A.D., but of these Camulodunum alone was a *colonia.* The others were only *municipia* (*Ann.* XIV. 33). Hence the plural *coloniae* is a rhetorical licence. The *veterani* of this passage formed the garrison of Camulodunum (*Ann.* XIV. 31).

intersepti, 'separated,' 'isolated.' Puteolanus has *intercepti,* but cp. *Hist.* III. 53 *intersepta Germanorum Raetorumque auxilia.* Technically there was but one *exercitus* in Britain ; the plural denotes its isolated units, for which see on c. 16, 1—2.

4. alterius, 'of another,' common in place of the rare genitive *alīus,* cp. 6. 5.

summa rerum, 'supreme command,' 'chief responsibility.'
The phrase may also mean 'the general situation,' as in *Hist.* II. 81,
III. 50.

in...cessit, 'fell to.' Earlier writers use *cedere* with a dative of
the person in this sense.

artem et usum, 'skill and experience.'

temporibus, either dative (cp. 31. 4), or ablative of point of
time, like *quibus*; 'times when a sinister construction was put upon
distinction.'

CHAPTER VI

1. degressus, the reading of the best MSS., unusual for *digressus*. The date of his return seems to be 61 A.D., of his
marriage 62.

Domitiam Decidianam, daughter of Decidius Domitius, who, as
we know from an inscription, had been a treasury official (*quaestor
aerarii*) and afterwards praetor under Claudius. See Furneaux *ad
loc.* The use of *natales* = 'descent' is post-Augustan.

decus ac robur, 'a source of prestige and material support.'
Some think that *robur* is to be explained in the same way as *subsidium* in § 3, where see note.

per mutuam caritatem et in vicem se anteponendo,
'through their mutual affection and by each putting the other
first.' The two expressions, though differing in construction,
are syntactically co-ordinate (cp. 41. 2) and explain *vixerunt
mira concordia.* With *in vicem se anteponendo* cp. *dial.* 25. 5 *in vicem
se obtrectaverunt.* See also 37. 5.

nisi quod. Tacitus' lust for epigram and brevity has led him to
omit important links in the thought. The passage may be filled out
thus: (each equally deserving the preference) except in so far as a
good wife merits greater praise (than a good husband), just as a bad
one merits more blame (than a bad husband). The balance, Tacitus
implies, is slightly in favour of Domitia. "By this observation,"
remarks Kritz, "Tacitus clearly wished to please his mother-in-law,
who was still living"; see 44. 4, 46. 3. *nisi quod*, often to be
translated by 'only,' 'but,' 'though,' limits a preceding statement
(cp. 16. 6, *Germ.* 17. 3, 25. 2) or, as here, something to be supplied
therefrom.

2. sors quaesturae. Each proconsular governor of a senatorial province was attended by a quaestor (in the case of Sicily
by two), who managed the finances of the province and acted as the

governor's deputy in both military and civil affairs. The distribution of provinces among the quaestors was determined by lot.

Salvium Titianum. L. Salvius Otho Titianus, elder brother of the emperor Otho, was proconsul of Asia in 63—64 A.D. The legal age for the quaestorship was 25. Agricola was born in 40 A.D. and was quaestor in 64. The fact that he had a son born to him in the previous year probably enabled him to stand a year earlier under the *lex Papia Poppaea.* See note on § 3.

parata, 'exposed to,' sc. *esset,* easily supplied from below. The wealth and temptations of Asia are often referred to, cp. Cic. *Epp. ad Q. F.* I. I. 19, *pro Mur.* 5. 12, 9. 20, Livy XXXIV. 4, XXXIX. 6.

pro consule, here in the nom., above in the accus. case. (The MSS. read *proconsul* and *proconsulem,* contrary to Tacitean usage.)

quantalibet, etc., 'by any degree of indulgence was willing to purchase a mutual concealment of crime,' cp. *Hist.* I. 72 *vices impunitatis.*

3. auctus, not infrequent in the sense of 'having an addition to one's family.' See *Ann.* II. 84 and Plaut. *Truc.* 384, Cic. *ad Att.* I. 2 *filiolo me auctum scito,* Seneca, *Oed.* 881.

ibi. See *Ann.* III. 33—34 for a debate in the Senate on a motion that no magistrate should be accompanied to his province by his wife. The motion was defeated.

in subsidium, probably with reference to the provisions of the *lex Papia Poppaea de maritandis ordinibus* of 9 A.D., whereby a married magistrate or candidate was given precedence over an unmarried, and one who had more children over one who had less; cp. *Ann.* II. 51 and XV. 19 (where fictitious adoptions to circumvent the law are mentioned). See Furneaux, appendix to *Ann.* III.

sublatum. By formally lifting the new-born child the father showed that he acknowledged it and intended to rear it. *suscipio* is similarly used.

inter quaesturam ac tribunatum plebis, qualifying *annum* to be understood from *tribunatus annum,* an awkwardness due to a desire to avoid repetition. For the adjectival use of a prepositional phrase cp. *sub Nerone temporum* below. A year was the usual interval between the tenure of the quaestorship and the tribunate. Agricola's tribunate seems to have fallen in 66 A.D.

quiete et otio, a favourite collocation, see 21. 1, 42. 2. Modal ablatives are employed with great freedom by Tacitus, Draeger, § 60. In this passage, as Stuart points out, Tacitus may be thinking of the contrast between Agricola's discreet inactivity and the rashness of

Arulenus Rusticus, who was probably his colleague in the tribunate. See on 2. 1.

4. **torpor**, adopted by Fossataro (cp. *Hist.* II. 99), is perhaps the best, though hardly a convincing, suggestion for *certior* of the MSS., *torpor et silentium* balancing *quiete et otio*. *tenor* (Rhenanus) is not a Tacitean word and is less likely than *torpor* to have been corrupted into *certior*. The date of Agricola's praetorship is 68 A.D.

iurisdictio. At this period besides the *praetor urbanus* and the *praetor peregrinus*, whose functions were still primarily judicial, as many as 16 other praetors were sometimes appointed, only part of whom engaged in judicial work. Their chief duty was to celebrate public games at their own expense.

inania honoris, 'the vain shows of office'; cp. *inania famae*, *Ann.* II. 76, *inania belli*, *Hist.* II. 69.

rationis, presumably meaning 'economy' (cp. its primary sense of 'calculation'), but the sense seems unexampled. Gudeman reads *moderationis*, supposing that *mode-* has fallen out after *medio* (written m̄d̄o). But we should have expected Tacitus to describe Agricola's expenditure as 'moderate,' not as 'half way between moderation and profusion.' The singular expression *ludos...medio... duxit*, 'conducted games in a course between,' seems modelled on the analogy of *funus, pompam ducere*.

uti longe, etc., either 'because avoiding extravagance, winning closer to distinction,' extravagance in public shows being regarded as vulgarity, or, if the comparative *propior* is not pressed, 'while avoiding extravagance, yet not missing distinction.' The latter sense, though perhaps less naturally derivable from the Latin, is probably what Tacitus intended. Note the irregular combination of positive and comparative, *longe...propior*, for the sake of euphony.

5. **tum**, in 68 A.D., the year of his praetorship. Agricola was commissioned to examine the temple treasures with a view to tracing and recovering what had been stolen. After the great fire at Rome in 64 A.D. Nero had despoiled the temples in the city, as well as in the provinces (*sacrilegium Neronis*; cp. *Ann.* XV. 45 *inque eam praedam etiam di cessere, spoliatis in urbe templis*); and it appears that other persons had availed themselves of the licence of the times to plunder on their own account (*cuius alterius sacrilegium*). It was the objects stolen by these individuals that Agricola succeeded in recovering.

fecit ne instead of *fecit* (*effecit*) *ut non*, a not uncommon construction occurring even in Cicero, cp. *de fin.* IV. 4. 10 *ars efficit ne*

necesse sit. ne...sensisset 'proved not to have felt,' 'entirely ceased
to feel,' cp. Pliny, *paneg.* 40 *effecisti ne malos principes habuissemus,*
'that we as good as never had bad emperors.' Such rhetorical
pluperfects express the completeness of the result attained.

CHAPTER VII

1. **sequens annus**, 69 A.D., the year which saw four emperors,
Galba, Otho, Vitellius, Vespasian. Tacitus often, as here, personi-
fies *annus*, cp. 22. 1.

2. **classis Othoniana**, etc. In March 69 Otho's fleet was
operating against the district of the Maritime Alps, which had
declared for Vitellius. Otho's troops roamed through the country
and, exasperated by the resistance of a body of mountaineers,
vented their rage upon Intimilium,—*municipium Albintimilium*, as
it is called in *Hist.* II. 13, now Vintimiglia, some 30 miles east of
Nice.

suis, more emphatic than *eius*; 'on her own estate.'

3. **sollemnia pietatis**, 'the customary rites which affection
demands,' funeral observances, not the funeral itself. (Cp. Catullus,
CI.) His mother probably died in March; Agricola could not have
reached Intimilium from Rome for a month or so. Indeed Tacitus'
words suggest that Agricola was only on his way when the news
of Vespasian's elevation reached him.

nuntio, etc., 'overtaken by the news of Vespasian's attempt
upon the empire.' On July 1st the legions at Alexandria swore
allegiance to Vespasian, and on July 3rd the army in Judaea took the
oath to him in person (*Hist.* II. 79).

4. **Mucianus.** M. Licinius Crassus Mucianus, appointed
governor of Syria in 67 A.D., had urged Vespasian to make himself
emperor and secured for him the allegiance of Syria (*Hist.* II. 76, 80).
He was commissioned to act against Vitellius (*Hist.* II. 82) and
arriving in Rome shortly after Vitellius' death (Dec. 21st, 69) took
complete control of affairs (*Hist.* IV. 11).

iuvene admodum Domitiano. He was 18. After Vitellius'
murder Vespasian's younger son, Domitian, was saluted Caesar at
Rome, and 'paying as yet no attention to public affairs played the
part of emperor's son by debauchery and intrigue' (*Hist.* III. 86,
IV. 2). Domitian's name headed despatches and edicts, but the
real power was in the hands of Mucianus (*Hist.* IV. 39).

fortuna, 'elevation,' cp. 13. 5; common in the sense of 'imperial rank.'

5. **integre**, 'honourably,' i.e. he was not to be bribed by persons wishing to escape military service. The levy, apparently held in Italy (a rare proceeding—see Furneaux's note), would be necessary to repair the losses in the year of confusion.

vicesimae legioni, stationed in Britain, at Chester. The other legions then in Britain were the Second and the Ninth. The Fourteenth, which had been recalled in 68 and sent back by Vitellius about May 69, was finally withdrawn in the summer of 70, perhaps before Agricola's arrival. For *tarde...transgressae* cp. *Hist.* III. 44. The Second legion, which had been commanded by Vespasian in the Claudian invasion, was chiefly responsible for attaching Britain to Vespasian's cause 'not without some disturbance among the other legions which contained a number of centurions and soldiers promoted by Vitellius.' Detachments of three British legions (II, IX and XX) had fought against the Vespasianists at Cremona (*Hist.* III. 22).

ubi, = *apud quam legionem*, 'where the retiring officer was reported to be acting disloyally.' The *decessor*, below called *legatus praetorius*, was Roscius Caelius, who early in 69 quarrelled with the governor, or *legatus consularis*, Trebellius Maximus (cp. 16. 3—5) and was charged by him with disloyalty (*seditio*) and the subversion of discipline. Caelius gained so strong a following that Trebellius had to flee for safety to Vitellius (*Hist.* I. 60). After Vespasian's accession Caelius was still reported disloyal, this time to the new emperor. But, adds Tacitus, 'as a matter of fact' (*quippe*) the trouble was perhaps due more to the unruliness of the legion and the weakness of the commander than to the commander's disloyalty.

legatis quoque consularibus nimia, 'too much even for the consular legates,' viz. the governors of the province, Trebellius and his successor Bolanus (8. 1). Imperial provinces occupied by more than one legion were governed by ex-consuls. Ex-praetors were put in command of single legions (cp. Agricola's own case) or of provinces occupied by single legions or containing no troops. For the sense of *nimia* cp. Vell. Paterc. II. 32 *Pompeium nimium iam liberae reipublicae*.

incertum...an, a favourite parenthetical formula in Tacitus, with *utrum* omitted; *Hist.* IV. 6, *Ann.* I. 11, XIV. 51, XV. 38.

6. **rarissima**, etc., i.e. Agricola 'with singular modesty' said very little about his measures for restoring discipline, thereby giving the impression that he had found the troops loyal and obedient (*bonos*) on his arrival.

CHAPTER VIII

1. Vettius Bolanus appointed by Vitellius to succeed Trebellius in the summer of 69. He had seen service in the East under Corbulo in 62 (*Ann.* XV. 3) and after his British command was pro-consul of Asia.

feroci, 'warlike.'

ne incresceret. Agricola is the subject; 'to avoid becoming conspicuous.'

peritus. The use of adjectives with explanatory infinitives, doubtless due in part to Greek influence, is classical only in poetry but occurs not infrequently in later prose. Draeger, *S. und S.*, § 152 b cites *certus, properus, manifestus, suspectus, facilis, suetus* as thus used by Tacitus.

utilia honestis miscere, 'to combine interest with duty'; i.e. he never studied his own advantage at the expense of his duty to his superiors.

2. brevi, etc. Agricola probably reached Britain in the latter part of 70, while Petilius Cerialis arrived early in 71. Cerialis had already seen service in Britain as commander of the 9th legion which was cut up by the Iceni in Boudicca's rebellion of 61 (*Ann.* XIV. 32). He was one of Vespasian's most trusted generals and had just suppressed the revolt of Civilis (*Hist.* V. 21). For *consularem* see note on 7. 5.

virtutes, sc. *Agricolae*. *spatium exemplorum*, 'a field for display,' wanting under Bolanus' regime.

in, 'with a view to,' cp. *in famam* below, 5. 2, 10. 1, etc.

ex eventu, 'on the strength of the result.'

3. auctorem, 'his director,' 'chief.' *fortunam*, 'his success.' For the sentiment cp. *Germ.* 14. 2.

extra, as in *Hist.* I. 49 *magis extra vitia quam cum virtutibus.* Cp. the use of *citra*, 1. 3.

nec, 'but not.' Cp. note on *et*, 3. 1.

CHAPTER IX

1. revertentem, 'on his return,' instead of *reversum*, cp. *ingredienti*, 18. 6. The aoristic use of the present participle occurs sporadically in prose writers as well as in poets, e.g. in Cicero, Livy, and especially Sallust (*Iug.* 15. 1, 35. 10, 113. 1). Agricola seems to have returned in 73 A.D.

inter patricios adscivit. Julius Caesar in 45 and Augustus in

29 B.C. had in accordance with legislative enactment replenished the depleted patrician class by the admission of new families. Claudius and Vespasian did the same in virtue of their censorial powers. See *Ann.* XI. 25. The patriciate was now mainly a social distinction. The offices still confined to it (e.g. that of *rex sacrificulus*) were quite unimportant.

Aquitaniae. As delimited by Augustus, the province extended from the Pyrenees and Narbonese Gaul to the Loire.

splendidae...dignitatis, genitive of description, cp. 4. 1; 'a post of the very highest distinction in respect of its administrative duties and because of the prospect of the consulship which it held out.' Aquitania was an imperial province administered by a legate of praetorian rank. There are several recorded instances of governors of Aquitania receiving the consulship, e.g. that of Galba, the future emperor (Suet. *Galba* 6).

destinarat, sc. *eum,* not infrequently omitted in Tacitus, cp. 4. 5.

2. subtilitatem, 'a nice discernment.'

secura, 'unconcerned,' i.e. 'summary.'

obtusior, 'somewhat blunt,' neglectful of fine distinctions. *ac,* contrasted with *et* above, shows that the following words amplify *obtusior.*

manu, 'with a high hand,' cp. *Germ.* 36. 1.

3. naturali prudentia, 'thanks to his natural good sense,' (or the ablative may be one of quality, cp. 4. 1).

togatos, 'civilians,' as opposed to soldiers, who wore the *sagum* or *sagulum,* cp. *Hist.* II. 20. The point is that a soldier, used to the rough and ready methods of military justice, might well have been a failure in civil affairs; not so Agricola, who 'conducted business in a deft and equitable manner.'

iam vero, 'further,' 21. 2, *Germ.* 14. 2, a Ciceronian phrase.

tempora curarum remissionumque, 'his periods of business and relaxation.'

conventus, 'courts.' Provincial governors went on circuit through the towns of their provinces and held assemblies for the transaction of judicial (cp. *iudicia* here) and other business. Cp. Caes. *B. G.* I. 54, V. 1.

poscerent, subjunctive in a frequentative sense, common in Livy and Tacitus, though very rare in earlier writers. See note on 13. 1.

et, 'and yet,' as in 3. 1. Cp. *nec,* 8. 3.

nulla...persona, 'he no longer wore the mask of officialdom.'

tristitiam...exuerat, a difficult and perhaps spurious passage. *exuerat,* 'had rid himself of' is loosely used for 'had kept free from.' It implies, not that Agricola had ever actually possessed these vices, but that as a provincial governor he might naturally be expected to have possessed them. So in *Ann.* VI. 25 the words *Agrippina feminarum vitia exuerat*, 'A. had put off all feminine weaknesses,' do not mean that she had ever manifested these weaknesses. *avaritiam* is very awkward, as it anticipates *abstinentiam*, etc., in § 4. Moreover, the sentence comes in very abruptly and spoils the run of the passage. For we can hardly take *tristitiam*, etc., as explanatory of *nulla ultra potestatis persona*; that would make Tacitus say of his hero, 'he showed he was no longer the official by ceasing to be moody, conceited and grasping'! A full-stop, it seems, must be placed at *persona*, and the following words, in spite of their abruptness, regarded as an entirely new thought. One is tempted to follow Wex in expelling the clause as an unintelligent marginal gloss on *nulla...persona*.

4. facilitas, 'easy manner,' 'affability.' *amorem*, 'his popularity.'

fuerit. Cp. *haud fuerit longum*, *Hist.* II. 2; *neque dici decuerit*, *Ann.* III. 39; *non decorum fuerit*, *Ann.* XIV. 56. The usage is late and illustrates a growing fondness on the part of Silver Latin for the perfect subjunctive. See notes on 3. 1 and 2.

Tac. means that to call Agricola honest would be to suggest that that was the best that could be said about him.

5. famam, 'that last infirmity of noble mind' (Milton). Cp. *Hist.* IV. 6, *etiam sapientibus cupido gloriae novissima exuitur.* Even Stoic professors, at least the later ones, admitted it to be *propter se praepositam et sumendam*, Cic. *de fin.* III. 17. 57.

per artem. Governors often employed underhand methods to procure complimentary addresses and votes of thanks. See *Ann.* XV. 20—22, Dio Cass. LVI. 25.

collegas, governors of neighbouring provinces.

procuratores, the emperor's financial agents, one in each province, cp. on 4. 1. The plural perhaps denotes successive procurators during Agricola's governorship. As the procurator was directly responsible to the emperor and so more or less independent of the governor, friction constantly arose between the two. The governor and the procurator belonged to different orders, the senatorial and the equestrian, rivalry between which is a marked feature of the imperial civil service. Cp. note on 16. 3.

atteri, 'to suffer loss of authority,' 'to be flouted,' a strange use of the word, which does not appear to be elsewhere applied to persons in this metaphorical sense. Cp. however, Sallust *Cat.* 16

ubi eorum famam atque pudorem attriverat. Here indeed *atteri* seems almost to be put for *famam* or *auctoritatem atteri*, 'to have his dignity impaired.' For another sense of the word see *Germ. 29. 2.*

6. minus triennium, A.D. 74—77. Note the idiomatic omission of *quam.* Augustus made it a rule that the governors of imperial provinces should not hold office for less than three years except in case of misbehaviour, or for more than five years (Dio Cass. LII. 23). Tiberius liked to prolong commands indefinitely (*Ann.* I. 80).

statim, a very remarkable use of an adverb where we should have expected an adjective agreeing with *spem*; 'with the immediate prospect.'

dari, vivid present for future, 'was waiting to be given him.'

in hoc, 'to this effect.' *hoc* is accusative.

7. aliquando et eligit, 'sometimes it actually makes the choice,' i.e. hits upon the right man and leads to his appointment. Note that the epigram forms an iambic senarius.

egregiae tum spei, 'then a maiden of noble promise'; cp. *per spes surgentis Iuli,* Verg. *Aen.* VI. 364, X. 524. Born in 64 A.D. she was about thirteen years old at the time of her marriage. Roman girls frequently married at thirteen, generally before sixteen. Tacitus must have been some ten years older than his wife.

post consulatum. Under the Empire the consulship was not tenable for the whole year, but for two-monthly or four-monthly periods. The *consules ordinarii,* who assumed office on January 1st, held it, at least under the Flavian emperors, for four months, the rest of the year being parcelled out among *consules suffecti.* Agricola was *consul suffectus* in 77 A.D., perhaps in the latter part of the year, and according to the common and most probable view took up his British command in the summer of 78 (*media iam aestate transgressus,* 18. 1). Another view places the beginning of his governorship, as well as his consulship, in 77. If he was consul in May and June, 77, he might well have reached Britain by the following August, supposing that he was not long detained by his daughter's marriage or by pontifical duties (see R. K. McElderry, *Class. Rev.* XVIII. 459).

pontificatus. The college of pontiffs normally comprised fifteen members under the presidency of the emperor as *pontifex maximus.* The emperor had the right of selecting members, his nominations being formally ratified by the Senate. The pontiffs had a general supervision of religion, the calendar, state archives, wills and adoptions.

CHAPTER X

1. scriptoribus, dative of agent, cp. 2. 1. Descriptions of Britain were given by Caesar, Pomponius Mela (about 45 A.D.) and the elder Pliny (d. 79 A.D.), in addition to Livy and Rusticus. The earliest writer on Britain was the famous Greek traveller, Pytheas of Massilia, who visited Britain and parts of northern Europe about 325 B.C. His work exists only in fragments. Other Greek authors who dealt with Britain are the Stoic philosopher, Posidonius (d. 51 B.C.), who wrote from personal knowledge, Diodorus Siculus (40 B.C.), and Strabo (d. about 24 A.D.).

in comparationem, etc., 'to provoke comparison of diligence or ability.' *in,* as in 5. 2, *in iactationem.*

ita, because the conquest resulted in more accurate knowledge.

quae priores...eloquentia percoluere, 'matters which my predecessors have treated with a brilliant literary finish.'

rerum fide, 'on the guarantee of facts,' or 'with truth of facts' (Furneaux).

2. spatio ac caelo, 'in respect of its extent and geographical position.' *caelum,* the quarter of the sky under which a cou try lies, a term of astronomical geography.

in occidentem, etc. So Caes. *B. G.* v. 13, *alterum (latus) vergit ad Hispaniam atque occidentem solem.* Strabo, the chief geographical authority of the time, ignoring the peninsula of Brittany and the Bay of Biscay, regarded the coast of Gaul as stretching south-west in almost a straight line from Germany to the north-east corner of Spain, more or less parallel to the coast of Britain, the south-west angle of which lay opposite to, and not a great distance from, the end of the Pyrenees, conceived as running from north to south. The north coast of Spain, which he supposed to have a decided north-westerly inclination, thus lay somewhat west of Britain.

Gallis, dative of agent.

etiam inspicitur, 'is actually in sight of.'

nullis contra terris, sc. *positis,* ablative of description, cp. 16. 4, *nullis castrorum experimentis.* Caes. *B. G.* v. 13 gives the same account.

3. Livius, in the lost book, where he described Caesar's invasions.

Fabius Rusticus, a favourite of Seneca (*Ann.* XIII. 20), wrote a history of Nero's reign (*Ann.* XIV. 2, XV. 61). His account of

Britain would naturally find a place in the story of Boudicca's revolt (see c. 16). The belief that Rusticus also wrote on Claudius is apparently due solely to the notion that his description of Britain would come more naturally in an account of Claudius' invasion, the first since the time of Caesar. (See Schanz, II. 2, p. 340.)

eloquentissimi, the highest compliment that could be paid to a Roman historian, who was judged by his 'style' rather than his fidelity to fact. See Quint. X. 1. 31—34, where the poetic quality of historical composition is brought out.

oblongae scutulae vel bipenni, 'to an oblong dish or axe-head,' a difficult passage. *bipennis*, properly a double-headed axe, is here commonly taken as a general term for axe. Britain *citra Caledoniam*, i.e. south of the Forth and Clyde, is not at all like a double axe, but may be roughly compared to a single one, which from its narrow end at the handle gradually widens out towards the cutting edge. (See however note on § 4.) *scŭtula* is a dish, probably of quadrilateral form, and as *vel* indicates, must bear some sort of resemblance to a *bipennis*. The probability is that Livy and Rusticus realised that Britain, exclusive of Caledonia, was four-sided, not triangular as Caesar supposed, Livy thinking of it as an oblong with the north side more or less equal to the south, Rusticus, with later and more accurate information, as a hatchet-shaped figure with the north side considerably shorter than the south. Ancient geographers are fond of making comparisons with common objects. Thus Strabo compares the world to a chlamys or Greek mantle (II. 5. 14, p. 118), the Peloponnese to a plane leaf (II. 1. 30, p. 83 *ad fin.*), and Spain to the outstretched hide of an animal (III. 1. 3, p. 137).

scutula is a technical term of geometry in Censorinus (3rd cent. A.D.), *scutula, id est rhombos, quod latera paria habet nec angulos rectos*, frag. 7, *de figuris*; and it possibly has a similar sense in Vitruvius VII. 1 (speaking of a pavement), *nulli gradus* ('uneven-nesses') *in scutulis aut trigonis aut quadratis seu favis exstent*, where *scutulis* seems to mean lozenge-shaped plates. The meaning rhomb is improbable in the present passage, because (1) Britain does not in the least resemble a rhomb, and (2) a rhomb and an axe are too dissimilar to be joined by *vel*. The notion that *scutula* means a trapezium is ruled out by the extreme unlikelihood that a word meaning dish would come to be used of so irregular a figure. For another, to me improbable, explanation of *scutula* here see T. G. Tucker in *Class. Rev.* 1901, p. 46.

4. et est, etc., 'and it has that shape' (i.e. is axe-shaped) 'this side of Caledonia, whence the report that it also has it as a whole.' If we take *bipenni* in its strict sense of a double-headed axe, with which Rusticus compared the whole island, we must suppose that Tacitus agrees to the simile so far as regards the southern portion of the island, but not as regards the northern, which, he adds, is like a wedge. Even so, we should have to take *ea facies* to mean the shape of an axe, not of a double-axe. For the adverbial *in universum*, cp. 11. 3.

sed. E, owing to its double version of the passage (see note on text), gives both *est* and *sed*. *sed* is almost certainly right, for *est* is much better away, while an adversative particle is urgently wanted.

transgressis, 'if you cross,' i.e. into Caledonia, an instance of the so-called 'dative of the person judging,' common in both Latin and Greek, particularly in topographical contexts.

procurrentium, etc., 'of lands jutting out with what now actually is the furthest coast-line.' *litore* is probably ablative of description, meaning the shore of the projecting lands, which *iam* contrasts with the expected ending at the isthmus between the Forth and the Clyde (cp. J. W. E. Pearce, *ad loc.*). Others take *extremo iam litore* as a local ablative referring to the isthmus itself, 'where the shore seems already to end' (D. R. Stuart), but it is difficult to get the idea of 'seeming' out of the Latin.

5. novissimi, 'remotest,' as in *Ann.* 11. 24, *novissimum ac sine terris mare.*

adfirmavit, 'definitely proved.' The belief that Britain was a triangular island goes back to Pytheas. Cp. H. F. Tozer, *History of Ancient Geography*, p. 156. For the circumnavigation, which however was not complete, see 38. 4.

Orcadas, the Orkneys. *incognitas*, 'unexplored' (F.) rather than 'unknown,' for Pytheas seems to have touched there (Elton, *Origins of English History*, p. 71). Mela III. 6 says they are thirty in number, *angustis inter se diductae spatiis*, while Pliny, *H. N.* IV. 30. 103, with a similar comment, reckons them as forty.

6. Thyle. What the Romans saw was doubtless Mainland, the chief of the Shetland Islands. This they naturally identified with Thule, the half-mythical land, which Pytheas, apparently on hearsay, described as the northernmost of the British Islands, six days' sail from Britain, on the Arctic circle and near the frozen ocean (Tozer, *op. cit.*, p. 159). Pytheas' Thule some identify with Mainland, others with Iceland, and Mr Rice Holmes with Scandinavia (*Ancient Britain, etc.*, p. 226).

hactenus iussum, 'their orders went only so far,' a reason why Thule was only 'seen at a distance.'

sed, 'but to proceed,' after the historical digression. Cp. the use of *ceterum,* II. I.

mare pigrum, etc., cp. *Germ.* 45. 1, perhaps partly explained by the strong tides and adverse currents which still make navigation difficult in the Orkneys. But the notion of the sluggishness of northern seas is ultimately derived from Pytheas who, according to Strabo II. 4. 1, said that there land, sea and air were all confused together into a mass resembling the πλεύμων θαλάττιος, or jelly-fish, which could neither be walked over nor sailed through. Pytheas was perhaps thinking of rotten ice. The rhetoricians of the Empire adorned Alexander's adventures in the Far East with tales of a *mare pigrum.* See the elder Seneca's first *suasoria, passim,* and Curt. IX. 4. 18, *immobiles undas in quibus emoriens natura defecerit.*

perhibent, etc., 'they say is not even raised by winds so much (as other seas).' The second member of a comparison is often omitted after *perinde.* Cp. *Germ.* 5. 4 and examples in Lewis and Short's Dict.

rariores, sc. *sunt.* Seneca *Quaest. Nat.* V. 13. 2 enlarges on the effect of obstacles in the production of strong winds. The Atlantic is perhaps less liable to sudden squalls and less 'choppy' than the Mediterranean. Caesar noticed that the waves in the Channel were smaller, though he put it down to the constant change of tide (*B. G.* V. 1).

7. neque...ac, a very uncommon collocation.

multi rettulere, e.g. Aristotle, Pytheas, the first Greek to note the influence of the moon on the tides, and Posidonius, who produced a fairly complete theory of tides.

addiderim, 'I may add,' see 3. 1.

fluminum, 'currents.' *mare* is probably subject to *ferre,* though others take *ferre* intransitively, 'set in different directions.'

litore, etc., 'flow or ebb only on the coast.'

ambire, 'winds in and out.'

velut in suo, 'as though in its own realm.'

CHAPTER XI

1. ut inter barbaros, 'as is usual among barbarians,' cp. 18. 5.

habitus corporum, 'physical characteristics,' *Germ.* 4. 2.

ex eo argumenta, 'from that fact (i.e. the variation) arguments are drawn.'

2. rutilae...comae, etc., see *Germ.* 4. 2, where the Germans are similarly described. We should have expected the Caledonians to have been Celts, and Tacitus' description of them as tall and red haired is quite in harmony with this view. Tallness and fairness, according to the unanimous testimony of the ancients, were characteristic of both Gauls (or Celts) and Germans, the only difference between the races being that the Germans were the taller and the more red-haired of the two (Strabo VII. 1, 2, p. 290). If the Caledonians possessed Celtic attributes in an exaggerated degree, a Roman would naturally describe them as Germans. However, it is not impossible that some of the Caledonians came from Germany or Scandinavia (see Rice Holmes, *op. cit.*, p. 418).

colorati, 'swarthy,' the regular word for dark-complexioned races, e.g. Indians (Verg. *Georg.* IV. 293). *torti*, 'curly.' The Silures occupied the south-east corner of Wales with Herefordshire, Monmouthshire and the Forest of Dean. Tacitus' theory that they came by sea from Spain is certainly wrong and is due to the erroneous notion that Spain lay near the west coast of Britain (see on 10. 2). They were probably a Celtic tribe with a large admixture of an earlier, dark-featured, non-Aryan population, 'Iberian' only in the modern ethnological sense of the term, as indicating a small, dark, long-skulled race which inhabited various parts of the Mediterranean basin, Spain included, in the later Stone Age (see Rice Holmes, *op. cit.* pp. 398-9).

proximi, etc., 'those nearest to the Gauls' (viz. those living in the south-east of Britain) 'also resemble them.' Caesar *B. G.* V. 14 remarks on the similarity between the customs of Gaul and Kent.

seu, etc., 'whether because the effect of their (common) origin persists, or whether...' Note the change of construction from participle to finite verb after the second *seu*, as in *Ann.* II. 21, etc.

procurrentibus...terris, ablative of reason, 'the two countries projecting different (i.e. opposite) ways,' Gaul towards Britain, Britain towards Gaul,—an extremely awkward and artificial method of denoting proximity.

positio caeli, 'their geographical position,' cp. on 10. 2.

habitum, 'their (similar) characteristics.'

3. in universum...aestimanti, so in *Germ.* 6. 4. See 10. 4 for the dative and for *in universum*. *tamen* introduces what Tacitus regards as the most probable explanation—of course, the true one. Celtic immigrations began possibly as early as the 7th century B.C. The notion that the Celts came in two well-defined waves of invasion, first the Goidels who at the time of the Roman occupation populated Ireland, the Scottish Highlands, most of Wales, and the West of England, and secondly the Brythons who inhabited the rest of England (see Prof. Rhys' map in his *Celtic Britain*), does not appear so certain as was once thought, though of course the existence of two Celtic dialects, Goidelic and Brythonic, is incontestable (cp. Rice Holmes, *op. cit.*, p. 228).

4. **deprehendas**, understand 'in Britain.' The subjunctive (cp. *videas*, *Germ*. 30. 3) seems to express logical necessity rather than mere potentiality; 'you shall detect,' to use a somewhat archaic idiom. See Prof. Sonnenschein's *Unity of the Latin Subjunctive*, p. 14, where the close parallelism between the pres. subjunct. and the fut. indic. in such expressions is pointed out. Tacitus is here thinking of Druidism, which Caesar believed to have originated in Britain, *B. G.* VI. 13.

superstitionum persuasiones, 'superstitious persuasions.' The Romans frequently applied *superstitio* to foreign religions.

in deposcendis, etc. Cp. Caesar, *B. G.* III. 19, *ut ad bella suscipienda Gallorum alacer ac promptus est animus, sic mollis ac minime resistens ad calamitates perferendas mens eorum est*. See also Livy X. 28. Mommsen's classic description of the Celts (*Rom. Hist.* Book II. chap. 4) should be read.

5. **accepimus**. Editors quote *B. G.* VI. 24, *fuit antea tempus cum Germanos Galli virtute superarent, ultro bella inferrent*. Cp. Sall. *Cat.* 53, *cognoveram...gloria belli Gallos ante Romanos fuisse*, etc. (See on *Germ*. 28. 1.)

olim victis, to be taken together. The reference is to the subjugation of southern and central Britain in the time of Claudius.

CHAPTER XII

1. **curru proeliantur**, cp. 35. 3, 36. 3, where the chariot-fighters are called *covinnarii*. Caesar, *B. G.* IV. 24, calls them *essedarii*. The *covinnus* can hardly have been scythed in spite of Mela III. 6. 52 and the Roman poets. No trace of chariot-scythes has been found in any Gallic or British interments. The Brigantes appear to have made much use of *covinni*. Of twelve British chariot burials all but two were found in Yorkshire (Rice Holmes, *op. cit.* 676).

honestior, etc., meaning that a noble drove the chariot and his dependants fought from it, or, perhaps, fought for him, cp. *Germ*. 14. 2. Caesar's account is that the *auriga* after depositing the fighting man (*essedarius*) drove the chariot out of the battle and waited near by for his return, *B. G.* IV. 33, a different procedure from that described by Tacitus. In Gaul, too, each chariot contained one driver and one fighting man (Diod. V. 29. 1). Cp. the town *covinnus* of Martial XII. 24, which only had room for two. The present passage can hardly mean that only the noble rode in a chariot and his dependants fought *on foot* round it. There must have been at least *two* in each chariot.

regibus parebant. See Caesar, *B. G.* v. 22.

per principes, 'owing to the chieftains they are distracted by factions and rivalries.' *trahuntur* is for *distrahuntur* (read by Heinsius; an easy correction after *studiis*), the simple verb for the compound. See Draeger, *S. und S.* § 25. Britain had now reached a stage of political development similar to that of Gaul when Caesar conquered it. Cp. for instance, *B. G.* v. 3—7.

2. pro nobis, used instead of a simple dative to point a contrast with *adversus.*

in commune, etc. Cp. Curt. VIII. 14. 21, *nihil in medium consulebatur.*

tribusve, more correct than the better supported reading *tribusque*, which would mean 'aye and even three,' implying a good many. On the other hand, *duo tresve* suggests fewness. Cp. *unus aut alter*, 15. 5, 40. 4, 'one or at most two,' i.e. quite a few. The distinction was pointed out by Bentley on Hor. *Epodes* v. 33.

3. asperitas, etc. Caesar found Britain warmer than Gaul, *B. G.* v. 12.

nostri orbis, 'our (Mediterranean) latitude.' He is speaking only of summer. Pliny, *N. H.* II. 77. 186, says with approximate correctness that the longest day in Italy lasts fifteen hours, in Britain seventeen hours. (See Furneaux.)

internoscas, apparently a subjunctive of the kind noted in 11. 4, here in a dependent clause.

4. transire, i.e. passes along the horizon. Cp. *Germ.* 45. 1. It seems natural to supply *solem* as the *subject* of *occidere*, etc. Others take *solis fulgorem* with all the verbs, to avoid making Tacitus assign the midnight sun to Britain.

scilicet, etc., 'the fact is that the flat edges of the world, casting only a low shadow, do not throw the darkness up, and night falls below the level of the sky and stars.' Night is rightly conceived as the shadow thrown by the earth (cp. Pliny, *H. N.* II. 7. 47). When the sun is only a little below the rim of the earth, the shadow it casts does not extend sufficiently high above our heads to darken the sky. Tacitus probably regarded the sky as a kind of inverted bowl with the stars set in it. The words *extrema et plana* suggest that he is thinking of the world as a disc, not as a sphere, though conceivably they might refer merely to the absence of mountains or the level expanse of sea (*terrarum* need not be pressed) in the distant north. It is strange if Tacitus was unaware of, or disbelieved, the earth's sphericity, which was taught by the Pythagoreans, proved by Aristotle and held by the Romans generally.

5. praeter, 'except.' The olive and vine are thus included under the term *fruges*, which generally means corn, pulse, etc., 'crops' as distinguished from tree-fruit, *fructus*. Cp. Cic. *Rep.* 3. 9, *oleam frugesve ferre*, but *frugiferarum arborum*, *Germ.* 5. 1; cp. Curt. VIII. 10. 14.

calidioribus terris, local ablative without *in.*

fecundum. *pecudumque*, the reading of E and T, is, in spite of Leuze, *Philol.* Suppl. VIII. 530, at once ruled out by the following words. *fecundum* itself seems a somewhat abrupt amplification of *patiens frugum.* In view of the asyndeton we should have expected a balanced expression like Doederlein's *arborum patiens, frugum fecundum. fecundumque*, a combination of the readings of text and margin of E and T, might possibly stand. With the whole passage cp. *Germ.* 5. 1.

cito proveniunt, adversative asyndeton; 'though they sprout up quickly.' The natural order is reversed.

6. aurum. "Clear traces of Roman gold-mining survive near Dolaucothy [about 12 miles north of Llandilo in Caermarthenshire]— well-wrought drainage tunnels, extensive workings, a rock-hewn reservoir, and an aqueduct cut for five miles along the side of the Cothy valley to bring it a constant water supply." Prof. Haverfield in *Class. Rev.* 1914, p. 43.

alia metalla. In Roman times tin was worked in Cornwall, iron in the Weald (Caes. *B. G.* V. 12), and lead in the Mendips, Flintshire, and Derbyshire. In all the three last-named districts inscribed pigs of Roman lead have been found, and some of the old workings, for instance those on the Mendips, have been reopened in recent years.

margarita. The usual classical form is of the 1st declension. Pliny, *H. N.* IX. 57. 116, says, *uniones...in Britannia parvos et decolores nasci certum est.*

7. rubro mari, a name primarily applied to the Persian Gulf, but often used of the Indian Ocean; cp. Curt. VIII. 9. 6 *uterque* (the Indus and the Ganges) *rubro mari accipitur*; Hor. *carm.* I. 35. 32.

viva, etc., the pearl-bearing animals, not the pearls. See *Germ.* 45. 7 for a similar confusion.

expulsa, 'cast up' by the sea. By what follows Tacitus means that it is more probable that the pearls are really of bad quality than that human avarice should fail to adopt the means of obtaining them at their best. The love of pearls as a mark of human degeneracy is a commonplace of the rhetorical style. See Curt. VIII. 9. 19, quoted in Introd. p. xxvii.

naturam, 'quality,' denoting, like φύσις, the proper essence and true characteristics of a thing.

Chapter XIII

1. ipsi, the inhabitants as opposed to their country, cp. *Germ.* 2. 1.

imperii munia, 'imperial services,' for which see 31. 3. Tacitus uses *munia obire* in four other places, *munera obire* never. See note on text.

obeunt, si...absint. For similar conditional sentences with pres. subjunct. in the *si*-clause and pres. indic. (expressed or implied) in the main clause see *Germ.* 7. 1, 14. 3, 17. 1, 35. 4. The union of a protasis having properly a *shall*-meaning (see note on 11. 4) with an apodosis denoting present fact is remarkable. The subjunctives in this usage may perhaps be classed as subjunctives of indefinite frequency (cp. note on 9. 3).

2. igitur, 'to explain,' introducing an account of the conquest.

litore potitus sit. See on 3. 1 *ad init.* for the subjunctive. In his second invasion of 54 B.C. Caesar did somewhat more than occupy the coast, crossing the Thames and penetrating into Hertfordshire.

potest videri, etc. Tacitus' judgment on Caesar's achievement is the fairest to be found in any ancient author and can hardly be improved upon.

3. etiam in pace, i.e. after the civil wars were over. In 34 B.C. and again in 27 and 26 Augustus seems to have contemplated the invasion of Britain (Dio C. XLIX. 38. 2, LIII. 22. 5, 25. 2), and the prayers and prophecies of Virgil (*Georg.* I. 30) and Horace (*Carm.* I. 35. 29, III. 5. 3) point in the same direction. Besides, the presence of British princes and embassies in Rome hardly allowed the Romans to 'forget Britain.' The motives for the policy (*consilium*) which Augustus ultimately adopted are clearly set forth by Strabo. Britain was no longer dangerous and its conquest would be difficult and unprofitable; while the duties imposed on certain British imports and exports at the harbours of Gaul produced greater revenue than would the tribute resulting from its conquest, when deduction was made for the expenses of its military establishment (Strabo, II. p. 116 *ad init.*, IV. p. 201).

praeceptum, cp. *Ann.* I. 77, *neque fas Tiberio infringere dicta eius* (sc. *Augusti*), and IV. 37.

4. agitasse, etc. In A.D. 40 Adminius, the exiled son of the powerful British monarch Cunobelinus (Cymbeline), put himself under the protection of Caligula, who at once sent a grandiloquent dispatch to the Senate, *quasi universa tradita insula.* According to Suetonius' story, Caligula's army on reaching the coast of Gaul was ordered, not to invade Britain, but to gather shells (Suet. *Cal.* 44, 46).

ni, etc., understand 'and would have invaded it, unless.' Cp. 4. 4 and Livy V. 36 *mitis legatio, ni praeferoces legatos...habuisset. paenitentiae* depends on *velox*, with which supply *fuisset.* Tacitus similarly uses *acer, impiger, strenuus, pervicax, ignavus, segnis* with the genitive. *ingenio mobili* is ablative of cause, 'owing to his fickle temperament.'

ingentes, etc. The German expedition took place at the close of 39 A.D. Cp. *Germ.* 37. 5 and *Hist.* IV. 15 where it is said of a prince of the Canninefates, a German people at the mouth of the Rhine, that *multa hostilia ausus Gaianarum expeditionum ludibrium impune spreverat.* Suetonius, *Cal.* 45, enlarges on the farcical side of the operations. See however Merivale's *History* VI. 80—81.

5. auctor iterati operis, i.e. was responsible for the second invasion (43 A.D.). The reading is conjectural. Leuze, following T and Puteolanus, reads *auctor operis*, thinking *auctor* contrasted with *agitasse.* But this reading fails to account for the corruption in E A B. Dio LX. 19. 1 says that a British exile named Bericus persuaded Claudius to undertake the invasion. Bericus' flight was perhaps due to troubles consequent upon the death of Cunobelinus, whose kingdom passed to his sons Caratacus and Togodumnus. Some have thought Bericus to be a fourth son of Cunobelinus.

transvectis legionibus, four in number, II Augusta, XIV Gemina, XX Valeria Victrix, IX Hispana. The whole force, including auxiliaries, may well have amounted to 50,000 men.

in partem rerum, 'to share the campaign.' In reality Vespasian only held a subordinate command as legate of the Second legion, though he greatly distinguished himself in the operations (in the south and west), fighting 30 battles and reducing 20 towns as

well as the Isle of Wight (*Hist.* III. 44, Suet. *Vesp.* 4). Prof.
Haverfield suggests that a tile of the Second legion, found at
Seaton, may date from these operations. The commander-in-chief
was Aulus Plautius. The emperor himself spent 16 days in
Britain, being present at the final battle and entering Camulodunum,
which became the capital of Roman Britain (Dio C. LX. 19).
Vespasian was of obscure Sabine parentage.

fortunae, 'elevation,' cp. 7. 4.

domitae gentes, etc. An inscription on the triumphal arch of
Claudius, dedicated in 51 A.D., is thus restored, *quod reges
Britanniae XI devictos sine ulla iactura in deditionem acceperit
gentesque barbaras trans oceanum primus in dicionem populi Romani
redegerit.* This record of course includes the successes of Claudius'
generals up to date.

fatis, ablative, 'marked out by destiny.' Cp. *Hist.* I. 88
Dolabella...vetusto nomine et propinquitate Galbae...monstratus.

CHAPTER XIV

1. consularium. Provinces containing more than one legion
were regularly put in charge of ex-consuls.

Aulus Plautius, consul 29 A.D., governor of Dalmatia and
Pannonia 41—43, of Britain 43—47. On returning to Rome he
was awarded an ovation, an honour seldom accorded to anyone but
a member of the imperial house. Plautius seems to have extended
the dominion, or at least the suzerainty, of Rome as far as a line
extending from the neighbourhood of Bath (Aquae Sulis) along
the Fosse Way, with possibly an outpost at Gloucester (Glevum),
and thence across to the Wash (see Mr Bernard Henderson,
"The Roman Legions in Britain" in *English Historical Review*,
XVIII. 1—23). The Icěni or Eceni of Norfolk and Suffolk came
over voluntarily, *societatem nostram volentes accesserant, Ann.* XII. 31.
Plautius probably subdued Somerset. Pigs of lead found on the
Mendip Hills and inscribed with the names of Claudius and his
son Britannicus prove that the mines there were worked as early
as 49.

Ostorius Scapula, governor 47—51, had at once to quell a rising
of the Iceni. He then subdued the Decangi, who lived somewhere in N. Wales, and may have been the first to garrison
Chester (see Prof. Haverfield in his edition of Mommsen's *Provinces of the Roman Empire* II. p. 348). His most important
achievement was the conquest of the Silures and their general

Caratacus, who after his defeat by Plautius, and the death of his brother Togodumnus in battle, organised resistance in the west. For the well known story of Caratacus' surrender by the faithless Carti-mandua, queen of the Brigantes, and his dignified bearing when a prisoner at Rome, see *Ann.* XII. 36—38. Worn out by his labours Ostorius died at his post in 51. The Roman frontier, as he left it, probably extended from near Isca Silurum (Caerleon-on-Usk), the headquarters of leg. II, northwards to Viroconium (Wroxeter near Shrewsbury) or Chester (see above) and then eastwards to the Humber or at least to Lindum (Lincoln), the headquarters of leg. IX. (That Ostorius occupied Viroconium is perhaps somewhat conjectural. Recent excavations suggest that the earliest remains date from 80—90 A.D. Anyhow, leg. XIV and leg. XX must at this period have been watching N. Wales.)

colonia, Camulodunum (Colchester), officially known as Colonia Victrix.

2. Cogidumno. The so-called Goodwood inscription, found at Chichester, records the dedication of a temple by a guild of smiths on the authority of a certain *Tiberius Claudius Cogidubnus rex*(?) *legatus Augusti in Britannia*. The inscription, which according to Prof. Haverfield pretty certainly belongs to the middle or third quarter of the first century (*Class. Rev.* 1914, p. 43), probably refers to Tacitus' Cogidumnus, who for his loyalty was rewarded with the honorary title of *legatus Augusti*. The *civitates donatae* doubtless include the Regni of Sussex.

consuetudine, ablat. of manner, 'according to the custom.' With *haberet* sc. *populus Romanus*. The constr. is a little awkward, but Rhenanus' transposition *vetere...consuetudine ut haberet*, where *ut haberet*, etc., explains *consuetudine*, seems hardly justified.

et reges, 'even kings.' *instrumenta* is predicative. Editors illustrate by such kings as Masinissa, Attalus, Eumenes, Juba, Herod. See also *Germ.* 42. 2.

3. Didius Gallus had seen service in South Russia about 46 and governed Britain 52—57, where his first duty was to punish the Silures who had defeated the 2nd legion. He also interfered in the affairs of the Brigantes (dwelling in the north of England). See *Ann.* XII. 40 and XIV. 29, where Tacitus again says that he merely retained what had been won.

paucis, etc. Mr Henderson, *op. cit.* p. 20, thinks that it was probably Didius who moved forward the 14th and 20th legions to Deva (Chester). But see note on Ostorius, § 1.

fama aucti officii, 'the credit of enlarging his sphere of duty.'

Veranius, consul in 49, legate of Britain 57–8. He made raids on the Silures and in his will stated that he would have conquered the province for Nero, had he lived two years longer, *Ann.* XIV. 29.

4. biennio, 59—60. For Suetonius see on 5. 1.

firmatis...praesidiis, 'posting strong garrisons,' so *firmando praesidio, Ann.* XIII. 41. Cp. 35. 2.

Monam. For Suetonius' landing and victory on the shore of Anglesea see *Ann.* XIV. 29, where the island is described as *incolis validam et receptaculum perfugarum.*

terga, etc., i.e. gave the enemy an opportunity to attack him in the rear. The personification of *occasio* is remarkable.

CHAPTER XV

1. conferre, 'communicated' or 'compared.'

interpretando accendere, 'inflamed their wrongs by the construction which they put on them.'

tamquam=ὡς, giving the oppressors' point of view.

ex facili, a not uncommon periphrasis for *facile.* Cp. *ex aequo,* 20. 3. So Greek uses ἐκ or ἀπό with an adjective.

2. procurator. See on 4. 1. In *Ann.* XIV. 32 Tacitus says that the avarice of the procurator Catus Decianus had driven the province into war.

aeque...aeque, an emphatic variant on *aeque ac.* For the relations between legate and procurator (*praepositorum*) see note on 9. 5.

alterius...alterius, the legate...the procurator.

manus, acc. plur., 'the tools'; cp. Cic. *Verr.* II. 10. 27 *comites illi tui delecti manus erant tuae. centuriones* is in appos. with *manus,* which must be supplied before *servos.* The passage is echoed in *Ann.* XIV. 31 where Prasutagus, king of the Iceni at the time of the revolt, is said to have had his kingdom plundered by centurions, his house by slaves (see C. and B.'s note).

3. exceptum, 'exempt from.'

nunc, 'as things are.'

ab ignavis, i.e. by the Romans. The reference is in particular to the *veterani* at Camulodunum who *pellebant domibus, exturbabant agris, Ann.* XIV. 31. Cp. the *senum coloniae* of 32. 5.

tamquam, etc., 'as though it was only for their country that they did not know how to die.' *iniungi dilectus* suggests that they would die for the Romans (see Prof. Walter's note).

4. enim, elliptical; the Romans must think thus of us Britons, *for* what a small body of troops have come over, if we compare our numbers with theirs. (So Furneaux.)

sic, i.e. as we intend to do.

Germanias, Upper and Lower Germany. The plural is somewhat rhetorical. Varus' defeat in A.D. 9, here referred to, took place in Lower Germany. *flumine* is the Rhine. It was Claudius who made the Lower Rhine the Roman frontier.

5. divus in a barbarian's mouth is a slight violation of dramatic propriety (Gudeman compares *dictatorem Caesarem* on the lips of Caratacus, *Ann.* XII. 34); or else it is ironically intended, in which case cp. Arminius' sarcasm in *Ann.* I. 59 *ille inter numina dicatus Augustus.*

modo, more commonly *dummodo.* Note the change of subject with *aemularentur.*

impetus, 'dash.' *felicibus* is omitted by A B. Editors had long suspected that a word was missing, e.g. *integris*, inserted by Acidalius.

6. relegatum, 'banished,' a rhetorical exaggeration.

fuerit, representing *fuit* of *oratio recta*; 'a thing which has been in the past most difficult.' See 12. 2.

porro adds a reason for carrying their deliberations into effect.

CHAPTER XVI

1. in vicem=*inter se*; 'having inflamed one another with such thoughts as these.'

Boudicca. This spelling is generally adopted from *Ann.* XIV. 31; the traditional Boadicea has no manuscript or philological warrant. The root of the word is the Celtic *boudi*, 'victory.' Boudicca, queen of the Iceni, and her daughters had been outrageously treated by Roman officials.

in imperiis, 'in military commands'; cp. *Ann.* XIV. 35. Sir John Rhys thinks that it was unusual for a woman to exercise the power of king among the Celts of Britain (*Celtic Britain*³, p. 66). Boudicca's position was exceptional as the widow of the deceased monarch Prasutagus (see on 15. 2), and much of the opposition to Cartimandua (see on 14. 1) was due to dislike of a woman ruler, *Ann.* XII. 40.

coloniam. Camulodunum was as yet unfortified. The temple of Claudius, whither the garrison retired, was stormed after a two days' siege, and the 9th legion, which marched to the relief of the place under Petilius Cerealis, was cut to pieces.

Prof. Haverfield (*Class. Rev.* 1914, p. 42) makes the interesting suggestion that a bronze head, closely resembling Claudius, which was found by itself near Woodbridge in Suffolk, may have been torn from the temple of Claudius in the Colonia by British pillagers and thrown away later on.

in barbaris ingeniis. Note the adverbial phrase attached attributively to a substantive. The adjectival nature of the words is here made clear by their position between *ullum* and *saevitiae genus.* In *Ann.* XIV. 33 we are told that the enemy was intent not on making prisoners, but on slaughter, the gibbet, the fire and the cross. 70,000 Romans and persons friendly to Rome perished in the massacres.

omisit, etc. Cp. Curt. VIII. 14. 29 *nec quicquam inexpertum non mortis modo sed etiam in ipsa morte novi supplicii terror omittebat.*

2. quod nisi, 'and unless,' the negative of *quod si.* Suetonius with the 14th and the 20th legions marched along Watling Street from North Wales to Londinium. In spite of the supplications of the inhabitants he had to abandon Londinium to the foe. Verulamium (St Albans) also fell into the enemy's hands. The final battle is generally supposed to have taken place between London and Colchester. Mr B. Henderson, however, thinks that Suetonius fell back into the Midlands and that the site of the battle is to be looked for on the line of Watling Street. See his brilliant reconstruction of the campaign in his *Life and Principate of the Emperor Nero*, pp. 209 ff. Henderson, p. 477, following Asbach, dates the rebellion in 60 A.D. Tacitus, it is true, distinctly states that the *clades* occurred in the year of Turpilianus' consulship, i.e. 61 (*Ann.* XIV. 29); but in *Ann.* XIV. 39 he implies that Turpilianus succeeded Suetonius soon after his consulship (*qui iam consulatu abierat*), i.e. in the spring or early summer of 61. Suetonius' campaign, the mission of Polyclitus, etc., would certainly occupy more time than Tacitus seems to allow.

fortuna, probably nominative.

patientiae, 'submission.'

tenentibus, concessive, 'though a considerable number retained their arms.'

proprius, etc., 'personal fear of the governor.' *metus ex* is common in Tacitus. The old reading *propius*, to be taken with *agitabat*, would mean 'touched them more closely,' i.e. than the knowledge of their complicity in the revolt.

cetera, adverbial accus. with *egregius*.

ut, connected only with *suae*, 'avenging every wrong as though it were a personal matter.'

3. Petronius Turpilianus, consul at the beginning of 61, governor of Britain 61—63, put to death by Galba in 68 as a partisan of Nero.

tamquam in later Latin often introduces a real, not merely a pretended, reason. Suetonius' recall was largely due to the intrigues of his procurator, Julius Classicanus, who gave out that hostilities would never end as long as Suetonius remained in command. Nero sent out his freedman, Polyclitus, to investigate, and shortly afterwards Suetonius was recalled, *Ann.* XIV. 38, 39.

paenitentiae, 'to the penitent,' abstract for concrete.

prioribus, 'the previous trouble,' neuter, cp. 41. 4. Gudeman points out that Tacitus has no objection to these ambiguous forms. In earlier writers such forms are generally masculine.

Trebellio Maximo, consul in 56 A.D., governor of Britain 63—69.

4. et nullis, for *neque ullis*, as often in Tacitus, cp. § 6. For the ablative of description see on 4. 1.

curandi, 'of administration,' used absolutely as in Sallust.

didicere, etc., 'the natives too now learnt to tolerate engaging vices,' ironical. The Romans knew how to do it already.

civilium armorum, the wars of Galba, Otho, Vitellius and Vespasian in 68—69.

discordia, mutiny in the Roman army. For the facts see on 7. 5.

5. pacti sc. *sunt*, 'they bargained as it were, the army for insubordination,' etc.

stetit, 'ended.' Note the alliteration.

6. Vettius Bolanus, governor 69—71. See on 8. 1.

nec...agitavit, etc., 'did not disturb Britain by the quality of his discipline,' i.e. he did not discipline his troops by operations against the Britons.

nisi quod, 'the only difference being that,' see on 6. 1.

innocens, 'had clean hands' (Fyfe), unlike Trebellius, see *Hist.* I. 60.

CHAPTER XVII

1. reciperavit, implying that he was the lawful owner, or perhaps that he 'reclaimed' it out of the turmoil of civil war. See on 7. 5 for the attitude of the British legions to Vespasian.

magni, sc. *fuerunt*.

2. Petilius Cerialis, governor 71—74. See on 8. 2. Cerialis probably brought with him from Lower Germany the newly raised Legio II Adiutrix (*Hist.* IV. 68), which in place of the 14th, recalled in 70 (see on 7. 5), was stationed with the 20th at Deva.

Brigantum. The Brigantes seem to have occupied the whole of the north of England beyond the Humber and the Mersey. In 69 their queen Cartimandua (see on 14. 1), attacked by her former husband Venutius, had been rescued by Roman detachments; *regnum Venutio, bellum nobis relictum, Hist.* III. 45.

aut victoria, etc., 'embraced within the range of his victories or his wars.' It seems to have been Cerialis who occupied Eboracum (York), making it the headquarters of the 9th legion (hitherto stationed at Lincoln), and throwing out an advance-post at Isurium (Aldborough). Professor Haverfield thinks that Cerialis' annexations did not extend beyond latitude 54.

3. alterius, 'any other' than Frontinus. Cp. 5. 4.

obruisset, 'would have utterly eclipsed.'

Iulius Frontinus, consul in 74 (again in 98 and 100), governor of Britain 74—77, proconsul of Asia 93, the author of *strategemata*, 'Tactics,' and of *de aquis urbis Romae*, 'On the aqueducts of Rome.' He was *curator aquarum*, 'inspector of aqueducts,' in 97.

quantum licebat, best taken with *vir magnus*, 'a great man, so far as the age allowed'; cp. *Ann.* XIV. 47 *Memmius Regulus...in quantum praeumbrante imperatoris fastigio datur, clarus.* Gudeman prefers to take the words with *subiit sustinuitque*, 'sustained, so far as he could.'

super=*praeter.* For the Silures see on 11. 2.

eluctatus, 'having surmounted,' as in *Hist.* III. 59 *nives eluctantibus.*

CHAPTER XVIII

1. media iam aestate, July 78 A.D. But see on 9. 7. The doubt about the year is unfortunate, as it affects the dating of all Agricola's campaigns. *iam* suggests that the new governor was late in arriving.

velut omissa expeditione, 'in the idea that operations had been abandoned.' Cp. § 3.

ad occasionem verterentur, 'were turning their thoughts to their opportunity.'

2. Ordovicum, occupying Central and North Wales, formerly allies of Caratacus, *Ann.* XII. 33.

alam, a regiment of auxiliary cavalry.

agentem, 'quartered,' 'stationed,' a common military use of the word.

erecta, 'was intensely excited.' Cp. *erecta multitudine, Hist.* IV. 81.

3. quibus, etc., 'those who wanted war'; cp. *Ann.* I. 59 *ut quibusque bellum invitis aut cupientibus erat,* a Graecism apparently first introduced into Latin by Sallust in imitation of Thucydides; cp. Thuc. II. 3 τῷ πλήθει οὐ βουλομένῳ ἦν ἀφίστασθαι.

probare, historic infin., 'approved the example (of the Ordovices) and yet waited to see the temper...'

numeri, 'detachments,' whether of legionaries or auxiliaries.

praesumpta...quies, 'the anticipation of repose.' These words with *transvecta aestas* and *sparsi...numeri* are best taken as subject to *tarda et contraria* (*erant*). Others regard *transvecta* (*est*) etc. as finite verbs, and *tarda* as in apposition to the preceding phrases. *tarda* here is actively used, 'causing delay,' a poetical sense, cp. *tardum onus,* Sen. *Phoen.* 568.

suspecta, 'suspected points.'

potius, 'preferable,' adjective.

statuit, indicative, because *cum* here = *et tum*; 'the coincidence in time is vividly expressed by an inversion,' Roby, § 1733.

vexillis, 'detachments.' The name *vexillum* or *vexillarii* indicates a corps detached from the main body for special duty, because it served under a *vexillum* or flag instead of under the manipular *signum,* a pole decorated with discs, half-moons, figures of animals, etc.

quo. For the absence of a comparative with *quo = ut eo* cp. 38. 4.

par, equal to his own.

simili periculo, 'as they both took equal risk.'

erexit aciem, 'led his troops up the hill,' cp. 36. 2.

4. instandum famae, 'he must follow up the prestige he had won.'

prout prima cessissent, 'in proportion to the result of his initial operations.'

possessione, 'seizure' not 'possession.' For the facts see 14. 4 ff.

5. ut in, 'as is usual in the case of.' Note the abbreviation of the thought.

ratio et constantia, 'skill and determination.'

lectissimos, etc. Batavian auxiliaries (cp. 36. 2) are probably meant, for whose skill in swimming see *Hist.* IV. 12, *Ann.* II. 8.

They could obtain knowledge of the fords from prisoners. Others suppose *nota vada* has a general reference, 'they knew all about fords.' The account of Paulinus' passage into Mona in *Ann.* XIV. 29 should be compared, *naves fabricatur plano alveo adversus breve et incertum. sic pedes; equites vada secuti aut altiores inter undas adnantes equis tramisere.*

mare, i.e. an attack by sea. Stuart happily compares *Hist.* II. 12 *possessa per mare et naves maiore Italiae parte.*

6. quippe cui, 'being indeed a man whom,' not found else-where in Tacitus.

ingredienti, see on 9. 1.

officiorum ambitum, 'courting attentions.' See on 9. 5 and for *ambitus* cp. the use of *ambio* in *Germ.* 18. 1.

7. victos continuisse, 'his having kept the conquered in check,' object of *vocabat.* Note the alliteration in this clause.

laureatis, sc. *litteris.* Dispatches announcing victories were wreathed in laurel leaves.

prosecutus est, 'adorned,' from the notion of complimentary attendance upon a person.

aestimantibus, either ablat. abs. or dat. of the person judging (see on 10. 4).

quanta futuri spe. The emphasis falls on these words; 'how great his aspirations for the future must be, seeing that....'

CHAPTER XIX

2. domum, 'household,' freedmen, slaves, etc.

nihil...publicae rei, sc. *agere* (historic infinitive). For the phrase cp. *Germ.* 13. 1.

studiis privatis, 'according to his personal predilections.'

ascire, 'attached to his staff.' Such soldiers, called *beneficiarii,* were exempt from ordinary military duties and formed part of the governor's *cohors,* acting as his orderlies, clerks and executive officers. Cp. the *centuriones* of 15. 2.

3. omnia exsequi, 'follow up, i.e. take action in, all cases.' *exsequi* here comes near the Livian use of the word, 'to punish,' a sense not actually found in Tacitus.

poena. Supply *uti* from *contentus esse,* which is only appropriate to *paenitentia* (Furneaux). Note the assonance *poena...paenitentia.*

non peccaturos, 'men not likely to do wrong.'

4. frumenti, etc., 'the collection of corn and tribute he rendered less offensive by equalising the burdens,' i.e. by bringing the amount of any district's contribution into equitable relation to its resources. According to Wex, Agricola introduced *aequalitas* by allowing a state unable to supply its quota of corn to pay the market value of the corn instead, a custom existing in Cicero's time, see *Verr.* III. 82. 189. Tacitus' words are hardly definite enough to justify this interpretation of Agricola's reform. The *frumentum* was for the army and the governor's establishment.

quae in quaestum reperta, 'the devices for making profit which...'

namque, etc., 'for the Britons were mockingly compelled to sit at the doors of the granaries, which were never opened, and actually to buy the corn and so meet their obligations by a payment.' *adsidere, tamquam mendicantes,* says Wex comparing Seneca, *Ep.* IV. 10 *superbis adsidere liminibus. luere* is used absolutely, or *imperata* may be supplied as object. If the Britons could not supply the corn demanded by the government, they had to purchase corn already stored in the Roman granaries and deliver this as their quota. During this operation the corn never left the granaries, hence perhaps *clausis horreis*—the doors were never even opened. The great grievance would of course be the extortionate price which the Roman officials put upon the corn in store.

5. divortia itinerum, 'road forks,' probable places for the delivery of corn, but a meaning inconsistent with *avia* below, which is clearly intended to balance the phrase. Many therefore read *devortia,* a word which Lipsius invented for the benefit of this passage, and take the phrase to mean 'out of the way routes' or 'places away from roads.'

et longinquitas, etc., 'and far-off districts (cp. 22. 2) were named in order that, although there were winter encampments close at hand,....' Note the sing. *indicebatur* in spite of the plural *divortia. proximis hibernis* is a very difficult ablative absolute and Ritter's *proximae* is tempting.

donec, 'till what was easy for all' (i.e. the delivery of the corn, had there been no artificial obstacles) 'became a source of profit to a few.' The Britons could only avoid these inconveniences by bribing the officials.

CHAPTER XX

1. famam...circumdedit, a favourite Tacitean metaphor, cp. *dial.* 37. 6; 'invested peace with a glorious name.'

intolerantia, 'arrogance,' lit. 'impatience.'

2. aestas, the summer of 79 A.D. Agricola perhaps started his campaign from Chester. A piece of lead piping has been discovered there with the inscription 'in the 9th consulship of Vespasian, the 7th of Titus and the governorship of Julius Agricola.' But of course this does not prove Agricola's own presence at Chester.

multus in agmine, 'constantly in the line of march,' copied from Sallust, *Jug.* 96 and an imitation of Greek expressions like πολλὸς ἦν ἐν τοῖσι λόγοισι, 'he took a great part in the discussion,' Herod. VIII. 59.

modestiam, disiectos. Note the rhetorical collocation of abstract and concrete and the chiasmus. *disiectos,* 'stragglers.'

aestuaria, perhaps those of Wales and Lancashire. Others think that in this year Agricola may have advanced to the aestuaries of the Tees, the Wear and the Tyne, and perhaps also to the Solway Firth.

et nihil, for *neque quidquam,* cp. 16. 4.

nihil...quietum pati, again from Sallust, *Jug.* 66; 'allowed the enemy no rest from his sudden plundering forays.'

quo minus is not uncommon in Tacitus where *quin* would be usual. Cp. 27. 3.

3. ex aequo egerant, 'had lived on an equality,' so 'had been independent'; cp. *Hist.* IV. 64 *aut ex aequo agetis aut aliis imperabitis.*

praesidiis castellisque, frequent in Wales and the north of England (see Haverfield, *op. cit.* II. p. 349). Some of Agricola's forts may have been between Tyne and Solway on the line of the future wall of Hadrian.

et tanta, etc., 'and that too with such systematic thoroughness.' Others read *sunt* for *et.*

ut, etc., 'that never before did a new part of Britain come over (to the Romans) so little harassed,' sc. by its neighbours who objected to its defection but could not make any armed protest owing to the fortifications (Furneaux). This interpretation, which depends upon the insertion of *pariter* after *pars,* seems to put a considerable strain upon *inlacessita,* for which see *Germ.* 36. 1. It is still more difficult to understand *pariter inlacessita* to mean 'equally unharassed by the Romans.' There is much to be said for Susius' *inlacessita transiit sequens hiems* (see note on text), with which cp. **22. 3** *intrepida ibi hiems.*

Agricola's system of *castella* was thoroughly successful. In Wales at least there was no serious trouble after this date.

CHAPTER XXI

1. adsumpta, 'devoted to.' *consiliis* is dative. Cp. 23. 1. Puteolanus' *absumpta* is the generally accepted reading, but as Fossataro points out, *absumere* means 'to waste' as applied to time.

privatim, 'unofficially.'

publice, 'with government assistance.'

templa fora domos. Temples, though hardly of Agricola's date, have been found at Bath, Silchester, Caerwent, Lydney and elsewhere. Good examples of *fora* are those at Silchester and Caerwent, rectangular colonnaded courts with shops and offices on three sides and a *basilica* or market hall on the fourth. By *domos* are meant stone buildings like the town houses and the 'villas' which are found in various parts of central and southern England.

castigando, sc. *verbis,* 'censuring.' The gerunds are equivalent to present participles.

honoris, etc., 'rivalry for distinction took the place of compulsion.'

2. iam vero, 'further,' as in 9. 3.

ingenia, etc., 'expressed a preference for the natural ability of the Britons over the trained industry of the Gauls,' i.e. he encouraged the Britons by saying that they would do better with their native wit than the Gauls with their laborious study. Plutarch writing about this time mentions a rhetorician, Demetrius of Tarsus, as teaching in Britain (*de def. orac.* 2). Martial XI. 3. 5 (written before 100 A.D.) says *dicitur et nostros cantare Britannia versus.* According to Juvenal XV. 111 (about 120 A.D.) 'Gaul has taught the Britons to be pleaders and Thule now talks of hiring a rhetorician.' See Prof. Haverfield's *Romanisation of Roman Britain*[2], 24—29, and his note in *Class. Rev.* 1914, p. 43, where he points out that the appearance of *legati iuridici* in Britain about A.D. 80 indicates an extension of Roman law courts in the island.

3. habitus nostri honor, 'our dress came to be esteemed.'

balinea, such as those of Silchester, Wroxeter and Bath (which was a spa then as now). It should be remembered that the Roman, like the modern Turkish, bath was primarily a hot-air bath.

humanitas, 'civilisation.'

Chapter XXII

1. tertius...annus, 80 A.D. For *aperuit* cp. Curt. IX. 6. 20, *aliam naturam, alium orbem aperire mihi statui.*

Tanaum, unknown, but almost certainly on the east coast and not higher than the Firth of Forth. The inferior reading *Taum* has been taken to mean the Tay, but Agricola could hardly have reached so far north this year. Agricola must have advanced along the line of Dere Street, a Roman road leading through Corbridge-on-Tyne (*Corstopitum*) over the Cheviots and thence across hill and dale to Cappuck and the important base fort of Newstead under the Eildon Hills (see Curle's *Newstead*, p. 7, with the authorities there cited). Archaeological evidence goes to prove that all these places were occupied by Agricola (cp. the *castella* mentioned below). Other forts on Dere Street have yet to be excavated. The idea that Agricola's main advance was by way of Carlisle seems untenable in view of the fact that no Roman relics have been found on any of the possible routes from Carlisle to Newstead (Curle, *loc. cit.*). There is little doubt, however, that Carlisle itself was occupied by Agricola, as Samian ware of his date has been found there. At Birrenswark, near Ecclefechan, some 20 miles N.W. of Carlisle, "a native hill-fort encircled by Roman blockading lines...can best be assigned to the Agricolan age. This was perhaps Agricola's furthest on that side of Scotland " (Haverfield, *Class. Rev.* 1914, p. 44).

2. opportunitates locorum, for *opportuna loca*, 'suitable positions.' Cp. *longinquitas regionum*, 19. 5.

pactione ac fuga, 'capitulation or retirement.'

crebrae eruptiones ; nam. The sequence of thought seems to be, 'on the contrary they frequently took the offensive (instead of having anything to fear from the enemy), for they were constantly secured by a year's supplies against the tedium of a siege.' The passage is very awkward, and Halm boldly transposes *crebrae eruptiones* after *hiems*. See, however, Gudeman.

annuis copiis. Pairs of large granaries, standing side by side, have been found at Corbridge and at Newstead. These, however, belong to a later date.

3. intrepida, 'was without alarms.' Cp. Susius' reading in 20 *ad fin.*

quisque, every commander of a *castellum*. *inritis*, 'baffled.'

iuxta = *pariter*, 'alike.'

4. praefectus, a commander either of a cohort of allied infantry or of a regiment (*ala*) of allied cavalry.

incorruptum...testem habebat, 'found in him an impartial witness.'

ut erat. There is asyndeton (Purser suggests *et ut*). *ut...ita* are correlatives.

5. ceterum, etc., 'but no relics of his anger lurked in reserve, so that one had not to fear his silence.' The subjunctive *timeres* has a kind of past jussive sense; cp. 11. 4, 12. 3.

CHAPTER XXIII

1. quarta aestas, A.D. 81.

obtinendis, 'securing,' dative with *insumpta*, cp. 21. 1.

pateretur, the imperfect because indicating a general principle of Roman conquest in Tacitus' time.

inventus, sc. *erat*, rhetorical for *esset*. Cp. on 4. 4.

in ipsa Britannia, i.e. without crossing into Caledonia.

2. Clota et Bodotria, the estuaries of the Clyde and Forth.

diversi, etc., 'carried a vast distance inland by the tides of opposite seas.'

angusto...spatio, a little over 30 miles.

praesidiis. The line of Agricola's forts clearly coincides with that of the later wall of Antoninus. The Antonine system of fortification comprised some nineteen stations placed at intervals of about two miles. Excavations have proved that at least three of these stations, Bar Hill, Castlecary, and Rough Castle, were occupied in the first century, i.e. by Agricola, and this is probably true of the majority of them. At Bar Hill the remains of the Agricolan fort were found concealed in a larger Antonine fort. As in the case of the contemporary German *limes*, the ramparts of Agricola's forts were of earth, not of turf or stone. There must have been a road connecting them, though no certain indications of it have yet come to light, and between the forts there were probably wooden watch towers, *burgi* or *praesidia*, similar to those on the German *limes*. The fortress of Camelon, which lies three-quarters of a mile north of the *limes*, near Rough Castle, and was certainly occupied by Agricola, probably belongs to the offensive operations of 83 or 84. (See Dr George Macdonald's *Roman Wall in Scotland*, pp. 383 ff. and *passim*.)

propior sinus, 'tract of country on the nearer side,' i.e. to the south. For this sense of *sinus* cp. *Germ.* 1. 1; 37. 1.

velut in aliam insulam, i.e. Caledonia.

CHAPTER XXIV

1. quinto...anno, 82 A.D.

nave prima transgressus, 'crossed with the first ship,' a difficult phrase, meaning perhaps, 'for the first time crossed the sea in his operations,' *prima* being used as equivalent to the adverb *primum*. Other suggested renderings are, 'in the leading ship' and 'in the first ship to sail that spring.' Prof. Haverfield (*Class. Rev.* IX. 310) would take *prima* as neut. plural, 'as regards the first part of the journey.' Of the many emendations proposed *vere primo* is the most obvious.

ignotas...gentis. Gudeman, following Pfitzner, supposes that Ireland is meant by these *ignotas gentis* and by *aliam insulam* above. He is supported by Prof. R. K. McElderry in *Class. Rev.* XVIII. 460; "The new emperor Titus [acceded Sept. 13, 81 A.D.] saw a way to win for his reign a distinctive renown, and the conquest of Ireland was planned." He thinks that the reference in Juvenal II. 159, *arma quidem ultra litora Iubernae promovimus* is not simply rhetorical. But it seems inconceivable that Tacitus should have alluded to so epoch-making an event in a manner so obscure. Cp. Prof. Haverfield in his paper, 'Ancient Rome and Ireland,' *Eng. Hist. Rev.* Jan. 1913: "Tacitus does not suggest by even the merest phrase that an invasion actually took place, and the total absence in Ireland of Roman remains of Agricola's time, save for one single coin [of Vespasian, found in co. Down], is fairly conclusive." Sir J. H. Ramsay, *Foundations of England*, I. 69, suggests that this season Agricola sailed across the Solway from Cumberland (where Agricolan, or at least Flavian, antiquities have been found, e.g. at Carlisle), and subdued Kircudbright and Galloway.

eamque...aspicit. "The district might be either Wales or the Cumberland coast, or possibly Wigton and Galloway, but here remains of Roman forts are entirely absent, and even Roman smaller objects are rare. The idea that it was the Mull of Cantire is geographically and archaeologically absurd." Prof. Haverfield, *op. cit.* The words *in spem* refer to the hope of conquest.

si quidem...miscuerit, 'if indeed it should prove to unite,' or causally, 'since it might prove to unite.' *miscuerit* is probably perf. subj., see on 3. 1.

medio...sita. Cp. on 10. 2, 11. 2, for the geography.

opportuna, 'conveniently situated for,' so 'easily accessible from.'

valentissimam imperii partem, the western provinces, Gaul, Spain, and Britain, as supplying the best soldiers. In *Hist.* III. 53 Tacitus calls Gaul and Spain *validissimam terrarum partem,* and in c. 12. 2 describes the Britons as *validissimas gentis.*

magnis in vicem usibus, 'to great mutual profit.'

2. nostri maris, the Mediterranean. Ireland is a little more than three times the size of Sicily, the largest of the Mediterranean islands.

a Britannia, 'from those of Britain,' a *comparatio compendiaria.* Tacitus' brief notice of the Irish marks an advance upon Strabo and Mela, who regarded them as the lowest of savages. Ptolemy, writing some two generations later than Tacitus, shows considerable acquaintance with the geography of north-east Ireland.

⟨**ni**⟩ **in melius,** see note on text; 'unless it be for the better.' The emendation is palaeographically easy, though it must be admitted that we have no other evidence for a belief in Ireland's superiority in these respects. Ritter's first proposal, adopted by Halm, *in⟨teriora parum⟩, melius,* etc., seems too obvious a remark for Tacitus.

per commercia. The trade was between North Ireland and Britain, but Prof. Haverfield thinks it must have been small. Almost all the Roman finds in Ireland are coins, and of these only two or three belong to the first century. No fragment of Roman pottery has been discovered. In prehistoric times there seems to have been some trade in gold ornaments between Ireland and the mainland of western Europe.

3. in occasionem, 'for a favourable opportunity,' when the fugitive might be used as an excuse for, or an assistance in, invasion. See notes on 13. 4 and 5, 14. 2.

eo, Agricola. This, 4. 4 and 44. 5 are the only places where Tacitus quotes Agricola's utterances.

legione una et modicis auxiliis, say 8,000 men. Agricola was "the first of the countless optimists who have planned a future for Ireland" (Haverfield).

arma, sc. *essent.*

CHAPTER XXV

1. ceterum, 'But to proceed,' after the digression, cp. 11. 1.

sextum...annum, 83 A.D.

amplexus, sc. *animo,* 'embracing in his designs. Cp. the use in 17. 2.

ultra, used adjectivally.

infesta, etc., lit. 'the marches of an invading army beset with dangers,' i.e. 'the dangers besetting the march of....' With the reading in the margin of E, *hostili exercitu*, the passage means, 'marches beset by the enemy's troops,' viz. by the Caledonians, though, as Furneaux points out, a Roman would hardly call a gathering of Caledonians an *exercitus*. Bekker's *hostibus* for *hostilis* seems unnecessary.

portus, on the coast of Fife, in particular the estuary of the Tay.

in partem virium, 'as part of his force' for offensive purposes. He had already used ships on the west coast (see 24. 1), but apparently only for transport. A *classis Britannica* with head-quarters at Gesoriacum (Boulogne), and stations on the Kentish coast, dated from the Claudian invasion.

bellum impelleretur, 'war was being pushed on,' a unique variant for *bellum inferretur*. This vivid and sonorous passage finely illustrates Tacitus' skilful application of rhetoric to historical writing and prepares us for the impressive military pictures of the Histories and the Annals.

isdem castris, local ablative without *in*; cp. *calidioribus terris*, 12. 5.

mixti, etc., 'mingling together in their food and their merriment,' i.e. 'sharing their food and their merriment,' a remarkable union of concrete and abstract. For *copiis* cp. 22. 2.

suos casus attollerent, 'magnified their own dangers.'

terra et hostis, to be joined with *victus*.

2. **tamquam** for *tamquam si*.

aperto...clauderetur, an intentional play upon contradictory words (oxymoron) emphasised by their positions.

3. **ad manus et arma,** 'to armed resistance.'

magno paratu, etc., 'with large preparations, largely exaggerated' (Stephenson).

uti mos est de ignotis, cp. 30. 4, *omne ignotum pro magnifico est.*

ultro, often of taking the initiative. *adorti*, 'having undertaken,' a common Livian use. The *castella* may well be the forts between Forth and Clyde.

ut provocantes, 'as challenging their foes.'

pellerentur, to be explained as an oblique jussive subjunctive; 'advised that a retirement should be made rather than that they should be driven back.'

specie, 'posing as.' The *ignavi* are of course Romans.

cognoscit, sc. Agricola.

pluribus agminibus, 'in several columns,' ablative of manner.

4. superante, etc., 'owing to their superior numbers and their acquaintance with the district.' Both ablatives are causal.

et ipse, 'he on his part,' to be closely connected with the ablat. absol. The words stand for *divisit et ipse...exercitum et incessit.* Cp. *Germ.* 37. 4.

CHAPTER XXVI

1. mutato...consilio. They attacked *universi* not *pluribus agminibus,* 25. 3.

invalidam. The Ninth Legion had been cut up in the Boudiccan revolt (see on 16. 1), and though gaps had been filled by drafts from Germany (*Ann.* XIV. 38), was perhaps never restored to its full complement. Others think its weakness may have been due to the absence of a detachment in Germany. (See Furneaux' note.) This unlucky legion is not heard of after 108 A.D., when its name occurs on an inscription found at York, its headquarters. It was probably annihilated by the Brigantes. (Macdonald, *op. cit.* p. 3.)

2. vestigiis, 'on their tracks,' a local ablative as in *ire via,* 'to go along a road.' Cp. Livy IX. 45 *pergunt hostem vestigiis sequi.*

signa, of the legions which were following the light troops.

3. pro with *securi,* instead of *de.* Cp. the common construction *cura pro.*

ultro. See on 25. 3. For the position of *quin etiam,* cp. *Germ.* 3. 3.

utroque exercitu, the relieving force and the beleaguered Ninth Legion.

4. quod nisi. See 16. 2.

CHAPTER XXVII

1. cuius, sc. *victoriae.*

fama, 'report,' because all the army had not been present at the battle.

ferox, 'inspirited.'

fremebant, 'clamoured that,' a word generally used of complaint, but cp. *fremitu,* 33. 1.

2. illi, see 25. 3 *ignavi specie prudentium.*

3. occasione, 'by a lucky chance'; see 26. 2 *ab exploratoribus edoctus.* For *quo minus,* see on 20. 2.

CHAPTER XXVIII

1. cohors. An auxiliary cohort generally consisted of 500 men (*cohors quingenaria*).

Usiporum. The Usipi, for whom see note on *Germ.* 32. 1, at this time dwelt on the right bank of the Rhine, north of the Ruhr. They were probably subjugated in Domitian's German campaign of 83 A.D., and a detachment of them sent at once to Britain (Mommsen, *Provinces*, I. 150. See, however, R. K. McElderry, *Class. Rev.* XVIII. p. 460). Forcible enlistment and deportation were a common method of pacifying disturbed districts. (See Macdonald, *op. cit.* 56.)

2. militibus, i.e. legionary troops. The drill sergeants who trained recruits were known as *campi doctores* or *exercitatores.*

habebantur, 'were employed.'

liburnicas. *liburnica*, or *liburna*, was properly a light war-vessel with two banks of oars, named after the piratical Liburni of the Illyrian coast. Later the word came to be used for any sort of warship.

remigante. It is very doubtful whether this can be strained to mean, 'directing the rowing,' hence W. R. Paton (*Class. Rev.* XVI. 283) suggests *regente remigantes*. Other emendations (*renavigante*, Mützell; *retro remigante*, Gudeman) involve the assumption that the Usipi performed their voyage without *any* pilot (cp. § 4), the defection of the first causing the other two to be suspected and slain. In the case of the latter suggestions the present participle is used aoristically, cp. 9. 1.

ut miraculum, because no one who saw them could account for their presence.

praevehebantur. Tacitus frequently uses *prae* for *praeter* in compound verbs.

3. ad aquandum...plerisque. The reading can hardly be regarded as more than a makeshift to give sense to a thoroughly corrupt passage, though Selling's *utilia* ('supplies,' a Sallustian use) for *ut illa* seems certain, as Furneaux points out.

raptum, supine co-ordinated with *ad aquandum.*

ad extremum, 'finally.' *inopiae* depends upon *eo.*

vescerentur, often construed with the accus. in later writers by an archaism which had survived in poetry and in Sallust. So Tacitus construes *potior* and *fungor* with accus.

4. circumvecti. It seems clear that the Usipi started on the west coast, perhaps from Galloway (cp. 24. 1), and coasted round the north of Scotland, whence they sailed to Holland. For had they gone round the south of England, they would have reached the Rhine before Holland (see § 5), and Dio Cassius, LXVI. 20, lays special stress on the fact that their voyage first suggested to Agricola the possibility of circumnavigating Britain, with the south and west coasts of which Agricola must have already been familiar. Dio's account is different and must derive from an inferior authority. According to him certain soldiers (unnamed) mutinied and killed a tribune and some centurions.   They then sailed aimlessly round Britain *from east to west* till they came to the Roman stations on the west coast.   Dio does not mention the voyage to Holland (see Furneaux' note).

Suebis, a widespread German race, cp. *Germ.* 38. 1.   Augustus had settled some near the mouth of the Rhine (Suet. *Aug.* 21), and these may be meant here.   Strabo VII. 1, p. 290, makes them spread from the Rhine to beyond the Elbe.   Prof. Chadwick (*Origin of English Nation,* p. 203) is inclined to think that the Suebi mentioned here lived north of the Elbe, in which case the Usipi must have reached the Danish peninsula.

Frisiis in the north of Holland (Friesland), *Germ.* 34. 1.

5.   nostram...ripam, the left bank of the Rhine.

mutatione ementium, 'by changing hands among the purchasers.'

indicium, etc., 'the disclosure of their remarkable adventure made them famous.'   The indicative after *sunt qui* is rare in prose (only once elsewhere in Tacitus, *dial.* 31).

CHAPTER XXIX

1.   initio aestatis, not the same, but the next summer, 84 A.D. See 34. 1 *proximo anno.*

ictus, aoristic, contemporaneous with *amisit.*   Cp. notes on 2. 2, 5. 1.

fortium, a name dear to the Stoic sage, cp. Hor. *Sat.* II. 3. 97.

ambitiose, 'ostentatiously,' 'with a view to effect,' cp. *ambitiosa morte* 42. 5.   The Stoics made a parade of their freedom from emotion (ἀπάθεια).   Some of the later eclectic Stoics like Panaetius realised that the doctrine of 'apathy' was overdone and protested against it.   Cp. A. Gellius, *N. A.* XII. 5. 10.

2.   incertum, 'vague,' because the enemy did not know where the next attack would be.

expedito, 'without heavy baggage.'

exploratos, 'tried.' Gudeman wonders how Tacitus can reconcile *longa pax* with *fortitudo* in view of 11. 5. History is revenging itself upon rhetoric.

Graupium. The name 'Grampians' is due to a misspelling in Puteolanus' edition. This year Agricola advanced along the route which the Caledonian railway now follows, past Stirling, Dunblane, Ardoch, where an enormous Roman fort of the first century guards the road, Perth, where Agricola would be in contact with his fleet which was doubtless operating on the tidal waters of the Tay, and then up Strathmore to the confluence of the Tay and Isla. Near here is the large camp of Inchtuthill on a plateau rising abruptly from the plain. This was certainly occupied by Agricola, and Sir J. H. Ramsay places the scene of the battle here (see his plan *op. cit.* I. 74). Prof. Haverfield, who observes that Inchtuthill looks like a campaigning base, is inclined to think that the battle was fought further north. There are other encampments, probably Roman, in Eastern Scotland, the most northerly being in the uplands of north Aberdeenshire. This camp, which was examined in 1913, can hardly have been the scene of Agricola's battle (see Haverfield, *Class. Rev.* 1914, p. 44), and may be a relic of the expedition of the emperor Septimius Severus, who about 208 A.D. penetrated far into Caledonia.

3. pugnae prioris, c. 26.

tandemque docti, etc., cp. 12. 2, 27. 3.

4. adhuc, 'in addition.'

cruda ac viridis senectus, from Virg. *Aen.* VI. 304. *crudus*, connected with *cruor*, hence 'full of blood' (a rare sense), so 'fresh,' 'vigorous.'

praestans, 'one who excelled.' In four other places in Tacitus *vir* (or *femina*) is omitted in expressions with *nomine*.

Calgacus is not heard of elsewhere. His sole function is to make a speech. The harangue put into his mouth does not pretend to be historical (cp. the vague *in hunc modum locutus fertur*). It is a piece of imaginative rhetoric and is betrayed as such by its elaborate use of rhetorical figures and its echoes of generals' addresses in other writers.

CHAPTER XXX

1. causas, see 31. 1.

animus, 'confidence,' hence it takes the construction of *spes*.

initium, etc. Caratacus (see on 14. 1) addresses his troops in similar terms, *Ann.* XII. 34.

universi colitis, 'you dwell all together,' i.e. as one people. Contrast *Germ.* 16. 1.

terrae, sc. *sunt*.

securum = *tutum*, a somewhat rare meaning. Calgacus insists that they *must* conquer, as they have no retreat by land or sea.

3. priores pugnae...habebant, 'previous battles saw a hope and a refuge still left in us.' *priores pugnae* is rhetorically put for 'those who fought in previous battles.'

eoque, 'and therefore'; presumably that in their 'innermost sanctuary' they might be furthest from debasing influences. There seems to be an inversion of the natural order of ideas, *in ipsis penetralibus siti eoque nobilissimi.*

servientium litora, 'the shores of slaves,' i.e. of Gauls, visible from the south-east coast of Britain.

a contactu. For the preposition instead of the simple ablative, cp. Livy XXXIX. 40 *invictus a cupiditatibus animus.*

4. nos, etc. 'Dwelling as we do on the confines of the world and of liberty, our very remoteness and the seclusion of our glory...' cp. Hor. *Odes*, I. 35. 29 *ultimos orbis Britannos. sinus* may contain the notion of safekeeping (*tutela*), derived from the meaning, 'fold in a garment,' or 'bosom.' Cp. Seneca, *Ep.* 103 *illa* (sc. *philosophia*) *te sinu suo proteget.* So here, perhaps, 'the seclusion which kept safe our fame.'

atque omne ignotum pro magnifico est, 'and indeed there is always a sublimity in the unknown,' strengthening the statement that their isolation had been their defence. [In the MSS. these words occur after *patet*, the passage running, *in hunc diem defendit. nunc terminus Britanniae patet, atque omne ignotum pro magnifico est ; sed nulla iam ultra gens,* etc. If this order is correct we must regard the words in question as giving a motive which *will draw the Romans on*, now that the door is open (*patet*). The following *sed* will then mark a return to the Caledonian position, 'The Romans will inevitably advance, attracted by the unknown, *we* have no retreat open to us.' This interpretation is certainly difficult, and Calgacus would hardly have represented the unknown as attractive to the Romans, cp. 32. 3. Brüys' transposition therefore seems justified.]

5. patet, sc. to the Roman advance.

infestiores, than waves and rocks.

effugias, 'one tries to escape' (potential subjunctive with indefinite subject), better than the perfect *effugeris* read by the inferior MSS.

6. mare scrutantur, referring to the operations of the fleet. Cp. *Germ.* 45. 4 for the phrase.

ambitiosi, 'eager for glory,' i.e. the glory of conquest.

quos...satiaverit. The subjunctive is generic (i.e. ' men whom,' etc.) or perhaps potential (cp. 3. 1).

omnium with *soli. inopiam* implies that not even the poor escape.

7. imperium, sc. *appellant.*

pacem. The expression *pax Romana* had become an official euphemism for subjugation (Gudeman). Cp. *Ann.* XII. 33, *Hist.* IV. 17 *servitutem falso pacem vocarent.*

CHAPTER XXXI

1. voluit, 'has ordained.'

alibi servituri. Nero had sent British contingents to the East (*Hist.* I. 6). Britons took part in the operations of A.D. 69 (*Hist.* I. 6, 43, 70, III. 41), and we know from inscriptions that British auxiliaries raised about the time of Agricola's governorship served in several parts of Central Europe. See note on 28. 1.

nomine amicorum, 'under the name of friends,' i.e. by those who profess to be friends.

2. ager atque annus, to be closely connected, 'the yearly produce of the land.' For *annus=annona* cp. *Germ.* 14. 5.

in frumentum, sc. *exiguntur* out of *conteruntur,* 'are requisitioned for the provision of corn.' For *frumentum* see on 19. 4.

emuniendis, 'in constructing roads through.'

semel, 'once for all,' contrasted with *cotidie.*

atque ultro, 'and what is more.'

servitutem, etc., 'every day purchases (by tribute), every day supports (by corn) its own slavery.'

3. novi nos, etc., 'we new acquisitions—and worthless ones— are marked out for destruction.' The parallel between the two clauses, *sicut...sic...,* is not exact. The newly enslaved Caledonians will not be derided, but killed.

nobis, Caledonians, as distinct from the other Britons.

quibus exercendis, dative of purpose. The words involve a zeugma, for *exercere* can hardly be joined with *portus* in the sense of 'working at,' i.e. 'constructing' harbours.

4. ferocia, 'spirit.'

secretum, 'isolation.'

5. Brigantes. As we find no other mention that the Brigantes took part in the rising under Boudicca and the sack of Camulodunum (*coloniam*, cp. 16. 1), it is best to suppose that Tacitus, by a dramatic inaccuracy, makes Calgacus employ the name of his nearest British neighbours as a general term for Britons.

castra, of uncertain reference. Possibly the temple precinct held by the troops at Camulodunum is meant.

potuere, 'were able,' with *exurere* and *expugnare*, but 'would have been able' with *exuere*. In the apodosis of unfulfilled conditional expressions the indicative of words like *debeo*, *possum*, *oportet* is regularly used instead of the subjunctive.

in libertatem, etc., 'about to fight to win liberty, not to regret our action' (as the Britons did), certainly an awkward expression in view of the ordinary meaning of *arma ferre in*, but none of the other emendations seems more satisfactory.

CHAPTER XXXII

1. dissensionibus. See 12. 2 and contrast 30. 1.

nisi si, ironical, introducing an absurd alternative. *nisi forte* is commoner in this sense.

pudet dictu, without parallel according to Draeger (*S. und S.* § 218), instead of *pudendum dictu*, as only adjectives are used with the supine in -*u*.

plerosque, not 'most,' but 'a great many,' cp. 1. 3.

diutius, etc., 'yet having been enemies longer than slaves.'

adfectu, 'affection,' cp. *Ann.* XIV. 27, a late meaning, which is approached in 30. 6.

2. terror, 'intimidation.'

nullae...accendunt. Celtic and German women were accustomed to encourage their menfolk on the battlefield; *Ann.* XIV. 34, *Germ.* 7. 4.

nulla...patria, because their national existence had been destroyed by Rome, or because they were homeless mercenaries. For the phrase cp. Sallust, *epistula Mithradatis* 17 (*frag. hist.* IV. 61), *convenas*, sc. *Romanos, olim sine patria parentibus* (asyndeton). Calgacus' speech seems to contain several echoes of Mithradates' letter.

alia, other than Rome.

3. circumspectantis, 'anxiously surveying,' a common shade of meaning.

vinctos, 'chained to the spot,' similarly used in *Hist.* I. 79. *Ann.* I. 65, cp. 34. 3.

4. nostras manus, i.e. troops whose cause is ours.

ultra, beyond the present enemy.

coloniae, Camulodunum and Lindum (Lincoln), which was founded in A.D. 70—80. [Glevum (Gloucester) was made a colony in 96—98, Eboracum (York) about the beginning of the third century.]

inter, 'between reluctant subjects and tyrannical governors the free towns are weak and disaffected.' This use of *inter* to give a reason is common in Tacitus. Cp. *Hist.* II. 92 *inter discordes* ('since they were at variance') *Vitellio nihil auctoritatis.*

municipia were native towns which received Roman civic rights and a municipal constitution based on the Italian model. Municipal status was only granted to towns where the Romanisation was already fairly thorough. In imperial times it was less honourable than that of the *coloniae*, which were often, like Camulodunum, the direct foundations of the emperor. The only *municipium* known to have existed in Britain is Verulamium (established before A.D. 60), though the *coloniae* also had municipal rank. The less privileged towns of Britain, like Calleva Atrebatum (Silchester), Venta Silurum (Caerwent), Viriconium, etc., were the capitals of tribes or cantons and were governed by native chiefs or nobles, though even here the Roman organisation was imitated. "The cantonal *civitas* had its *duoviri* and quaestors and so forth, and its *ordo* or senate, precisely like any municipal *colonia* or *municipium*." (Haverfield, *Romanisation, etc.*, p. 50.)

5. in hoc campo est, 'depends on this field.'

CHAPTER XXXIII

1. alacres, 'with enthusiasm.'

ut...moris, common for *ut mos*; literally, 'as belongs to' or 'is part of the custom.' The words modify what follows.

cantu, cp. *Germ.* 3. 1.

agmina, 'moving bodies of troops.' A verb like *conspiciebantur* must be supplied.

audentissimi, etc., 'as all the boldest spirits rushed forward.' *procursu* is ablat. of attendant circumstances. The rare superlative *audentissimus* occurs in Gellius, VI. 2.

adhuc, 'yet more.'

2. septimus, reckoning inclusively from A.D. 78. *octavus* of the MSS. cannot be right.

auspiciis would naturally be followed by the emperor's name. But Agricola had served under three emperors: Vespasian, Titus, and Domitian. Tacitus, too, was doubtless unwilling to mention the hated name of Domitian in this connexion. So *imperii Romani* is substituted. (Cp. *auspiciis populi Romani*, Livy XXX. 14.) On the strength of the personification Gudeman retains the MS. text, *virtute et auspiciis imp. R.* The reading is at least improbable, and Gudeman's objections to the commonly accepted emendation do not seem well founded. (See, however, Warde Fowler in *Class. Rev.* XVIII. 43.)

fide, 'loyalty.'

expeditionibus...proeliis, locative ablatives, to be construed with *paenituit.*

3. non fama nec rumore, 'not by mere report or rumour.' Our grasp of Britain's extremity is not mere visionary talk and gossip, it is an actual armed occupation.

inventa, 'discovered'; previously it was only half known.

4. acies. See note on the text. Stuart's *adimus* (vivid present for future) is ingenious.

vota, etc., 'your prayers and your prowess have an open field, and all is easy if you conquer.' See on 1. 2 for *prona* and *in aperto. omnia...adversa* is a reminiscence of Sall. *Cat.* 58. 9 *si vincimus, omnia nobis tuta erunt. sin metu cesserimus, eadem illa adversa fient.*

5. in frontem, 'while we face forwards,' a harshly elliptical expression (sc. *progredientibus*), balancing *fugientibus.*

in his omnia, 'all depends on them.'

6. mihi decretum est, 'I have made up my mind,' 'been convinced.'

terga, i.e. retreat.

et...et, 'while...yet.' In sense *et honesta mors...potior* is subordinate to *et incolumitas...sunt,* and *proinde* ('therefore') really introduces the latter clause. Nipperdey transposes the clauses.

decus, 'glory,' i.e. a glorious resistance.

eodem loco sita sunt, i.e. go together.

fuerit, probably fut. perf. indic. See on 3. 1.

ac naturae, 'and indeed of the world,' cp. *Germ.* 45. 1.

CHAPTER XXXIV

1. constitisset, 'had taken up its position,' sc. against you.

decora, 'glorious deeds,' Livy III. 12, XXI. 43.

furto noctis, 'by a night surprise,' cp. Curt. IV. 13. 9, Livy XXXI. 31, *furto insidiarum.* For the facts see c. 26.

S.   8

clamore, 'merely by a shout.'

ceterorum fugacissimi, a confusion between *omnium fugacissimi* and *ceteris fugaciores*, in imitation of a common Greek idiom, e.g. Thuc. I. 10 μεγίστην τῶν πρὸ αὐτῆς. *Hist.* I. 50 is similar, *solusque omnium ante se.* Cp. Milton, *P. L.* IV. 324 'the fairest of her daughters, Eve.' Shakespeare, *Midsummer Night's Dream* V. 256 'This is the greatest error of all the rest.' The idiom is not uncommon in Elizabethan writers.

2. quo modo, answered by *sic.*

penetrantibus, sc. *nobis,* either dative (cp. on 10. 4) or abl. abs.

ruere, historic infin., used several times by Tac. in temporal clauses in combination with the imperf. indic., *Ann.* II. 4, III. 26, XI. 37, XII. 51, XIII. 57, *Hist.* III. 31. There is particular force in the contrasted imperf. here, 'while the frightened ones were being driven away.' Others take *ruere* to be aorist indic. The passage seems to echo Curt. III. 8. 10 *delituisse inter angustias saltus ritu ignobilium ferarum, quae strepitu praetereuntium audito silvarum latebris se occulerent.*

numerus, contemptuous, 'a mass of,' cp. Hor. *Ep.* I. 2. 27, apparently an imitation of the Greek use of ἀριθμός.

3. quos, etc. 'As to the fact that you have found them at last, (you must know that) they have not turned to bay.' For a similar use of *quod* cp. Ovid, *Trist.* III. 1. 15, *littera suffusas quod habet maculosa lituras, laesit opus lacrimis ipse poeta suum.*

novissimae res, 'their extremity' (Furneaux).

extremo metu torpor. See note on text. Ritter's emendation, which I adopt, involves only the change of *corpora* to *torpor* and gives perhaps a slightly better-sounding sentence than Gudeman's *extremus metus corpora defixere* [*aciem*].

defixere, 'have rooted to the ground.'

ederetis, final, 'might exhibit.' The phrase is on the analogy of *edere spectaculum.*

4. transigite cum, 'have done with,' cp. *Germ.* 19. 3.

quinquaginta annis, really from 43 to 84; 'crown 50 years with one great day.' Cp. *extremam* or *summam manum imponere,* 'to put the finishing touches to.'

CHAPTER XXXV

1. et...et, 'both...and.' For *alacritas,* cp. 33. 1.

2. ruentis, clearly not actually 'charging,' but 'full of dash.'

mediam aciem firmarent, 'made a strong centre.' cp. 14. 4.

adfunderentur, 'were spread out on.'

legiones, II Augusta, IX, XX and II Adiutrix (for the last see on 17. 2; its headquarters were Chester in Agricola's time). The legionary troops engaged are estimated at 15,000.

ingens...decus, in apposition with the preceding clause or rather with the whole account of the disposition; 'to add to victory the great glory of carrying on hostilities without the shedding of Roman blood (i.e. the blood of the legionaries), and to act as a reinforcement in case they (sc. the auxiliaries) were beaten.'

victoriae, dative, is parallel to *si pellerentur.* For *citra* see on 1. 3.

3. **in speciem,** 'to make an imposing show,' further explained by *in terrorem.* Cp. *Germ.* 38. 4.

in aequo, sc. *esset.*

per adclive, etc., 'sloping over the hillside appeared to tower up (against them).' The change to *conexi,* 'in close lines,' seems unnecessary. Indeed no instance of *conexus* used of troops is quoted. For *convexus* cp. Ovid, *Met.* XIII. 911 *convexus* (='sloping down') *ad aequora vertex* and *Met.* XIV. 154 *convexum* (probably = 'sloping up') *per iter.* Cp. too Claudian *VI. cons. Honor.* 613, cited by Wex. *velut* is inserted because *insurgere* would be more appropriately used of the hill itself than of the troops upon it, or perhaps it apologises for the whole phrase, including the somewhat strained use of *convexi.*

media campi, 'the intervening level ground.'

covinnarius eques, 'chariot squadron' (*eques,* collective), a strange circumlocution for *covinnarii,* 36. 3. *covinnarius et eques* is a tempting emendation. For the *covinnus* see on 12. 1. Cp. also Mr James Curle, *Journ. of Roman Studies,* 1913, p. 101, for remains of wheeled vehicles, possibly of native manufacture, found on Roman sites in Scotland.

strepitu ac discursu, 'with the clatter of their hurrying to and fro.'

4. **diductis,** cp. Livy v. 8 *instruunt aciem diductam in cornua.*

porrectior, 'too extended.'

promptior, etc., 'always quite ready to hope and unshaken in the face of danger.' *adversis* is dative, a variant on *firmus ad* or *f. adversus.*

ante vexilla, i.e. in the front line of the auxiliaries. In battle the Roman 'colours' were placed in the *rear* of the first line. For *vexilla,* here the flags of the auxiliary detachments, see on 18. 3.

CHAPTER XXXVI

1. constantia, 'with steadiness,' ablat. of manner.

gladiis...caetris, instr. ablat. Note the chiasmus; 'to avoid with their small targes and to parry with their huge claymores.' For the latter operation cp. Veget. I. 4 *obliquis ictibus venientia tela deflectere.*

quattuor Batavorum cohortis, attached to Leg. XIV (8 such were attached to it in 69). Cohort I saw service on the English Wall and one of them may have been at Castlecary (note on 23. 2). See Macdonald, *Rom. Wall*, 328. The home of the Batavians was at the mouth of the Rhine, *Germ.* 29. 1. See on 18. 5.

Tungrorum duas, each perhaps 1000 strong (cp. Macdonald, *op. cit.* 326). We hear of them first in 69, *Hist.* II. 14. Cohort I was at Castlecary and at Housesteads on the English Wall, Cohort II at Birrens. The Tungri lived in eastern Belgium, *Germ.* 2. 5.

quod, i.e. this kind of fighting.

vetustate...exercitatum, 'drilled into them by long experience of warfare,' for the Germans naturally used spears rather than swords; *Germ.* 6. 1, *Ann.* II. 21 (where the Germans are described as subject to the same disadvantage in fighting Romans as the Britons in this passage). *exercitatus,* generally of persons, is here used in a very forced sense.

inhabile, 'awkward.'

enormis gladios. Celtic swords have been found more than 3 feet long with only slightly tapering points (*sine mucrone*), intended for cutting, not for thrusting. With their small targes and large cutting swords the Caledonians could not face troops armed in the Roman fashion with large shields and small stabbing swords (cp. *ad mucrones* above).

complexum armorum, 'clash of arms,' 'mêlée,' only occurring here.

in arto, i.e. at close quarters.

2. miscere ictus, 'to exchange blows' (or perhaps 'to rain blows indiscriminately'), like *vulnera miscent*, Verg. *Aen.* XII. 720.

erigere, cp. 18. 3.

aemulatione et impetu, 'in impetuous rivalry.'

3. equitum, sc. of the Romans. Following Wex's suggestion, after *fugere* I have inserted *enim*, which may have been omitted by a scribe and wrongly replaced after *equestris ei* below (see note on text). Others read *ut* or *ubi fugere*.

peditum, the Roman foot. The cavalry first put to flight the *covinnarii* and then assisted the infantry.

recentem, 'fresh,' in addition to that caused by the infantry.

cum, etc., 'since they could scarcely keep their footing on the slope and were jostled by the horses' bodies.' Schoemann's *aegre clivo instantes*, though perhaps hardly more than a makeshift, gives a reasonable sense to the unintelligible words of the MSS. But the absence of a subject for *impellerentur* is very awkward (though the Romans are probably meant), and the *cum* clause as restored is not a lucid or natural explanation why the fight was not like a cavalry engagement.   Wex boldly reads *minimeque* aequa nostris iam *pugnae facies erat cum.*

vagi currus, etc. Cp. Curt. VIII. 14. 9 *ut dissipatos tota acie currus vagari sine rectoribus vidit.*

transversos aut obvios, 'on flank or front,' referring to the advancing Romans.

CHAPTER XXXVII

1. vacui spernebant, 'idly despised.' Cp. *animo vacuus = securus,* Sall. *Jug.* 52. Here perhaps *vacui* takes some of its colour from *pugnae expertes.* Gudeman wrongly brackets the word.

ni, sc. *et circumissent ni.* See on 4. 4.

equitum, distinct from those of 35. 2.

subita, 'emergencies.'

2. consilium, i.e. of taking the Romans in the rear.

aversam, lit. 'when turned away,' so 'in the rear.' Cp. 36. 3 *ad fin.*

patentibus, etc. This passage down to *cruenta humus* is a very obvious imitation of Sall. *Jug.* 101. 11.

eosdem, i.e. *captos.*

3. hostium, going with both *catervae armatorum* and *quidam inermes.*

prout, etc., according as they were cowards or brave men.

terga praestare, exceptional for *terga dare.* Cp. Juv. XV. 75 *terga fugae celeri praestantibus omnibus.*

ruere, 'charge.'

aliquando, etc., an echo of Virg. *Aen.* II. 367 *quondam etiam victis redit in praecordia virtus.*

4. quod ni, 'and unless'; cp. 16. 2.

frequens ubique, 'constantly everywhere'; cp. 20. 2.

indaginis modo, 'forming a cordon.' *indago* is the process of

surrounding a covert with nets, dogs, etc., to prevent the game
escaping; cp. Virg. *Aen.* IV. 121 and for the military sense
Livy, VII. 37. With *cohortis* supply *silvas circumire* out of *silvas
persultare* below.

sicubi artiora, etc. Where the woods were close, part of the
cavalry dismounted and searched them; where they were thinner,
the cavalry kept their horses.

equitem, collective, cp. 35. 3, somewhat harshly contrasted with
equitum dimissis equis. If the manuscript reading *equite persultari*
be accepted, there is a very remarkable change from active to
passive construction, and with *cohortis* and *partem equitum* we must
supply from *persultari* an active infinitive (which may possibly have
dropped out of the MSS.).

vulnus, 'disaster.'

5. respectantes, 'waiting for.'

vitabundi in vicem, 'avoiding each other.' Cp. 16. 1.

CHAPTER XXXVIII

1. quidem contrasts *nox* with *proximus dies* § 2; 'night
indeed...but.'

miscere, etc., 'formed some sort of common plans together and
then decided separately for themselves.' *separare*, sc. *consilia*, is
concisely put for *separatim capere* to parallel *miscere*, for which
cp. *Ann.* XV. 68.

pignorum, sc. *amoris*, wives and children. Cp. *Germ.* 7. 3.

2. saevisse, to prevent their falling into the hands of the
Romans. For *tamquam* see on 16. 3.

proximus, etc., 'next day opened out in wider view the
spectacle of victory'; cp. 22. 1 for the personification.

vastum, 'desolate.'

secreti, 'lonely,' because deserted by the enemy, a striking use
of the word.

3. incerta fugae vestigia, sc. *erant*, 'the track of the enemy's
flight was uncertain.' The phrase is from Lucan VIII. 4.

spargi bellum, i.e. extended over a wide area; again from
Lucan III. 64 etc., who imitates Virgil's *spargam arma, Aen.* VII.
551.

Borestorum, unknown, though some think they lived in Foth-
reve, i.e. Kinross. (For the assumed phonetic change from Bor-esti
to Foth-reve cp. Bodotria—Forth.) Others place them in Strat-
hearn. See Sir J. H. Ramsay, *op. cit.* I. 75.

4. circumvehi. Note the infin. instead of *ut* after *praecipio* (cp. 46. 3), a constr. quite common in Tacitus with such verbs.

vires, 'troops,' to make landings, as on the Orkneys, 10. 5.

et, 'and besides,' introducing a further source of strength.

peditem...equites, collective and plural combined for variety, cp. 37. 4.

hibernis, presumably on the Clyde and Forth line; in particular, Newstead.

5. secunda used in different senses with the two ablatives, which themselves denote different kinds of 'attendant circumstances'; 'with fair weather and a fair name.' The operations of 10. 5 justify the latter expression.

Trucculensem portum, unknown; probably in or near the Firth of Forth.

unde, going only with *praelecto*; 'from which it had coasted along all the adjoining side of Britain and then returned to it.'

proximum latus is the east coast, see on 29. 2. The fleet did not circumnavigate the whole island. It probably doubled Cape Wrath and went far enough down the west coast to establish the insularity of Britain, returning the same way. It should be remembered that the Usipi had already sailed round the north of Scotland, c. 28.

CHAPTER XXXIX

1. epistulis = *epistula*, as often in Tac., the plural being on the analogy of *litterae*.

ut erat Domitiano moris, short for *Domitianus, ut ei moris erat.* For *moris* see on 33. 1.

2. falsum e Germania triumphum. In 83 A.D. Domitian made an expedition in person against the Chatti, whom he drove out of the Taunus range, and on the strength of his success assumed the title of Germanicus (Frontinus II. 11. 7). It was after this expedition that the German *limes* or system of frontier defences was begun. Tac. speaks slightingly of the operations in *Germ.* 37. 6, so does Pliny, *Pan.* 16, but their criticisms are discounted by their prejudice against the emperor.

emptis, agreeing with the unexpressed antecedent to *quorum.*

crines, long and red, cp. 11. 2. A similar story is told of Caligula; *nonnullos ex principibus* (sc. *Gallicis*) *legit ac seposuit ad pompam, coegitque non tantum rutilare et summittere comam, sed et sermonem Germanicum addiscere et nomina barbarica ferre* (Suet. *Cal.* 47).

formarentur, sc. 'as they said,' subjunct. of virtual *or. obl.*

3. privati hominis, 'a subject.'

studia fori, etc., 'the eloquence of the bar and the noble activities of political life.' Cp. 2. 2 and 3. 2.

alius, other than the emperor.

utcunque, 'somehow,' a Livian use.

dissimulari, 'disregarded.' Domitian might perhaps ignore other claims to distinction, but could not allow competition in the imperial quality of generalship. The successful general might be a potential emperor.

4. quodque. The antecedent of *quod* is the phrase *secreto suo satiatus*; 'having indulged to the full in his usual solitary reserve, the sign of his savage purpose.' Cp. Pliny, *Pan.* 48 *non adire quisquam, non alloqui audebat tenebras semper secretumque captantem.* For the 'den' of this *immanissima belua*, as Pliny calls him, see 45. 1.

in praesentia, neut. plur., less common in Tac. than *in praesens*, which appears in the margin of E. (Others comparing Sen. *Ep.* 52. 15 *differam hoc in praesentia* and a similar phrase in *Ep.* 72. 1 assert that *praesentia* here is ablat. sing.)

reponere, 'to store up'; so *odia recondere* (of Tiberius), *Ann.* I. 69.

impetus, 'the first burst.'

nam, etc., the reason why Domitian preferred to wait. Agricola, with four legions at his back, might have imitated the example of previous provincial governors, like Vitellius and Vespasian, and aspired to become emperor.

Chapter XL

1. triumphalia ornamenta, the *toga picta*, purple and gold-embroidered, the *tunica palmata*, worked with palm leaves, the *corona triumphalis* or bay wreath, and the curule chair. Since B.C. 14 the triumphal procession, *iustus triumphus*, had been reserved for the emperor and members of the imperial house. The victorious subject had to be content with the *insignia* instead (cp. *pro triumpho* below).

inlustris statuae. A complimentary statue of the successful general (*statua laureata, Ann.* IV. 23) was sometimes placed in the forum as an additional honour.

quidquid, etc., including perhaps a *supplicatio* or national thanksgiving.

in senatu. In theory the Senate alone had the right of awarding a triumph.

addique, etc., 'and the impression to be conveyed besides.' There is a slight zeugma; 'and (allowed) the impression to get abroad.'

Atilii Rufi. He had been legate of Pannonia in 80.

maioribus, 'persons of special eminence.' Syria was the most esteemed of the imperial governorships. Its legate commanded four legions.

2. ministeriis, abstract for concrete, cp. *servitia* for *servi* and see 44. 4; 'one of his confidential servants.'

dabatur, 'was offered.' The offer of Syria, it is implied, was in the nature of a bribe to induce Agricola to quit his province. As the freedman found that Agricola had already acted upon the order of recall, it was unnecessary to deliver the dispatch.

ne, etc., 'without even having speech with him.'

ex, 'according to,' 'to suit,' cp. *Germ.* 3. 4.

3. successori, apparently Sallustius Lucullus, according to Suet. *Dom.* 10 ff. put to death by Domitian *quod lanceas novae formae appellari Luculleas passus esset.*

celebritate, etc., 'by crowds thronging to meet him.' For *occurrentium* see on 4. 3.

officio, 'the attentions,' cp. 18. 6.

praeceptum erat, i.e. by the emperor.

brevi osculo. The kiss was the usual salutation bestowed by the emperors upon their intimate friends. Herein they only followed the example of their subjects. See Mart. XI. 98.

servientium, 'servile courtiers.'

inmixtus est, i.e. 'was lost in.'

4. grave inter otiosos, 'unpopular among civilians,' who might envy it. *otium* is constantly opposed to *bellum.*

penitus hausit, 'drank deeply of,' cp. 4. 4.

cultu, 'in his style of living,' including dress, household, etc.

facilis, 'affable,' cp. 9. 4.

uno aut altero, 'one or at most two,' cp. 12. 2. The simple ablative of accompaniment with *comitatus* is frequent in poetry (cp. Ovid, *Fasti,* III. 603) and occurs even in Cicero, *pro. Cael.* 14. 34. Cp. *stipatus* with ablat.

per ambitionem, 'by their ostentation.'

aspecto, 'surveyed,' more forcible than *viso.*

quaererent, 'inquired about,' or 'asked the reason of' his fame.

interpretarentur, 'understood,' sc. the reason for his unassuming demeanour. Do not supply *famam.*

Chapter XLI

1. absens, etc. Note the alliteration.

laudantes, 'namely panegyrists,' substantival, see on 4. 3.

2. et, 'and besides,' introducing an additional reason for his danger.

sileri, 'to go unmentioned,' cp. Pliny, *epp.* VIII. 22, *ille...sileatur.*

in Moesia, etc. In 85 the Dacian king, Decebalus, invaded Moesia and defeated and slew the legate Oppius Sabinus. Next year Cornelius Fuscus drove the enemy back across the Danube, only to suffer a terrible disaster in which he lost his own life (see Juv. IV. 111). In 89 these calamities were avenged by the Roman general, Julianus, at the battle of Tapae. Meanwhile Domitian had been operating with the army of Pannonia against the Marcomanni and Quadi (*Germ.* 42) who had contributed to the overthrow of Fuscus by failing to send the succours they had promised. Domitian himself received a defeat, which induced him to make peace with the Dacians. Later, about 91, one of the Pannonian legions was annihilated by the Sarmatian Jazyges (see Bury, *Rom. Emp.* 408—410). On the Rhine frontier too the Chatti had given trouble by assisting the revolt of L. Antonius Saturninus, the governor of Upper Germany, who had been proclaimed emperor by his troops (88 A.D.).

militares viri, 'military men,' 'officers.'

expugnati, 'had their positions stormed.'

limite. *limes* originally meant a field-path and so a boundary between fields, then a military road made through an enemy's country to help in the process of conquest, and finally a frontier road or frontier line protected with forts and towers at intervals, or with a continuous earthwork, wall or fence. The *limes* here mentioned is that constructed by Domitian after his expedition against the Chatti in 83. It was a chain of earth forts with intervening watch-towers and perhaps a fence, stretching from near Rheinbrohl, a few miles N.W. of Coblenz, in a south-easterly direction along the hills on the right bank of the Rhine to the Taunus range, thence north-east along its summit to Arnsburg, and thence southwards to Krotzenburg on the Main. From this point the frontier passed with a general southerly trend to Rottweil (*Arae Flaviae*), coinciding with the courses of the Main and the Neckar except between Wörth and Wimpfen, where it crossed the watershed between the two rivers. (The more easterly *limes*, marked on most of the maps, which extended from the Main S.E. to Lorch, and the so-called

Raetian *limes*, between Lorch and Hienheim on the Danube, are later. The second belongs to the reign of Trajan, and the first apparently to that of Hadrian, who constructed a lofty wooden palisade along the whole line from Rhine to Danube.)

The Chatti broke through Domitian's *limes* to assist Antonius Saturninus (see above). "Several of the earth forts on the *limes* and one at least of the stone base forts (at Okarben) bear traces of having been partially destroyed by fire and rebuilt." Stuart Jones, *Comp. to Rom. Hist.* p. 245.

ripa, the river—as opposed to the land-frontier; here the line of the Danube.

possessione, understand *provinciarum*; cp. Cic. *Acad.* II. 43. 132 *non de terminis sed de tota possessione contentio.*

3. **damnis.** For dat. cp. *Germ.* 45. 9.

constantiam, 'steadiness,' 'determination.'

ceterorum. See note on text. *eorum* of the MSS. is too awkward to stand.

4. **auris verberatas**, 'ears were assailed,' a Plautine expression.

dum, 'whilst,' several times thus used by Tac. with the imperfect indicative; cp. *dum...enumerabat, Ann.* XIII. 3.

amore et fide, sc. towards Domitian; causal ablatives. Owing to a zeugma, with these words supply from *exstimulabant* ('kept goading him on') a milder verb like *adhortabantur* (i.e. advised him to employ Agricola). See Furneaux.

malignitate et livore, sc. towards Agricola.

deterioribus, 'to the worse course,' neuter, cp. 16. 3.

vitiis aliorum, sc. of his envious detractors and of the unsuccessful generals.

in ipsam gloriam praeceps agebatur, 'was hurried headlong into actual fame,' which he most wished to avoid. *praeceps agi* suggests 'being driven to ruin,' and so is appropriately applied to Agricola, for whom fame meant ruin. Cp. 5. 4 *ad fin.* and 42. 4 *famam fatumque.*

CHAPTER XLII

1. **Africae et Asiae**, the two most important senatorial provinces, annually bestowed on the two senior ex-consuls, whose turn seems generally to have come some twelve years after their consulships. As Agricola was consul in 77, he may have been ripe for the governorship about 89.

sortiretur, 'was to ballot for,' past jussive subjunct.

Civica. C. Vettulenus Civica Cerialis, propraetor of Moesia in 82, put to death by Domitian on a charge of treason when proconsul of Asia. Suet. *Dom.* 10.

nec Agricolae, etc. 'A. did not want knowledge how to act, nor Domitian a precedent.'

ultro, 'on their own initiative.' *interrogarent* is a final subjunctive.

2. occultius, 'somewhat obscurely,' i.e. hiding their real meaning. Contrast *non iam obscuri.*

adprobanda, 'making good,' sc. to the emperor. Cp. on 5. 1.

3. paratus, etc., 'primed with hypocrisy and assuming a majestic air.'

excusantis. Gudeman inserts *se.* Two parallel accounts of persons declining the offer of one or the other of these two provinces are quoted (*Ann.* III. 35, *Acta Arvalia*, Inscr. Or. 1170), in both of which *se excusare* occurs.

agi sibi, etc. The way to live long at court was to return thanks for injuries received, see Sen. *de ira*, II, 33. 2.

invidia, causal ablative; 'at the hatefulness of the boon,' i.e. of the pretended indulgence to Agricola.

salarium...proconsulare. The payment of provincial governors was instituted by Augustus. Sometimes the salary was given without the office. In 217 A.D. a certain Aufidius Fronto, in lieu of receiving the province of Africa, was offered 1,000,000 sesterces or about £8800, the annual value of the post. Dio Cass. LXXVIII. 22.

offensus, rarely followed by the accus. and infin. Cp. Suet. *Aug.* 89.

sive ex conscientia, etc., 'or from a guilty conscience, fearing he might be thought to have secured by a bribe what he had forbidden.' Domitian had virtually forbidden Agricola to accept the province. He was afraid it might be said that he had only prevailed on Agricola to refuse it by bribing him with the salary.

4. odisse, etc. So Seneca *de ira* II. 33 *hoc habent pessimum animi magna fortuna insolentes: quos laeserunt et oderunt.*

vero, 'certainly,' introducing a particular application of the general rule.

quo obscurior, etc., 'no less implacable than it was reserved.'

famam fatumque. Cp. note on 41. 4. For the alliterative *f* cp. 33. 4 and 46. 3 *formam...figuram.*

5. sciant, etc., a splendid sentence, important as an indication of Tacitus' own political attitude.

inlicita, 'lawless conduct,' i.e. disloyalty to the emperor. See notes on 2. 1, 4. 4.

modestiam, 'restraint,' 'discipline.'

eo laudis excedere, etc., 'attain to that high degree of distinction to which many have attained by dangerous paths but with no benefit to the state, winning fame by an ostentatious death' (i.e. by suicide). *excedere* contains the idea of 'passing beyond ordinary limits,' as in *Ann.* II. 24 *tantum illa clades novitate et magnitudine excessit.*

quo, 'whither,' cannot appropriately be joined with *inclaruerunt*, 'have won fame'; with it supply perhaps *excedentes*. For *plerique* cp. 32. 1.

abrupta, 'precipitous,' so 'dangerous.'

CHAPTER XLIII

1. extraneis, 'strangers.'

vulgus...populus. *populus* is the more dignified term as indicating the people in their political aspect, *vulgus* suggests social degradation ; 'the common herd and this heedless people of Rome.' Cp. *dial.* 7 *vulgus imperitum et tunicatus hic populus*; so *populus et imperita plebs, Hist.* I. 35, cp. I. 40. *aliud* or *alias res agens* is frequent in the sense of *incuriosus*, 'indifferent.'

circulos, 'social gatherings.'

2. interceptum, sc. *fuisse*, a word used of premature death, particularly of murder.

nobis, etc., 'I would venture to affirm that we (i.e. the family) have no ascertained evidence of this,' a mild deprecation of hasty belief in the rumours, which, however, Tacitus after his manner does his best to drive home. Dio Cassius LXVI. 20 definitely states that Agricola was murdered by Domitian, though Suetonius shows an unexpected silence on the subject. (There is something strange in Tacitus *making bold to affirm* the absence of good evidence ; hence the suggestions to insert *quod, ut* or *nec* before *adfirmare ausim*).

visentis, agreeing with *principatus=principum*, abstract for concrete ; 'of the throne when paying calls by means of its emissaries.'

medicorum intimi. For the confidential physician cp. *Ann.* IV. 3 *Eudemus amicus ac medicus Liviae, specie artis frequens secretis.*

sive, etc., 'whether that implied anxiety or curiosity,' i.e. to see how the poison was working. Cp. *Ann.* II. 69, when Germanicus was ill, *missi a Pisone incusabantur ut valetudinis adversa rimantes.*

3. momenta, etc., 'the very changes in the dying man's condition.'

dispositos cursores, couriers placed at intervals on the 17 miles of road between Rome and the Alban villa (45. 1).

constabat, 'it was generally supposed.' Having been absent from Rome at the time, Tacitus has only hearsay authority for his statement.

quae tristis audiret, 'news which it distressed him to hear.'

animi vultu. The MSS. read *animo vultuque,* but it is hardly possible to 'assume the appearance of grief *with one's mind.*'

securus iam odii, etc., 'now relieved from the trouble of hating and being one who...'

4. coheredem, etc. Testators frequently made bad emperors, like Tiberius and Nero, heirs to part of their property, in order to secure their other legatees in the possession of the rest; cp. *Ann.* XVI. 11. Domitian at first refused legacies from persons who had children, but soon became as grasping as his predecessors (Suet. *Dom.* 9 and 12).

optimae...piissimae, the conventional epithets of the will. Cicero, *Phil.* XIII. 19. 43, carps at Antony for using the form *piissimus* (instead of *pientissimus*), but later it became the recognised superlative.

velut honore iudicioque, 'in what he took as a compliment due to a good opinion,' or 'as a deliberate compliment' (Fyfe). *iudicium* often = 'favourable judgment,' cp. Pliny, *Epp. ad Trai.* 4 *ut...gloriari iudiciis tuis possim.*

CHAPTER XLIV

1. Gaio, etc., i.e. on June 13, 40 A.D. At the beginning of this year Caligula was sole consul, his colleague dying just before entering upon office (Suet. *Cal.* 17); hence the exceptional indication of the year by a single name.

quarto. *sexto,* the reading of the MSS., is obviously wrong.

decumum, sc. *ante diem.* For the ellipse cp. *Ann.* VI. 25 and 50, *Hist.* I. 18. Agricola died on Aug. 23, 93 A.D.

2. habitum, 'personal appearance,' cp. 11. 1.

decentior quam sublimior, 'comely rather than imposing.' See on 4. 5 for the idiom.

nihil impetus, 'no sign of passion,' a far better reading than *nihil metus,* which is taken to mean 'nothing alarming.'

gratia oris supererat, 'his face showed a great deal of graciousness.' *superesse* here means 'be in abundance,' cp. 45. 6, *Germ.* 6. 1, 26. 2.

crederes, 'you would have thought.'

3. et ipse quidem, contrasted with *habitus.*

medio…aetatis, 'in the middle of his course, while still in his prime.' Construe, 'in the mid-career of his life, (which was) still vigorous.' *spatium,* like *curriculum,* is a racing metaphor.

quantum ad gloriam, sc. *attinet.* Cp. *Germ.* 21. 3.

vera bona, etc., a piece of orthodox Stoicism, which held that virtue was the only true good, all else that 'fools' call good deserving at most the name of *commoda,* 'advantages,' or in Greek parlance προηγμένα, 'things preferred.' Such 'advantages,' here treated as fortune's gifts, were, for instance, life, reputation, wealth, relatives and friends.

impleverat, 'had fully achieved.'

4. opibus…contigerant, 'in excessive wealth he found no pleasure, though his fortune was respectable.' For *speciosus* in a somewhat weak sense cp. Vell. II. 59 *fuit C. Octavius, ut non patricia, ita admodum speciosa* ('highly respectable') *equestri genitus familia,* and the common meaning 'good-looking.' The other reading, *speciosae non contigerant,* where *speciosae* is taken to mean 'magnificent,' gives a weak and artificial antithesis. As proofs of Agricola's comparative poverty editors quote 6. 2, 7. 2, 9. 4, 42. 3 and Dio C. LXVI. 20, who says, probably with some exaggeration, that A. lived in want (ἐν ἐνδείᾳ). Gudeman, accepting *non,* transposes *opibus…contigerant* between *peregit* and *quippe.* But the *vera bona* come naturally before the *commoda,* and with Gudeman's order, as Furneaux points out, *quippe* is awkward.

filia, etc., 'with his daughter and wife surviving him, he may be considered even happy to have escaped the future by dying with his rank secure.' Some editors wish to place *filia…superstitibus* after *fama* or *amicitiis,* but Tacitus' order has distinct point. It purposely separates the wife and child, whose safety was guaranteed by their political unimportance, from the probable objects of Domitian's rage. Note the poetical construction *beatus effugisse.*

dignitate, sc. *senatoria.* Cp. *Ann.* III. 17 *M. Piso exuta dignitate…relegaretur.*

adfinitatibus et amicitiis. See on 40. 2.

5. non licuit. Dahl's insertion at least restores sense.

Another device is to read *sicuti...quondam* instead of *quod* (Ritter), but the pres. infin. after *ominabatur* is improbable.

sicut...ita, 'though...yet.' Cp. the passage from Velleius quoted on § 4.

quod, etc., 'which he used to divine and long for.' There is a slight zeugma; understand *optabat* with *votis*. Trajan seems to have distinguished himself by his promptness in marching troops from Spain to assist in quelling the rebellion of Antonius Saturninus (see on 41. 2) and was made *consul ordinarius* for 91. Pliny tells a story how, when he was visiting the Capitol before leaving for his province, the crowd shouted out Imperator, meaning Jupiter Imperator, but the utterance was interpreted as a prophecy of Trajan's elevation to the throne (*Pan.* 5, 23, 94. Cp. Dio C. LXVII. 12).

festinatae mortis, hinting at murder.

grande, etc., 'it was a source of great consolation that he....'

per...spiramenta, 'with pauses,' lit. 'breathing-spaces.' *per* indicates manner.

continuo, probably an adjective. Tac. does not elsewhere use the adverb. The passage seems to echo Caligula's famous wish *ut populus Romanus unam cervicem haberet, ut scelera sua...in unum ictum et unum diem cogeret,* Sen. *de ira* III. 19.

exhausit, 'drained the blood of.' Statius, *Theb.* x. 168, has *exhaurit genas* in the sense of 'makes the cheeks bloodless.'

CHAPTER XLV

1. non vidit, etc., a common rhetorical formula of the *consolatio* (Gudeman). Cp. Cic. *de orat.* III. 2. 8, of Crassus, *non vidit flagrantem bello Italiam, non ardentem invidia senatum...non exsilium generi*; cc. 43—46 contain many reminiscences of Cicero's panegyric of Crassus.

obsessam curiam, as by Nero at Thrasea's trial, *Ann.* XVI. 27.

tot consularium. Suetonius mentions 12 persons put to death by Domitian, *in eis aliquot consulares.*

feminarum, e.g. Gratilla, wife of Arulenus Rusticus (see 2. 1), Arria, widow, and Fannia, daughter, of Thrasea (Pliny, *Ep.* III. 11. 3).

fugas, a wider term than *exilium*, including the milder *relegatio*.

Carus Mettius, a well-known *delator*, accuser of Senecio (see on 2. 1) and Fannia. The younger Pliny only escaped prosecution by him through Domitian's death (*Ep.* VII. 27. 14), after which he was himself accused by one Heliodorus.

censebatur, 'was estimated by,' so 'was credited with,' a late sense, cp. Martial I. 61. 3 *censetur* (i.e. 'is celebrated for') *Apona Livio suo tellus*; Juv. VIII. 74 *te censeri laude tuorum, Pontice, noluerim.* Until about 93 Domitian discouraged delation, hence *una,* 'only one.'

Albanam arcem, Domitian's country house on the shores of the Alban lake (apparently on the west side, at a spot still marked by ruins, where water-pipes stamped with his name have been found). This *villa,* Domitian's favourite residence, was popularly called 'the citadel,' as the headquarters of his tyranny (cp. Juv. IV. 145, Dio C. LXVII. 1). Hor. *Sat.* II. 6. 16 calls his Sabine farm his *arx.*

Messalini, L. Valerius Catullus Messalinus, another much-dreaded informer, Juvenal's *mortifer Catulius, grande et conspicuum nostro quoque tempore monstrum,* IV. 113—115. He was blind; see the striking description of him in Pliny, *Ep.* IV. 22. 5. This passage shows that he had not yet appeared *publicly* as an accuser.

Massa Baebius, procurator of Africa in 70, 'even then fatal to all good men,' *Hist.* IV. 50. In 93 he was accused of extortion by the people of Hispania Baetica and the Senate entrusted his prosecution to Pliny and Senecio (Plin. *Ep.* VII. 33). The trial was just coming on. *etiam tum* implies that Massa's day was commonly thought to be over. However, though condemned to loss of property, he was by no means crushed, and promptly brought a charge of impiety against Senecio *questus Senecionem non advocati fidem sed inimici amaritudinem implesse.*

nostrae, sc. of the senators; cp. Plin. *Ep.* IX. 13. 2 *in senatu senator senatori...reo iudex manus intulisset.*

Helvidium, son of the Helvidius mentioned in 2. 2, consul in 87, put to death by Domitian because in a dramatic sketch on the subject of Paris and Oenone he was supposed to have referred to the emperor's divorce from his wife Domitia (Suet. *Dom.* 10).

Mauricum Rusticumque, brothers, both friends of Pliny. Mauricus was relegated by Domitian and recalled by Nerva. Rusticus was put to death; see on 2. 1.

divisimus, 'parted,' cp. *Hist.* IV. 14. With the reading *Maurici Rusticique visus* (i.e. the sight of them at their trial) supply e.g. *foedavit,* 'dishonoured,' out of *perfudit.* But *visus* is difficult and the zeugma intolerable.

perfudit, metaphorical. The Senate condemned him. See on 2. 2.

S.   9

2. tamen, in spite of his being Nero, i.e. inhuman. For Domitian's fine sense of cruelty see Suet. *Dom.* 11.

videre et aspici, 'seeing and being observed.' *aspici* is the stronger word (cp. 40. 4), and anyhow Tac. could hardly have used *videri* = 'to be seen,' a rare use in prose, though occasionally found in Cic. and Caes. (See Munro on Lucr. I. 270.)

subscriberentur, 'were being recorded,' cp. Quint. XII. 8. 8 *subscribere audita*. The word has sinister associations, being used (1) of subscribing one's name to an accusation, hence of accusing, (2) of writing against a man's name in the census list the reason for affixing the *nota censoria*.

denotandis...sufficeret. Domitian's cruel flushed look 'was enough to cause the paleness on so many faces to be noted.' This is taken to be a compressed way of indicating (1) that a glance from Domitian would make a senator turn pale, and (2) that the informers would note his pallor with a view to a future accusation (cp. *subscriberentur* above, and for the sense of *denotandis* see *Ann.* III. 53). But the expression is so hard that it may reasonably excite suspicion, particularly in view of the numerous defects in the MSS. in chs. 44 and 45. Wex, p. 63, suggests *denotandis...pallore oribus*, 'was enough to make their faces turn pale,' *denoto* being used like *noto*, as in the Ovidian *rubor ora notavit* (*Met.* IV. 329).

rubor, etc. Before Domitian's character was known, his frequent blushing was put down to modesty (*Hist.* IV. 40). Now his permanently flushed complexion is a screen against shame, because it rendered any blush invisible.

3. tu vero, another recognised formula of the *consolatio*. Cp. Cic. *de orat.* III. 3. 12 *ego vero te, Crasse, cum vitae flore tum mortis opportunitate...et ortum et exstinctum arbitror.*

constans et libens, 'unflinchingly and cheerfully.'

tamquam, etc., 'as though, so far as a man could, you were granting the emperor acquittal from guilt.' For *pro virili portione*, a rare variant for *pro v. parte*, cp. *Hist.* III. 20.

4. valetudini, 'your sickness,' instead of the concrete *aegro*; cp. 16. 3.

5. animo, local ablative without *in*.

noster, emphatic, 'this is our special sorrow.'

condicione, 'owing to the circumstance of.'

ante quadriennium, a somewhat illogical variant on *quadriennio ante*. Cp. the common formula for dates, e.g. *ante diem quintum Kal. Jan.*, cp. 44. 1. For the reason why 'Agricola was lost to us four years before,' see Introd. p. xi.

6. superfuere, cp. on 44. 2.

aliquid, i.e. his daughter and son-in-law.

Chapter XLVI

1. ut sapientibus placet. The Stoic Chrysippus believed in
the survival of the souls of the wise only; those of fools were dis-
sipated at death. Cp. Cic. *Somn. Scip.* § 5 *omnibus qui patriam
conservarint adiuverint auxerint, certum esse in caelo definitum
locum ubi beati aevo sempiterno fruantur*; Tert. *de an.* 54 *subli-
mantur animae sapientes...apud Stoicos sub lunam.* Seneca, who
typifies the Platonising Stoicism of the Empire, frequently dwells
upon a happy after-life, when the hero *ad excelsa sublatus inter
felices currit animas, excepit illum coetus sacer, Scipiones Caton-
esque*, etc., *dial.* VI. 25. 1.

nosque, domum tuam. Some insert *et*, because Tac. does not
legally belong to Agricola's house. But affection may excuse the
inaccuracy.

muliebribus lamentis, cp. 29. 1, *Germ.* 27. 2.

2. inmortalibus, 'undying,' i.e. 'lifelong.' So *aeternus* is
used in a weakened sense=*perpetuus* in *Ann.* XIV. 55. Tac. is not
thinking here of the immortality given by literature.

decoremus, a reminiscence of Ennius, *nemo me lacrimis decoret
nec funera fletu faxit.* (See crit. note for the reading.)

3. praeceperim. For the mood see on 3. 1, and for the following infin. 38. 4.

formam...figuram, 'form and features,' a favourite alliterative
collocation. Pliny, *Pan.* 55, contains several resemblances to this
passage, cp. *formam principisque figuram non aurum melius vel
argentum quam favor hominum exprimat teneatque.*

non quia...sed, so *dial.* 37. 6, *Hist.* I. 15. Note the change
from dependent to independent constr. in these instances.

alienam, 'foreign,' 'of another,' opposed to *tuis ipse.*

possis, an instance of the common use of the subjunct. in the
2nd pers. sing., where the implied subject is indefinite (i.e. you=
one). Roby, § 1544.

4. fama rerum, 'by the glory of his deeds,' causal ablative.
Others emend to *in fama*, 'in the record of history.'

obruet, generally changed to *obruit*, but the future is perhaps
more forcible, 'though many even of the ancients will be forgotten,

Agricola will live.'   See the eloquent Wex *ad loc.*   The best
commentary on this closing passage is Hor. *Od.* IV. 9. 25:

> *Vixere fortes ante Agamemnona*
> *multi ; sed omnes illacrimabiles*
> *urgentur ignotique longa*
> *nocte, carent quia vate sacro.*

Had it not been for Tacitus' work, our only records of Agricola
would have been two brief notices in Dio C. XXXIX. 50, LXVI. 20,
and the inscription mentioned on 20. 2.

Calpurnius Agricola, who governed Britain about 162 A.D., in
the reign of Marcus Aurelius, and whose name occurs on inscriptions
found in the north of England, must not be confused with the hero
of this biography.

NOTES ON THE GERMANIA

CHAPTER I

1. Germania omnis, 'Germany as a whole,' free Germany (Ptolemy's Γερμανία μεγάλη), exclusive of the Roman provinces of Upper and Lower Germany west of the Rhine. Caesar's *Gallic War* opens similarly, *Gallia est omnis divisa.*

Gallis, the dwellers in the district of *Gallia.* There were Gauls living east of the Rhine, 29. 4.

Raetisque et Pannoniis on the Danube frontier. *-que* joins the composite phrase to *Gallis.* Raetia, properly the modern Tirol and eastern Switzerland, by this time included Vindelicia, which lay immediately south of the Danube. Pannonia lay along the Danube from Vienna to Belgrade, and extended southwards to Illyricum. Between Raetia and Pannonia lay Noricum, which Tacitus fails to mention.

Rheno...Danuvio, both Celtic words. The old name for the Danube, Ἴστρος, Latin *Hister*, came from the Thracians.

Sarmatis. The Sarmătae, or Sauromatae, a nomadic race of Iranian affinities, are conceived by Tacitus as living to the extreme east of Germany (cp. Mela III. 3. 25) beyond the Peucini, Veneti, and Fenni, 46. 1. They roamed the vast plains of central and southern Russia.

Dacisque. The Dacians bordered on the south-eastern corner of Germany, occupying part of the modern Hungary between the Carpathians on the north, the Danube on the south, and the Theiss on the west. At one time they had stretched further west to the long, southward-flowing reach of the Danube, but they had been expelled from the tract of country between it and the Theiss by a body of Sarmatae, the Sarmatae Iazyges, who thus intervened between Dacia and Pannonia. (These isolated Sarmatae are not, or at least not primarily, in Tacitus' thoughts here.)

mutuo metu, because there was no natural barrier between the Germans and their eastern neighbours, the Sarmatians.

montibus, the Carpathians between Germany and Dacia. The concluding words of this opening clause with their notable conjunction of abstract and concrete and their sonorous alliteration at once reveal the studied rhetorical tendency of Tacitus' monograph.

Oceanus, the North Sea, and the Baltic, *Suebicum mare*, which was not known to be a mere gulf.

sinus, curving tracts either of water, or more rarely of land, here usually understood of the latter (cp. 37. 1, *Agr.* 23. 2) to avoid a slight zeugma.

insularum inmensa spatia, 'islands of vast extent' (cp. Juv. IV. 39 *spatium admirabile rhombi*), e.g. the Danish Islands, Gothland and above all Scandinavia, which was regarded as an island by Mela (III. 6. 54) and Pliny (*H. N.* IV. 43. 96), a misconception which endured until the Middle Ages.

nuper cognitis, etc., ablat. absol. in somewhat vague connexion with the foregoing; 'a fact attested by the discovery of nations...' or simply 'where nations and kings have in recent times been found.' In A.D. 5 Tiberius reached the Elbe and the Roman fleet coasted up the Cimbric Chersonese (Denmark), a fact commemorated on the Monumentum Ancyranum; see note on 37. 1. Neither Germanicus in A.D. 14—16, nor Domitian in his operations against the Chatti, penetrated as far as Tiberius, to whose expedition *nuper* and *bellum* must apparently be referred. For this broad sense of *nuper* cp. 2. 5 and Cic. *N. D.* II. 50. 126 *nuper, id est paucis ante saeculis*.

aperuit, *Agr.* 22. 1.

2. Raeticarum Alpium, extending from Tirol westwards to Adula and St Gotthard, upon which mountains the two arms of the Rhine respectively take their rise.

modico flexu, etc., with reference to the north-westerly trend of the lower course of the Rhine.

3. molli et clementer edito...iugo, 'on the easy and gently rising ridge,' in studied contrast to *inaccesso ac praecipiti vertice. clementer* in this local sense is a Silver use, much affected by Tacitus, for *leniter*.

Abnobae, the Black Forest. The Danube rises near its southern end, in Baden.

pluris = *compluris*, 'a considerable number of.' Tac. imitates Pliny's account, *H. N.* IV. 24. 79 *per innumeras lapsus gentes Danuvii nomine*.

sex meatibus, 'by six channels,' cp. *ire via*, a usage in which the local and modal senses of the ablative seem to run into one another. For *meatus* applied to water cp. Mela III. 1. 2 *tantis meatibus*.

erumpat. Tac. prefers the subjunctive after *donec*, even to express a simple fact. The indic. however occurs in 37. 6; 45. 5. *erumpat* may refer to the river bursting its way through sandbanks (see Schwyzer). The Danube, like the Nile, with which, according to Herodotus (II. 33—34), it presents many astonishing points of correspondence, traditionally had seven mouths. Pliny, whom Tacitus follows, allowed it only six; the seventh *magna palude sorbetur, H. N.* IV. 79.

CHAPTER II

1. ipsos, the people as distinct from their country, cp. *Agr.* 13. 1.

indigenas, the aboriginal inhabitants.

crediderim, 'I am inclined to believe,' see on *Agr.* 3. 1. It appears that at the dawn of history the Germans inhabited the country between the Oder and the Elbe, Denmark with its islands and southern Sweden; they did not spread over the whole of the Tacitus' Germany (see Schwyzer). Anthropologists are still debating the question of the original home of the Aryans. The Baltic region has strong upholders, so that Tac. may be partly right.

hospitiis, 'friendly relations,' 'intercourse'; the ablat. is causal.

nec, answered by *et* before *inmensus. terra...advehebantur* involves a slight zeugma; sc. *adveniebant.* Tac. is perhaps thinking of Greek legendary migrations and Greek maritime colonisation. It is curious that he overlooks evidence against his view. Did he fail to recognise that the Gallic invasions of Italy were really migrations?

mutare...quaerebant, a poetical constr. adopted by Silver prose.

ultra, 'beyond,' i.e. to the north. Cp. *Agr.* 25. 1 for the adjectival use.

utque sic dixerim. See on *Agr.* 3. 2.

adversus, on the opposite side of the world, almost 'antipodal,' cp. Cic. *Acad. Pr.* II. 39, *Somn. Scip.* 13 and Pliny *H. N.* II. 68, 172. Others interpret 'hostile' to navigators.

orbe nostro, cp. *Agr.* 12. 3.

2. quis porro, etc., a second reason why the Germans were pure-blooded—Germany did not tempt immigrants.

praeter, 'to say nothing of,' cp. 44. 2.

quis...peteret, lit. 'who was to seek?' so 'who would have sought?' Cp. Sonnenschein, *Lat. Subj.* p. 12 ff.

informem terris, 'dismal in its scenery.'

caelo, 'climate.'

cultu aspectuque, supines; 'dreary to live in and to look at.'

nisi si patria sit, 'unless it be one's native land,' to be taken only with *tristem...aspectuque,* not as protasis to *quis peteret,* which would present difficulties.

3. **carminibus,** mythical and heroic lays of an alliterative character. So Arminius *canitur adhuc barbaras apud gentes, Ann.* II. 88.

memoriae et annalium, 'tradition and history' (Furneaux).

Tuistonem (or v. l. *Tuisconem*), said to mean 'twofold,' and referable to an earth divinity possessing the two sexes combined— a not uncommon figure in primitive mythologies.

Mannum, our word 'man,' Greek Μίνως—a Germanic Adam. We do not hear of Tuisto or Mannus elsewhere.

originem, similarly used of a person in *Ann.* IV. 9, *origo Iuliae gentis Aeneas,* in imitation of Virg. *Aen.* XII. 166.

Ingaevones...Hermiones...Istaevones. Pliny *N. H.* IV. 28. 99 mentions the same groups. See also *N. H.* IV. 96 for the Ingaevones and Mela III. 3. 32 for the Hermiones. The Ingaevones, says Pliny, comprised the Cimbri, Teutoni, and Chauci; they seem to have occupied Schleswig-Holstein, Denmark with its islands, and the coast westwards towards the Rhine. The Hermiones, consisting, according to Pliny, of the Hermunduri, Suebi (Tacitus' Semnones probably), Chatti, and Cherusci, occupied the basins of the Weser and the Elbe, exclusive of the coast tract between the rivers; and the Istaevones the territories near the Rhine. These three tribal groups leave a vast area of eastern Germany unaccounted for, and Pliny in fact adds two more groups, the Vandili in the basins of the Oder and the Vistula, and the Bastarnae in the modern Galicia. The tradition of the three eponymous heroes, preserved by Tacitus, appears again in a sixth century document, apparently of Frankish origin, which mentions three brothers, Ermenus, Inguo, and Istio, from whom thirteen nations are descended (see Chadwick, *Origin of English Nation*, p. 208). Of Istio nothing more is known. Ermen, or Irmin, is perhaps the being called by Tacitus Hercules (3. 1; 9. 1; 34. 2), and we hear of a personage called Ing belonging to Denmark. Names compounded of Irmin and Ing are common (*op. cit.* pp. 225 ff., 342). Such eponymous heroes are often mere inventions for providing a respectable origin for tribal names. It is possible that these three groups were religious confederacies. See Prof. Chadwick's arguments (pp. 225 ff.) based on the hypothesis that the name Hermiones is connected with *irminsul* (see note on 34. 2). The names are clearly very old and their infrequent occurrence suggests that they were already antiquated in Tacitus' time.

4. **quidam,** etc. 'Some, with the licence permitted by antiquity, maintain that there are more descended from the god and
more race designations...and these genuine ancient names' (as contrasted with the newly applied name *Germani*). For *ut*, 'as is
natural,' cp. 22. 1, *Agr.* 11. 1.

quidam, perhaps denoting Roman antiquaries who, realising that
the threefold classification in the *carmina antiqua* was not exhaustive,
enumerated (like Pliny) other stocks for which they claimed equal
antiquity and purity of descent.

deo, Tuisto, if any particular god is intended.

Marsos, etc. The Marsi seem to have lived round the sources
of the Lippe; they were roughly handled by Germanicus (*Ann.* 1.
50 and 56; 11. 25) and subsequently disappeared. The Gambrivii,
probably connected with the Sugambri, who dwelt on the Ruhr,
likewise vanished. See cc. 38, 39 for the Suebi, a confederacy in
the basin of the Weser, under the presidency of the Semnones. See
above for the Vandilii. From the fact that in the territory of the
Marsi there was a sanctuary called the temple of Tamfana (*Ann.* 1.
51), which was the special resort of the neighbouring tribes, "we
may infer with some probability that the Marsi had once occupied
a position, similar to that of the Semnones, at the head of a religious
confederation of tribes which claimed descent from a common ancestor" (Chadwick, *op. cit.* p. 225). From *Germ.* 43. 4 *apud
Nahanarvalos antiquae religionis lucus ostenditur*, Prof. Chadwick
is inclined to infer that the Vandilii represent a similar religious
confederacy. There is no evidence as to the Gambrivii.

5. **Germaniae.** The first clear evidence of the use of the
name *Germani* among the Romans dates from B.C. 73 when some
Germani joined Spartacus. Caesar uses it constantly. The word
is thought to be Celtic, not Teutonic, and is derived by some from
Celtic *gair*, 'shout,' in reference to the loud German war-cry; cp.
the Homeric βοὴν ἀγαθός. There are strong reasons for supposing
that the name was sometimes used vaguely for invaders from over
the Rhine, whether Gauls or Teutons, whose physical characteristics
were difficult to distinguish (see Rice Holmes, *Caesar's Conquest of
Gaul*, p. 313 f.). It should be remembered that Gauls were originally settled in large numbers on the east bank of the Rhine, and
that it was probably Teutonic pressure which forced them westwards
into Gaul.

qui primi, etc. The *locus classicus* upon the Germans in Gaul
is Caesar's account in *B.G.* 11. 3 and 4, based on the report of the
Reman envoys, who told him that most of the Belgae were descended

from Germans. (There seems, however, to have been a strong
Celtic element in the population.) He mentions four tribes—the
Condrusi, Eburones, Caerosi, and Paemani, *qui uno nomine Germani
appellantur.* The Tungri (cp. *Agr.* 36. 1), whose name survives in
the modern Tongres, occupied what had been the territory of the
Eburones, whom Caesar perhaps almost exterminated. With *ac nunc
Tungri* supply *vocentur* out of *vocati sint*; cp. 36. 2.

ita nationis, etc., 'thus what had been the name of a tribe, not
of a nation, gradually came to prevail, so that while at the outset it
was only by the conquerors that all were called Germans, to inspire
terror, later they were called Germans by themselves too, adopting
the invented name'—a sentence concise to awkwardness, meaning
that the invading Germans, to alarm the Gauls, represented that all
the people across the Rhine were Germans like themselves (and so
equally to be dreaded), and that later these, too, adopted as their
national appellation the name invented for them by the invaders of
Gaul. As a matter of fact there is no evidence that the Teutonic
tribes ever collectively adopted this or any other national name.
Still Tacitus' account of how the collective name arose is in its
essentials plausible enough. Tribal have frequently become national
names, as for instance the names Hellenes and Graeci. The distinction here drawn between *natio* and *gens* is usual, though not
without exceptions; cp. 4. 1, 27. 3. The use of *ob*, 'to cause,' is
noteworthy; contrast *Agr.* 5. 2 *ob formidinem.*

CHAPTER III

1. Herculem, here a hero, a god in 9. 1. In German mythology
the divine and the heroic are not always sharply distinguished, and
this particular confusion is rendered easy for a classical writer by the
frequent twofold treatment of Herakles as god and as hero. Thus
Herod. II. 43 discovered the first in the Egyptian pantheon, but the
latter, he tells us, he could nowhere find in Egypt. With this German
martial hero may be compared the Hercules discovered by Alexander's
troops in India; *Herculis simulacrum agmini peditum praeferebatur,*
Curt. VIII. 14. 11. The grounds upon which Greeks and Romans
identified foreign divinities with their own seem to have been somewhat arbitrary.

memorant, with vague subject; 'they tell us.' With *canunt* sc.
Germani. To take *Germani* with some commentators as the subject
of *memorant* and *eos* as equivalent to *se* seems impossible as well as
unnecessary. None of the Tacitean instances of the incorrect use of
the demonstrative for the reflexive pronoun is half so pronounced

as this would be; cases like *quamquam edicto monuisset ne quis quietem* eius *inrumperet, Ann.* IV. 67, so far from being parallel, present quite natural grammar.

primum, predicative, 'as the foremost.'

haec, difficult, either 'of this kind,' or 'the following' (instead of *illa*).

relatu, 'by the recital,' an uncommon word.

barditum, later in Ammianus spelt *barritus*, possibly through confusion with a word meaning the trumpeting of elephants. The interpretations proposed for the word, e.g. 'shield song,' are very doubtful. Note that a mode of singing, not a particular song, is meant.

ipso cantu, 'from the sound itself,' or 'simply from the sound.'

nec, etc., 'and it seems a harmony not so much of voice as of valour.'

2. fractum murmur, 'crashing roar.' Cp. Verg. *Aen.* III. 566 *fractasque ad litora voces*, of waves breaking, and Ammianus XVI. 12. 43 of the *barritus, paulatim adolescens ritu...fluctuum cautibus illisorum.*

repercussu, 'through the reverberation' from the shield.

3. ceterum, resuming after the parenthetical account of the *barditus.*

Ulixen, etc. This antiquarian invention may possibly be due to an accidental similarity of sound between some place-name and Ulixes, who is also credited with visits to Spain, Caledonia, and other countries; cp. Solinus 22 *Ulixem Caledoniae appulsum manifestat ara Graecis litteris scripta*, a passage which suggests that Ulysses was liable to be called in to explain any inscription in Greek, or supposed Greek, characters.

hunc Oceanum, the German Ocean, cp. on 1. 1.

Asciburgium, Ship-town (from *asc*, the ash, used for shipbuilding), is probably the modern Asburg on the western bank of the lower Rhine, now some little distance from the river.

hodieque, post-Augustan for *hodie quoque*, 'even to this day.'

nominatumque 'ΑϹΚΙΠΥΡΓΙΟΝ. This, the reading of most of the MSS., is, it must be admitted, unlikely to be correct; one MS. marks a lacuna. Possibly some name resembling Ulysses was lost and Ascipurgium repeated in Greek characters by a copyist, to fill the gap. The word is certainly not Greek.

quin etiam. For the poetical anastrophe, frequent in Tacitus, cp. 8. 2, 14. 5.

Ulixi, probably dat. of agent.

monumenta et tumulos, 'memorial barrows.'

Graecis litteris. The Gauls used Greek characters in Caesar's time, and Alpine peoples like the Raetians are known from inscriptions to have employed the north Etruscan alphabet which was borrowed from the Greek. The latter characters are probably meant. Tacitus' authority for these statements is probably Pliny's 20 books on the German wars.

4. ex ingenio, etc., 'each one must credit or discredit them according to his turn of mind.'

CHAPTER IV

1. ipse, etc., reverting to the subject raised in 2. 1.

aliis, apparently inserted for emphasis; cp. *dial.* 10 *ceteris aliarum artium studiis.*

nationum. Contrast *gentium* in 2. 1, and see on 2. 5.

propriam et sinceram, 'distinct and unmixed.' Cp. *sincerus et integer populus, Hist.* IV. 64.

2. habitus...corporum. See on *Agr.* 11. 1 and 2 for this phrase and for German characteristics. *ingens magnitudo corporum, incredibilis virtus, acies oculorum* (cp. *truces oculi* here) are mentioned in Caesar, *B. G.* 1. 39, as among their attributes.

caerulei. So Hor. *Epod.* 16. 7 *nec fera caerulea domuit Germania pube.*

rutilae comae, a trait especially obvious to Roman invaders, as the Germans when at war were accustomed to make their red or yellow hair still redder by smearing it with a red soapy substance (see Pliny, *N. H.* XXVIII. 51, 191).

ad impetum valida. So in *Ann.* II. 14 of the Germans *iam corpus ut visu torvum et ad brevem impetum validum, sic nulla vulnerum patientia. impetum,* 'sudden effort.'

3. non eadem, sc. *est,* not contrasted with *idem omnibus* above, but meaning 'no corresponding power of enduring,' i.e. corresponding to their big frames and power of effort, cp. 23. 2.

aestumque tolerare, sc. *adsueverunt,* and *tolerare* with the next clause. Tac. twice mentions the susceptibility to heat of the Germans serving in Italy, *Hist.* II. 32 and 93.

frigora, etc., adversative asyndeton; 'though they have become accustomed to support cold and hunger owing to their climate or soil.'

It is noteworthy that ancient writers attribute practically all the above qualities, physical and moral, to the Gauls as well as to the

Germans, though Tacitus does not seem aware that his description is equally applicable to both (cp. *tantum sui similem gentem*). As a matter of fact, Gauls and Germans seem to have been so closely related as to be almost indistinguishable except in respect of customs and language, the former speaking Celtic and the latter Teutonic. Cp. note on *Agr.* 11. 2.

CHAPTER V

1. **aliquanto**, 'to a certain extent,' ablative of measure, used for the most part only with comparatives.

specie, 'in appearance.'

in universum, 'in general,' 6. 4, *Agr.* 11. 3, etc.

silvis, etc., 'savage with forests or dreary with morasses,' e.g. the Hercynian, Teutoburgian, Abnoban (1. 3) and Asciburgian forests and the marshes of the northern lowlands. The woods and morasses of Germany were fraught with a sinister interest for the Romans since the disaster of Varus and narrow escapes like that of Caecina, so dramatically described in *Ann.* I. 63 ff.

satis, ablat. pl. of substantive; 'fruitful in crops,' e.g. barley, wheat (23. 1), and oats, the principal German cereal (Pliny, *N. H.* XVIII. 44. 149). The cultivation of the first two in Germany goes back to Neolithic times, of the last to the Bronze Age (see Schwyzer *ad loc.*).

frugiferarum arborum, cultivated fruit-trees, as distinct from those which bore *agrestia poma*, 23. 1. For the phrase *f. a. impatiens* cp. *Agr.* 12. 5.

pecorum, flocks and herds generally.

inprōcēra, 'undersized,' sc. *pecora sunt*—a remarkable change of subject.

2. **suus honor**, etc., 'their proper beauty or pride of brow,' poetical expressions, the latter referring to the small horns of the German cattle.

numero gaudent, etc., i.e. the *number* of their cattle is the only thing they care about, each man's wealth being estimated solely by the quantity of cattle he possesses. The old German word for cattle (*fihu*, now Vieh) meant property and money as well. Cp. the Latin *pecunia* from *pecus*.

3. **propitiine**, etc., one of the ethical reflections which are so salient a feature of the *Germania*, as indeed of practically all the literature of the time. They are the product of a rhetorical education. See note on *Agr.* 12. 7.

nec tamen, etc. Tac. subsequently ascertained that about 47 A.D. a discovery of silver, though in unimportant quantities, was made near Wiesbaden (*Ann.* XI. 20).

haud perinde, 'not so much,' sc. as others, or as might be expected, 'not particularly.' See on *Agr.* 10. 6.

4. est videre, a Greek construction common in poetry and occasionally occurring in later prose. Cp. *Ann.* XVI. 34.

non in alia vilitate, etc., 'held no less cheap than pottery,' doubtless an over-statement made with a view to edification.

proximi, sc. *Romanis.*

ob usum commerciorum, 'for the purpose of trade.'

formas, etc., 'certain types of our money they recognise and show preference for.'

5. serratos bigatosque, silver denarii 'with notched edges and stamped with a two-horsed chariot,' coins of the Republic (cp. *diu notam*), not plated or debased like Neronian and subsequent issues. *bigati* were struck from about 217 B.C., *serrati* from 104 B.C.

nulla adfectione animi, 'not from any special liking' (C. and B.).

promiscua, 'common articles,' a rare use, cp. *in promiscuo,* 44. 4.

CHAPTER VI

1. superest. See on *Agr.* 44. 2. Note how artfully *aurum* and *argentum* are made to suggest *ferrum*, and this again the arms and military organisation of the Germans. Tacitus' statement about the scarcity of iron is remarkable in view of the fact that the Iron Age had begun in Germany at least five centuries before.

rari, 'only a few,' mainly perhaps the nobility. Certain eastern tribes were armed with *breves gladii*, 44. 1. Archaeological discoveries seem to prove that swords were rarer in the Rhine than in the Elbe district.

maioribus lanceis, spears with large iron heads. With this passage cp. *Ann.* II. 14, where Germanicus, after referring to the huge shields and enormous spears of the Germans, proceeds: "the German has no cuirass or helmet; even his shield is not strengthened with iron or leather, but consists merely of osiers woven together or of thin and painted boards. Though their first line may be armed with spears, the rest have only darts burnt hard at the points (i.e. of wood) or else quite short" (*praeusta aut brevia tela*).

frameas, a German word of doubtful etymology. These *frameae,* the *brevia tela* of the above quoted passage, were used both for hurling and for thrusting.

2. scuto. See above. The shields were quadrangular, hexagonal, or round. The round sort, according to Tacitus, 44. 1, were characteristic of the eastern tribes.

contentus est, i.e. they were without swords.

missilia, small javelins (hardly arrows or stones, for in that case *pluraque singuli* would be pointless).

sagulo leves, 'lightly clad in a short cloak.' Schwyzer gives a photograph of a bronze statuette, now in Vienna, representing a running German, clad only in a short mantle which flies in the wind.

nulla cultus iactatio, 'no parade of adornment,' as for instance with the Caledonians, *Agr.* 29. 4.

coloribus, e.g. the Cimbri had white shields, the Harii (43. 6) black. Schwyzer mentions a pig-skin shield painted white and red, which was discovered at Lippe-Detmold.

3. cassis...galea, of metal and leather respectively. Excavations have produced very few German helmets.

equi, etc., *iumenta parva atque deformia,* Caes. *B. G.* IV. 2, cp. VII. 65.

sed nec variare, equivalent to *sed ne variare quidem,* as though *non modo non* had preceded. Cp. the positive form *sed et* 8. 3, 17. 3, 45. 4.

variare gyros, i.e. to describe complicated figures, riding first to the right, then to the left.

in rectum, etc., 'they ride them straight forward or to the right, their only flank movement, keeping line as they wheel so closely that no one drops behind,' i.e. the wheeling line (*orbis*) always presented an even front. The reason why the Germans in battle practised only the right and not the left wheel was that in the latter case the side unprotected by the shield would have been exposed to the enemy (Schwyzer).

4. in universum aestimanti, cp. *Agr.* 11. 3. The Tencteri (32. 1) and the Batavi (*Hist.* IV. 12) were distinguished as horsemen.

eoque, common for *ideoque,* which acc. to Draeger § 64 is not found in *Hist.* or *Ann.*

mixti, cavalry and infantry together.

peditum quos, etc. Acc. to Caesar, *B. G.* I. 48, each of the 6,000 horsemen in the army of Ariovistus had a footman, selected for his bravery and speed of foot, specially attached to him, to support him in battle and stand by him in case of need; these footmen kept up with the horsemen by clinging on to the horses' manes. Caesar himself employed this mode of fighting at Pharsalia.

aciem, the general body of infantry left, after each horseman had chosen his foot-companion.

5. numerus, sc. of the picked footmen.

pagis, sub-divisions of the tribal territory, 12. 3, 39. 4. Caesar, *B.G.* IV. 1, mentions 100 *pagi* of the Suevi, each annually sending a contingent of 1,000 men for the army.

idque ipsum, i.e. 'The Hundred.'

nomen et honor, 'a title of honour.'

6. per cuneos, 'in wedge-shaped formations,' one to each family or clan, 7. 3, though several of these small *cunei* often united to form one large one. The compact *cuneus*, fenced all round with shields and known to the Germans as the boar formation (Latin *caput porcinum*), proved dangerous to the Romans. Cp. *Hist.* IV. 20 *illi...in cuneos congregantur, densi undique et frontem tergaque ac latus tuti ; sic tenuem nostrorum aciem perfringunt.*

instes, 'one advances,' indefinite 2nd person.

consilii, etc., 'shows prudence rather than cowardice.' Note the omission of *potius.*

dubiis proeliis, 'indecisive battles' where risk would attend the recovery of the dead.

ignominioso, 'one so dishonoured.' For *concilium* see cc. 11—12.

CHAPTER VII

1. ex nobilitate, 'for their high birth.' Teutonic kings claimed divine ancestry from Wodan. *stirpes regiae*, royal families, were common among German tribes. It seems probable that "the distinction drawn by Tacitus between *reges* and *principes* [10. 4] was based not on a contrast between kingship and 'republicanism,' but on the presence of one or more ruling princes within the same tribe" (Chadwick, *op. cit.* 310). All the *principes* we hear of seem to have been of noble birth. Cp. the history of the *principes* of the Cherusci, including the famous Arminius, which ended in the appointment of a king Italicus (*Ann.* I. 55 f., XI. 16). *reges* were commoner in eastern than in western Germany. Near the Rhine "we find *stirpes regiae*, but very few actual kings...Next we come to the Frisians with kings who can scarcely be called kings" [see *Ann.* XIII. 54 *qui nationem eam regebant in quantum Germani regnantur*], "and to the Cherusci, where kingship is intermittent. Next the Suebi, where kingship is constant and, if we may judge from the history of Maroboduus [*Ann.* II. 26, 44, 46, 62, 63] and his successors, not entirely impotent. Beyond them we come to the Goths, where kingship is of a somewhat stricter form. Indeed, 'obedience to kings' is noted by Tacitus as one of the salient characteristics of the north-eastern tribes in general [*Germ.* 44. 1]. Lastly, when we reach the Svear [44. 3] we find absolutism" (Chadwick, *op. cit.* p. 319. Cp. 308 ff.).

duces, military leaders in time of war. In a monarchy the *rex* would presumably act as leader. A *dux* would perhaps be appointed by a state under the government of several *principes*, who would probably choose one of themselves, or by a number of states uniting in common action.

sumunt. See *Hist.* IV. 15 for the ceremony, *impositus scuto more gentis et sustinentium humeris vibratus dux deligitur.*

nec regibus, etc. Cp. 44. 1 and *Ann.* XIII. 54 quoted above.

exemplo...praesunt, 'maintain their position by force of example rather than by the exercise of authority (cp. 11. 5), owing to the admiration excited if they are energetic and conspicuous and fight in the van.' *agant* is subjunct. of repeated action, cp. 10. 2 and note on *Agr.* 13. 1.

2. animadvertere, 'punish with death,' as often in Tac. So we continually use our word 'execute' in its strongest sense.

verberare, a power permitted to any Roman centurion.

sacerdotibus, etc. The priests thus possessed in time of war judicial in addition to religious functions, though they veiled the fact by insisting upon the inspired character of their judgments. These judicial powers are indicated by one of the Teutonic words for priest, *ewart*, meaning 'shield of the laws.' For their powers in peace, see 11. 4. It seems as though the priests had usurped some of the civil as well as of the divine functions of the ancient king (for the latter see Chadwick, *op. cit.* 321). Caesar, *B. G.* VI. 23, attributes the power of life and death to the 'magistrates chosen to command in war.' We are perhaps to assume an increase in the power of the priests between the times of Caesar and Tacitus.

non quasi in poenam, 'and then not as a punishment.' The slaying of a man under such circumstances was a sacrifice to the tribal god, as Furneaux points out. For the custom of sacrificing victims in war to propitiate the gods see Westermarck, *Origin and Development of Moral Ideas,* I. 440 f.

3. effigies, cp. *Hist.* IV. 22 *depromptae silvis lucisque ferarum imagines,* animal figures like the snake and wolf of Wodan, the bear and goat of Donar, the ram of Tiu, the boar of Freyr (Schwyzer).

signa, the attributes of the various gods, like the lance of Wodan, the hammer of Donar, the sword of Tiu.

ferunt, sc. *Germani.*

quod. The antecedent of *quod* is the whole clause, *non casus,* etc. **cuneum.** See on 6. 6.

propinquitates, 'clans,' groups of *familiae.* Schwyzer aptly quotes *Il.* II. 362 κρῖν' ἄνδρας κατὰ φῦλα, κατὰ φρήτρας, 'Αγάμεμνον, ὡς φρήτρη φρήτρηφιν ἀρήγῃ φῦλα δὲ φύλοις.

pignora. Cp. *Agr.* 38. I. *unde* refers to *in proximo.* For the custom see Caes. *B. G.* I. 51, *Hist.* IV. 18 *Civilis...matrem suam sororesque, simul omnium coniuges parvosque liberos consistere a tergo iubet, hortamenta victoriae vel pulsis pudorem.*

audiri, historic infin. in a subordinate clause, cp. *Agr.* 34. 2. The use of the historic infin. to express an habitual occurrence is certainly uncommon, and Draeger (§ 172) denies it altogether, accepting here Kritz' *auditur.*

4. hi, sc. *feminae,* due to the attraction of the masculine *testes.*

exigere, 'to examine,' 'to estimate,' in respect of their honourableness, not merely 'to examine medically' (*inspicere*). The word implies appraisement in reference to some standard. Others translate, almost equally well, 'to demand' of their warriors.

cibosque et hortamina...gestant, a harsh zeugma. Cp. I. I for the mixture of concrete and abstract.

CHAPTER VIII

1. memoriae proditur, 'it is on record.'

inclinatas iam et labantis, 'when already giving way and wavering.'

obiectu pectorum, i.e. they presented their bare breasts to their own menfolk either in token that they preferred death at their hands to captivity, or, as Schwyzer suggests, to remind them that they were their wives and mothers.

comminus, 'close at hand.' The use of the word without any notion of contest seems late, except for a few instances in poetry, Lucr. VI. 904.

impatientius, 'more intolerably.'

nomine, 'on account of.'

puellae...nobiles. High rank was naturally a requisite in hostages. Augustus demanded female hostages from some states *quod neglegere marium pignora sentiebat,* the practice being regarded as an innovation (Suet. *Aug.* 21). See also *Hist.* IV. 79, where we read of the wife and sister of Civilis as hostages in the hands of the people of Colonia Agrippinensis (Cologne).

2. quin etiam. Cp. 3. 3 for the anastrophe.

providum, 'prophetic.' So the German matrons decided by means of lots and divinations the appropriate time for giving battle. Caes. *B. G.* I. 50.

3. Veledam, a prophetess of the tribe of the Bructeri, possessing extensive dominions and a supporter of Civilis. She dwelt in a tower on the Lippe and communicated only by messenger with those who consulted her (*Hist.* IV. 61, 65, V. 22, 24). She was ultimately taken prisoner by the Romans. See Statius, *Silv.* I. 4. 90, who scans her name Vělěda (but see note on text).

sed et. See on 6. 3.

Albrunam, a conjectural emendation of the manuscript spellings, taken to mean 'gifted with mysterious magical powers' (*alb* = English 'elf,' *runa* = 'secret').

compluris alias, e.g. Ganna, a prophetess among the Semnones in Domitian's time.

non adulatione, etc., 'not out of flattery nor as if they were making goddesses of them.' Still the Germans did regard some of their prophetic women as goddesses, as Tac. himself says, *Hist.* IV. 61, *vetere apud Germanos more quo plerasque feminarum fatidicas et augescente superstitione arbitrantur deas.* In the present passage Tac. intends to satirise the deification by the Romans of Caligula's sister Drusilla (Suet. *Cal.* 24) and Nero's wife Poppaea (*Ann.* XVI. 21). Though the Germans thought some women divine, they did not *make* them so, like the Romans.

CHAPTER IX

1. deorum, suggested by *deas.* For the studied character of the transition cp. 6. 1.

Mercurium, i.e. Wodan, whose name survives in Wednesday, Latin *dies Mercurii.* The identification rests on a similarity of attributes and functions, Wodan having a magic wand and a broad hat like the *caduceus* and *petasus* of Mercury, and being, like him, the god of trade and discovery and also a god of the dead. This sentence echoes the initial words of Caesar's account of the Gallic deities, *deorum maxime Mercurium* (? Teutates) *colunt, B.G.* VI. 17.

certis diebus, 'on appointed days.'

humanis...hostiis. Such sacrifices were not confined to the worship of Wodan, cp. 39. 2, 40. 5. Prisoners of war were often sacrificed, as the officers of Varus' army, *Ann.* I. 61, and the Chatti who were offered *en masse* to Tiu and Wodan by the victorious Hermunduri, *Ann.* XIII. 57.

Herculem, generally identified with the thunder god Donar (Norse Thor, cp. Eng. Thursday), whose hammer bore some resemblance to the club of Hercules. Prof. Chadwick (*op. cit.* 228 f.) is inclined to think that he represents a somewhat problematical being called Irmin; see on 34. 2.

Martem, the German war god Tiu (cp. Eng. Tuesday). See on 39. 4.

concessis, 'permissible,' from the Roman point of view, not human victims. Cp. *Hist.* v. 4 *concessa apud illos* (the Jews) *quae nobis incesta.*

2. Isidi. This Roman identification of the German goddess with the Egyptian Isis is due to the fact that a boat figured in the rites of both. On March 5th the Romans celebrated a festival called *navigium Isidis,* marking the beginning of the sailing season. The German goddess of the present passage was doubtless an earth goddess similar to Nerthus, **40.** 2, and in this respect, too, was comparable to Isis, cp. Servius *ad Aen.* VIII. 696 *Isis autem lingua Aegyptiorum est Terra.* Prof. Chadwick (p. 239) cites a sixteenth century ceremony at Ulm as evidence for the symbolical use of boats in plough ceremonies, but the case seems isolated.

causa, sc. *sit.*

nisi quod, cp. on *Agr.* 6. 1.

signum ipsum, etc., 'the symbol in itself...indicates an imported worship.' For *liburnae* see note on *Agr.* 28. 2.

3. neque in ullam, etc. For the absence of images cp. **43.** 5. Herodotus, I. 131, gives a similar account of the Persian religion. The most obvious example of imageless worship is, of course, Judaism.

ex magnitudine caelestium, sc. *esse,* 'to be consistent with the greatness of celestial beings.' For *ex* cp. 7. 1, *Agr.* 40. 2. It must not be supposed that an 'aniconic' religion *necessarily* involves any lofty religious conceptions, as Tacitus seems to imply, though it may well lead to them.

lucos et nemora consecrant, cp. 7. 3, 39. 2, 40. 2, 43. 4, also the *silva Herculi sacra, Ann.* II. 12, and the *lucus Baduhennae, Ann.* IV. 73.

deorumque, etc., 'and call by the names of gods that mysterious existence which they see by devotion alone.' Cp. what Tac. says of the Jews, *Iudaei mente sola unumque numen intellegunt, Hist.*

v. 5. Throughout this passage Tac. is giving a highly subjective
interpretation of certain phenomena of early Teutonic religion, which,
to judge from other evidence, can hardly have been of a more exalted
type than the generality of primitive worships. The awe-inspiring
effect of forests upon the educated Roman is very noteworthy. Cp.
Pliny *H. N.* XII. 2. 3 *nec magis auro fulgentia atque ebore simulacra
quam lucos et in iis silentia ipsa adoramus,* Quint. X. 1. 88 *Ennium
sicut sacros vetustate lucos adoremus, in quibus grandia et antiqua
robora iam non tantam habent speciem quantam religionem,* and the
well-known passage in Seneca, *epp.* 41. 3. In fact, forests seem to
have played the same part in the production of 'transcendental
feeling' in the Roman mind that mountains so often do in the
modern.

CHAPTER X

1. auspicia, properly divination by the flight of birds, but here
in a more general sense, see § 3.

ut qui, etc., sc. *observant ut ei qui maxime observant,* a common
type of expression, cp. Livy, XXIII. 49 *ex provincia ut quae maxime
omnium belli avida.*

simplex, 'uniform,' of one kind only.

frugiferae arbori, wild fruit-bearing trees like oaks, beeches
and hazels. Contrast the meaning in 5. 1.

in surculos amputant, 'they lop into small slips.'

notis, of unknown nature. Runic characters, borrowed apparently from the Greek or Latin alphabet, could hardly have been
in use so early.

temere ac fortuito, 'at random and as luck has it.'

2. si publice consultetur, 'if the inquiry is on the nation's
behalf.' Cp. 7. 1 for the subjunctive. Though the head of the
household draws the lots for the household, the king or head of
the state does not do the same for the state. It is conjectured that
we have here another instance of the transference of kingly preroga-
tives to the priests. Cp. on 7. 2.

ter singulos tollit, i.e. picks up three times, one each time, so
'picks up three, one at a time.' For the mystic number three cp.
Caes. *B.G.* 1. 53, where one of Caesar's officers reports that, when a
prisoner among the Germans, *de se ter sortibus consultum utrum
igni statim necaretur,* etc.

3. prohibuerunt, sc. *sortes.*

in eundem diem, 'for that day.'

auspiciorum, etc., 'the warrant of divination is further required,' i.e. the evidence of *sortes* is not sufficient in itself, *auspicia* must be invoked for confirmation.

illud quidem, etc., 'though the practice of consulting the cries and flight of birds is known here also, their distinctive method is,' etc. For this form of sentence, where *quidem* is practically equivalent to the Greek μέν, cp. 6. 2, and for *hic*='in Germany,' cp. *hunc Oceanum*, 3. 3.

equorum, etc. Divination by the neighing of horses was also a Persian practice, Herod. III. 86. Achilles' horse Xanthus was endowed with prophetic utterance by Hera, *Il.* XIX. 404 f.

4. isdem, with reference to 9. 3. For the ablat. without *in* cp. *Agr.* 12. 5.

et nullo, for *neque ullo*, cp. *Agr.* 16. 14. With these white horses 'undefiled by any earthly labour' compare the Persian white horses which drew the chariot of Ahura-Mazda, Herod. I. 189, VII. 40. Relics of the Teutonic veneration for the horse are still to be seen in the white horses cut on the chalk downs of Berkshire and Wiltshire. A white horse is the cognisance of Hanover and Brunswick and the symbol of Kent. Hengest and Horsa, the names of the legendary leaders of the Jutes, mean stallion and mare. (See Grant Allen's *Anglo-Saxon Britain*, p. 28.)

pressos, 'yoked to,' a poetical use.

rex vel princeps. See on 7. 1.

hinnitus ac fremitus, 'neighings and snortings.'

5. se enim, etc., 'for they (the priests) regard themselves as the gods' servants and the horses as cognisant of their (the gods') will.' Many editors, feeling it awkward to understand *sacerdotes* as subject to *putant*, read *apud proceres: sacerdotes enim*, and take *putant* to mean 'the Germans think.' If the third *apud* were inserted in error, the addition of *se*, particularly easy between *-es* and *enim*, would naturally follow. Still the manuscript reading seems intelligible enough.

6. committunt, 'they pit against,' a gladiatorial expression.

praeiudicio, properly a legal term meaning a 'previous judgment,' here a 'premonitory decision.' The struggle between the champions did not finally decide the issue.

CHAPTER XI

1. principes, local chiefs, like the magistrates elected to administer justice in the various *pagi* (12. 3) and those at the head of a *comitatus* (13. 3). We may contrast them with the tribal *princeps* or *principes*, who were equivalent to national kings; see on 7. 1.

maioribus, peace and war, treaties, grave crimes, etc.

omnes, all free men, forming the national assembly or *thing*; cp. *plebem* below.

pertractentur, 'are thoroughly considered.' The reading *praetractentur*, 'are discussed beforehand,' is not so well supported and involves the occurrence of a word not found elsewhere. With the council of the chiefs the Anglo-Saxon *witanagemot* may be compared.

2. certis diebus. The regular assemblies seem to have been held two or three times a year, especially in spring and autumn, and to have been connected with religious festivals. Prof. Chadwick (*op. cit.* p. 312) thinks that they met in sacred groves, for it was with these groves that the priests (§ 4) were specially associated. In *Ann.* II. 12 upon a call to arms the tribes met in a sacred grove.

cum...incohatur luna. So the Germans thought it lucky to fight at the new moon, Caes. *B. G.* I. 50.

numerum...noctium computant, like the Indians, Persians and Gauls (Caes. *B. G.* VI. 18). Cp. our sennight, fortnight, Twelfth Night. The custom naturally follows from the use of the moon as a measure of time.

sic constituunt, etc., 'so they make their appointments and their contracts.'

nox ducere, etc. In Norse, as in Greek and other mythologies, Day is the child of Night.

3. ut iussi, 'as though under orders.' Cp. *Hist.* IV. 76 *Germanos...non iuberi, non regi, sed cuncta ex libidine agere.*

4. ut turbae placuit, 'when the crowd thinks fit.' Others read without manuscript warrant *ut turba placuit*, 'when the crowd is thought sufficient.'

5. prout aetas, etc., words applicable to *princeps* (in the sense noted on § 1) rather than to *rex.*

auctoritate suadendi, 'through the influence of persuasion'; cp. 7. 1.

6. concutiunt, 'clash upon one another.' Cp. *Hist.* V. 17 *ubi sono armorum tripudiisque (ita illis mos) approbata sunt dicta.* So the Gauls were accustomed *armis concrepare* to show approval of a speech, Caes. *B. G.* VII. 21.

Two descriptions of Swedish assemblies are good illustrations of Tacitus' account. In one, described in Rembertus' *Life of St Ansgar*, c. 24, "the king is represented as bringing before his assembly the question whether the introduction of Christianity should be permitted. Previously to doing so he goes out with his nobles to cast lots [cp. 10. 2]. In St Olaf's Saga the king's policy is openly discountenanced by the assembly under the leadership of the lawman, and he is compelled to change his attitude by threats of violence, remarking as he does so that it has been the practice of all kings of the Svear to give way to the wishes of the commons," (Chadwick, *op. cit.* p. 313). It will be noted that priests play no part in these assemblies.

Chapter XII

1. **discrimen capitis intendere,** i.e. to bring a charge involving risk of capital punishment. Cp. *in aliquem periculum intendere* ('to threaten') and *litem* or *crimen intendere.* Grave crimes affecting the whole community were, it appears, tried in the national *concilium,* lesser offences in the courts of the various *pagi* (§ 3).

distinctio, etc., 'The punishment varied according to (cp. 3. 4) the crime.'

arboribus. Withered trees were selected for the purpose. An old Roman law condemned persons guilty of treason to be hanged on a barren tree (*infelici arbori*), Livy I. 26.

ignavos et inbellis, 'cowards and cravens.' On this passage see.Westermarck, *Origin and Development of Moral Ideas,* II. 477. Archaeological discoveries have verified T.'s statement that drowning in a marsh was a recognised mode of execution in early Germany, and literary evidence shows that for many centuries women were punished in this way (see Schwyzer).

iniecta insuper crate. The same detail occurs in an account of a similar Roman execution, *ut...crate superne iniecta saxisque congestis mergeretur,* Livy I. 51, cp. IV. 50. The purpose seems to have been to keep the dead man's ghost under.

2. **tamquam,** etc., explaining *illuc*; lit. 'looks to this, namely as if,' so 'points to the notion that crimes, in being punished, ought to be exposed.' *tamquam* frequently introduces a notion or motive in the minds, or supposed to be in the minds, of the doers of an action (cp. Furneaux *ad loc.*). Here of course T. is putting his own rhetorical interpretation upon the facts. *flagitia* are disgraceful or immoral actions (cp. *ignavos,* etc.) as opposed to *scelera,* crimes against society (cp. *proditores et transfugas*).

levioribus delictis. The 'lighter offences' include homicide (21. 1, cp. *propinquis eius* below).

pro modo, 'in proportion,' i.e. to the offence.

vel civitati, because some states had no kings. The share which went to the king or the community was used to defray the expenses of sacrificial feasts (Schwyzer).

3. in isdem conciliis, i.e. in the national assemblies.

principes, influential persons to whom judicial functions are assigned, cp. on 13. 1. They are represented later by the Anglo-Saxon *ealdormen.* It is not clear whether each *pagus* had a judicial *princeps,* chosen out of its own members, assigned to it, or whether the *principes* went on circuit through a number of *pagi.* Schwyzer holds the later view, thinking that Caesar's expression, *B. G.* VI. 23 *principes regionum atque pagorum inter suos ius dicunt,* refers to a different institution.

pagos vicosque. *pagi,* cp. 5. 5, seem to have been districts embracing a number of scattered homesteads, *vici* collections of homesteads or villages.

iura...reddunt. The *princeps* appears only to have acted as president of the court, the decision of the case really resting with the *centeni.*

centeni, probably not itinerant, as the *princeps* may have been, but drawn from the locality where the court was being held. It may well be that in these 100 assessors, who were perhaps the heads of 100 families of the district, we have an early hint of the Anglo-Saxon *hundred.* "The union of a number of townships for the purpose of judicial administration, peace and defence, formed what is known as the *hundred* or *wapentake,* a district answering to the *pagus* of Tacitus, the *haerred* of Scandinavia, the *huntari* or *gau* of Germany" (Stubbs). Still we cannot definitely assert that the *centeni* imply the existence of *hundreds* in early Germany, or even that the *hundred* is evolved out of the *pagus.* For the question whether the *hundred* court of later times is a lineal descendant of Tacitus' *hundred* court, see Medley, *English Constitutional Hist.* p. 322 f.

consilium simul et auctoritas, 'to act at once as his advisers and supporters.' See on *iura reddunt* above.

CHAPTER XIII

1. armati, cp. 11. 4. The Tencteri regarded it as a great grievance 'to men born to arms' that when in Cologne they had to appear 'unarmed and almost bare,' *Hist.* IV. 64.

arma sumere, an echo of the Roman phrase *togam virilem sumere.*

moris, cp. *Agr.* 33. 1.

suffecturum, sc. *armis* ; 'has satisfied itself that he will be competent to use them.'

probaverit, perf. subjunct. of repeated action. A similar example after *non ante...quam* occurs in *Ann.* XV. 74 *ad fin.* Cp. Draeger, § 170.

in ipso concilio, i.e. in the assembly of the whole people and only there.

vel principum aliquis. The performance of the ceremony by a *princeps* was specially honourable, as it meant admission to his *comitatus.* See on § 2. Tacitus probably means to distinguish the military *principes* of cc. 13—14 from the judicial *principes* of 12. 3, where *eliguntur* seems to imply that not all *principes* exercised judicial functions. The latter would doubtless be chosen from the ranks of the former.

haec...toga, i.e. the arming corresponded to the assumption by Roman youths of the *toga virilis*, the plain white *toga* for which at about the age of 17 they ceremonially exchanged the purple-edged *toga praetexta* of childhood.

mox rei publicae. They were now full members of the state, able to attend its councils and bear arms on its behalf.

2. principis, etc., 'secure the esteem of a chief even for striplings ; these are grouped with the rest, stouter and long proved warriors.' That is to say, in spite of his immaturity a stripling is often included in a *comitatus* simply on the ground of his rank or his father's services. This interpretation gives far the best sense, though involving a somewhat uncommon sense of *dignatio*, not found elsewhere in Tac.; cp. however Suet. *Cal.* 24. Others interpret, 'assign [cp. 14. 2] the rank [the usual meaning of *dignatio*, cp. 26. 1] of chief even to striplings, though (for a time) they join another chief's *comitatus*.' But to take *ceteris*, etc., adversatively seems very strained. (See Furneaux' full discussion of the passage.)

nec rubor, etc., 'and it is no shame to be seen in the ranks of followers.' *rubor est* (effect put for cause), or more commonly *rubori est,* occurs in Ovid and Livy; cp. *Ann.* XIV. 55. These military *comites* are of course to be distinguished from the *centeni comites* of 12. 3.

3. gradus, 'degrees,' determined at the discretion of the *princeps.*

quibus, sc. *sit,* similarly understand *sint* with *cui.* Cp. 9. 2.

4. id nomen, etc., explained by the *si* clause, just as above *haec dignitas* is explained by an infinitival expression.

comitatus, probably genitive.

expetuntur. The subject is to be supplied from *cuique*, 'each chief.'

ipsa, etc., 'often by their very fame decide wars.' For this weak post-Augustan sense of *plerumque* cp. 45. 6, and for *profligo*, practically equivalent to our 'break the back of,' Cic. *ad fam.* XII. 30. 2 *profligato bello ac paene sublato.* So Livy XXI. 40, etc., Tac. *Hist.* II. 4, III. 50.

CHAPTER XIV

2. iam vero, 'furthermore,' cp. *Agr.* 9. 3.

superstitem, etc. The notion that a follower must not survive the death of his lord in battle is illustrated by the sagas and the history of the Teutonic kings. "When Cynewulf had been slain by Cyneheard, the king's men unanimously refused the terms offered them by the latter and fought until all were killed except a British hostage who was badly wounded." Chadwick, *op. cit.* p. 166. If the lord was captured, his followers were expected to share his captivity. Thus in 357 A.D., when Chonodomarius, king of the Alemanni, was taken prisoner by the Romans, his 200 *comites* surrendered themselves (Amm. Marc. XVI. 12. 60).

praecipuum sacramentum, 'their principal oath,' or 'their most solemn obligation.'

3. torpeat, subjunct. of indefinite frequency, cp. 7. 1.

plerique, 'a large number,' cp. *Agr.* 1. 3 and *plerumque* 13. 4 above. The *nobiles adulescentes* are young men of rank in general, not merely the 'striplings' of 13. 2. They may or may not be leaders of a *comitatus*.

ancipitia, 'dangers.'

clarescunt, sc. the *adulescentes.*

tueare, indefinite second person, cp. § 5 *ad fin.*, 6. 6, *Agr.* 46. 3.

4. illum, 'the well-known,' 'usual,' here fairly represented by our English article 'the.' Note the poetical phraseology here, the Virgilian *bellator equus* and the anticipatory *cruentam victricemque*, '(that shall be) stained with the blood of victory.' "The standing epithets of a [Teutonic] king in poetry are words which signify 'giver of treasure.' In addition to bracelets and other ornaments we find mention of weapons and armour, especially swords, helmets and coats of mail" as gifts to followers. Chadwick, *op. cit.* p. 168.

nam, explaining why the presents in question are attributable to the *generosity* of the lord; the *pay* which he gives his followers is their **meals.** Many editors insert *a* between *enim* and *principis*. But *liberalitate* may be a causal ablative 'thanks to the generosity.'

apparatus, nom. plural, an amplification of *epulae*; 'feasts and entertainment of a rough though liberal character.' For *apparatus* in a somewhat different sense see 23. 1.

pro...cedunt, 'are equivalent to,' an uncommon phrase, cp. Columella VI. 38 *herba, quam veratrum vocant rustici, pro pabulo cedit.* Cp. also *cedere in* 36. 2.

5. annum for *annonam,* as in *Agr.* 31. 2.

vocare, i.e. *provocare,* the simple for the compound verb, as so often in poetry and later prose, cp. *Agr.* 12. 1.

vulnera mereri, 'to win wounds,' as the reward of valour. Cp. the sentiment of 7. 4.

quin immo, 'nay, on the contrary.' Cp. note on *quin etiam,* 3. 3.

CHAPTER XV

1. non multum, sc. *temporis.* This passage flatly contradicts Caesar, *B.G.* VI. 21 *vita Germanorum omnis in venationibus atque in studiis rei militaris consistit*; cp. also *B. G.* IV. 1. Tacitus may of course be intentionally correcting Caesar, though other evidence is all in favour of the latter's statement. On the other hand there is much to be said for excising *non,* which comes in somewhat awkwardly after *non ineunt* and may well owe its existence to dittography. Cp. a similar difficulty in *Agr.* 44. 4. [Some try to solve the contradiction by supposing that T. here is speaking only of the *comites,* not of the Germans in general.]

delegata...cura, ablat. absolute.

domus et penatium, 'house and home.'

ipsi, repeating *fortissimus quisque,* etc., and contrasting them with the women and weaklings.

mira diversitate, causal ablat.; 'by a strange contradiction in their character.' "Industrial activity is not infrequently looked down upon as disreputable for a free man. This is especially the case among warlike nations, nomadic tribes, and peoples who have many slaves" (Westermarck, *op. cit.* II. 272).

quietem, i.e. peace with their neighbours.

2. ultro ac viritim, 'voluntarily and by the contributions of individuals.'

armentorum vel frugum, partitive genitives depending upon the noun clause *quod...subvenit.* C. and B. compare *Hist.* II. 44 *superesse...militum quod trans Padum fuerit.* These offerings were complimentary gifts (cp. *pro honore acceptum*) voluntarily tendered. Anything in the nature of compulsory tribute was repugnant to the Germans, cp. 43. 1.

3. sed et for *sed etiam*, 35. 2.

phalerae, metal discs or medals worn on the breast, especially by Roman soldiers as military decorations. Archaeological discoveries prove that the Germans wore similar neck and chest ornaments.

pecuniam, etc., cp. 42. 2, *Hist.* IV. 76, *pecuniamque ac dona quis solis corrumpantur*, sc. *Germani*. There is clearly some allusion to bribery of Germans by the Roman government.

CHAPTER XVI

1. populis, dat. of agent, cp. *Agr.* 2. 1.

urbes, elaborately planned walled cities like those of Italy. Colonia Agrippinensis, with its walls and fortifications, the Germans associated with slavery, *Hist.* IV. 64. We hear of German *oppida* both in Caesar and in Tacitus, but these were only large stockaded villages, or strongholds used as places of refuge during hostile invasion. Such were *Mattium gentis Chattorum caput, Ann.* I. 56, and the numerous German πόλεις mentioned by Ptolemy.

inter se iunctas sedes, 'connected dwellings.'

colunt, etc., 'they live separate and scattered.'

ut fons, etc. A proof of this is the frequency in German place-names of endings like -*brunn* (spring), -*bach* (brook), -*wald* (wood), -*feld* (field). Schwyzer.

2. vicos, etc., 'they build villages, but not in our way with the buildings adjoining and in close contact.'

spatio, 'an open space.'

remedium, in apposition with the preceding clause.

inscitia, causal ablative. Note the 'inconcinnity' or co-ordination of different constructions. Tacitus' reasons for the isolation of their dwellings are fanciful; the real one was their independence and lack of tribal solidarity.

Seebohm (*English Village Community*, p. 339) regards the settlers by spring, grove, etc., as the chiefs and free tribesmen "who were in a very loose sense the landowners, while...the villagers must chiefly have been their servile dependants." He finds here an embryo manor with its village of serfs upon it. But while serfs may well have formed a considerable part of the population of the *vici*, the conjecture that they formed their sole inhabitants is hazardous and improbable.

3. **caementorum,** 'building stone' (from *caedere*, 'to quarry').

materia...informi, etc., 'timber unshaped and without beauty or attractiveness.' For *citra* see on *Agr.* 1. 3. Note the adjectival use of the adverbial phrase. Near Berlin the remains of a large Bronze Age village have been excavated. The four-cornered houses are built of timber uprights with horizontal logs between them. The Antonine column shows houses constructed of vertical logs bound together at intervals with bands of wicker. (See Schwyzer.)

quaedam loca, etc., 'some parts of them they daub with an earth so clean and brilliant that it looks like painting and designs in colour.' The *loca* are probably parts of the outside, which they covered with a white clay or ochre plaster or perhaps with combinations of coloured earths.

lineamenta colorum is equivalent to *lineamenta colorata*.

4. **subterraneos specus aperire,** 'to dig underground holes.' *aperire* is unusual for *fodere*. Virg. *Georg.* III. 376 says of the Scythians *ipsi in defossis specubus secura sub alta | otia agunt terra.* Certain Aethiopians (Herod. IV. 183) and the Armenians (acc. to Xenophon, an eye-witness, *Anab.* IV. 5) are credited with this mode of life, which the Greeks regarded as the essence of primitive barbarism. Cp. Aesch. *P. V.* 452 κατώρυχες δ' ἔναιον...ἄντρων ἐν μυχοῖς ἀνηλίοις (before the advent of Prometheus). Pit-dwellings were indeed a regular form of habitation in the Neolithic, Bronze and even the Iron Ages. Pliny *H. N.* XIX. 2. 9 says the Germans did their spinning in such underground dens.

insuper, 'above.' The holes were no doubt roofed with boughs, on which the 'muck' was plastered.

hiemi, dative of purpose, 'for the winter.'

locis, ablative of means, or perhaps of 'place where.'

advenit, perfect tense.

eo ipso, etc., 'are undetected for the very reason that they require to be searched for,' and this an enemy would not be inclined to do; a pointed but somewhat platitudinous expression.

CHAPTER XVII

1. **sagum,** cp. 6. 2, a mantle consisting of a square piece of cloth, usually fastened on the right shoulder and leaving the arms free. It was worn by Roman soldiers, artisans and farm-hands.

fibula, a brooch or large safety-pin, one of the commonest of antiquarian objects.

desit, cp. 7. 1 for the mood.

cetera, accus. of reference; 'otherwise uncovered.'

locupletissimi, contrasted with *omnibus* above.

veste, referring to the *tunica* and *braccae*, as opposed to the overgarment or *sagum*. The Germans wore *braccae* to the knee or sometimes to the ankle.

sic ut Sarmatae, etc., sc. *distinguuntur*, or rather *vestiuntur*. They wore wide-sleeved tunics and loose, baggy trousers.

stricta, 'tight.'

exprimente, 'exhibiting.' The plain meaning of Tacitus' words is that the *vestis stricta* was confined to the rich. The monuments, however, generally represent German fighting-men with *braccae* and often with *tunicae*. But see note on *sagulo leves* 6. 2.

2. gerunt et, 'they wear too,' sc. the Germans in general. Acc. to Caesar, *B. G.* IV. I, VI. 21, they wore nothing else but skins.

ripae, the Rhine and Danube frontier.

neglegenter, etc. Those near the frontier were careless about their skins, because familiar through traders with the superior clothes of civilisation. Those further off, in the north and east, 'took considerable pains' about them (cp. *eligunt*, etc.); for skins were the only, or at least the most splendid, clothes they knew.

nullus...cultus, 'none of the refinements of civilisation.'

eligunt, sc. *ulteriores*.

velamina, strangely put for *pelles*, perhaps with a proleptic allusion to the 'coverings' for the human body, which they were to become.

spargunt, etc., 'they variegate them with patches of skin from beasts,' such as seals. Note the hendiadys *maculis pellibusque* to avoid two genitives (Schwyzer). Others translate 'with speckled skins,' but it seems less easy to get this out of the Latin.

3. habitus, 'dress,' *Agr.* 21. 3.

purpura, with purple stripes or patches.

vestitus superioris, the tunic; see on *veste* § 1. Tac. clearly means, and probably wrote, *partem vestitus superiorem*. The transference of the epithet seems gratuitous and pointless.

bracchia ac lacertos, the forearm and upper arm respectively. Cp. § 1 for the accus. Roman women generally wore sleeved tunics.

sed et, as though *non modo* had preceded. Cp. on 8. 3.

Chapter XVIII

1. quamquam, 'and yet,' in spite of a costume which struck the Romans as immodest. For the curiously artificial transition cp. 6. 1, 9. 1.

laudaveris, Cp. on *Agr.* 3. 1.

prope soli barbarorum. As a matter of fact, many of the lowest savages are strictly monogamous. But it was with peoples higher in the social scale, where polygamy becomes common, that the Romans were mainly familiar.

non libidine, in harsh zeugma with *ambiuntur*, sc. 'take more than one wife.'

nuptiis, modal ablat., 'are courted in very numerous marriages.' Virg. *Aen.* VII. 333 has *conubiis ambire.* Ariovistus had two wives, one a Sueban, the other a Norican (Caes. *B. G.* I. 53). Polygamy is known to have existed among the Franks and Scandinavians.

2. dotem, etc. 'The dower which the husband brings to the wife, not the wife to the husband' (as in Rome), is commonly supposed to have been in reality the bride-price, which the husband paid to the bride's father in purchase of her father's rights over her and in remuneration for his loss. It appears indeed that in some Teutonic instances the price was paid to the bride herself (Chadwick, *op. cit.* 325), and acquaintance with such exceptional cases might explain the words *dotem...uxori maritus offert.* Still, the view that Tacitus has misinterpreted the common German practice of purchasing a bride from her father seems more probable. *dos* is properly the marriage portion which among the Romans, as among the Greeks, Jews and Gauls, was given by a man to his daughter upon her marriage.

intersunt, i.e. are present at the wedding.

munera probant, 'appraise the gifts.' The rhetorical repetition of *munera* is noteworthy.

non...quaesita, 'not designed to please a woman's taste' (Fyfe), like jewels and ornaments.

boves. Cp. the Homeric παρθένοι ἀλφεσίβοιαι, maidens who on their marriage bring their parents payments of oxen.

3. in haec munera, 'in consideration of these gifts.' For a similar use of *in* cp. Livy XXXIV. 35 *condiciones in quas pax...fieret has conscripsit.* The meaning 'with a view to' easily passes into 'on condition of.' Cp. the Greek ἐπί with dative.

ipsa, etc. Tacitus is held to be wrong here. It was the bride's

father who presented the bridegroom with a sword in token that he
delivered to him power of life and death over his daughter.

hoc, etc.   In Tacitus' view the interchange of presents took the
place of the solemn mystery (*arcana sacra*) of the Roman *confarr-
eatio*, in which the contracting parties made an offering of bread
together in the presence of the *pontifex maximus* or *flamen dialis*
and ten witnesses.

coniugalis deos, among the Romans, Jupiter, Juno, Venus,
Hymenaeus and many others.

4.   extra virtutum cogitationes, 'excluded from thoughts of
brave deeds.'

auspiciis, 'solemn preliminaries.'

paratus, i.e. *frenatus*, § 2.   Tacitus is reading a mystical
meaning into what was mainly at least a business transaction.

5.   sic, as described in § 4.   With *vivendum* sc. *esse*.

accipere se, depending on *admonetur*, § 4.   *hoc...denuntiant* is
parenthetical.

quae liberis, etc., somewhat rhetorical, as only the *arma* could
be transmitted to posterity.

quae, object of *accipiant*, subject of *referantur*.   It is co-ordinate
with the preceding *quae*, not connected with *digna*.

Chapter XIX

1.   saepta, 'fenced in,' so 'unassailable.'

inlecebris...irritationibus, 'seductions,'...'exciting influences.'
See Friedländer, *Roman Life and Manners*, I. 245 ff.

litterarum secreta = *litteras secretas*, 'clandestine correspond-
ence.'   There is no good evidence for the use of writing among the
Germans at this date.   The letters addressed by German princes to
Rome (*Ann.* II. 63 and 88) would probably be written in Latin by
Roman interpreters.

2.   praesens, 'immediate.'

maritis permissa.   In Rome, Athens, early England, Peru,
China and many countries which habitually prohibited self-redress,
the injured husband was permitted to kill the guilty pair (Westermarck, *op. cit.* I. 290).

abscisis crinibus, etc., apparently a later mitigation of the
extreme penalty.   'Among the Wyandots of North America a
woman guilty of adultery is punished by having her hair cropped,'
op. cit. I. 311.

enim, sc. 'this is not surprising, for,' the reference here being to unmarried women.

invenerit, sc. the offender. See *Agr.* 3. 1 for the perf. subjunct.

3. saeculum, 'the spirit of the age.' *vocatur* suggests that this was a fashionable sense of the word.

melius quidem adhuc, sc. *agunt*, 'actually do even better.' *adhuc=etiam*, as often in post-Augustan writers.

cum spe, etc., 'they once for all have done with the hopes and vows of a wife,' i.e. they can only marry once. For *transigitur* cp. *Agr.* 34. 4. The rule that widows shall not marry again is widespread. It held apparently among the early Greeks (Paus. II. 21. 7, where see Frazer's note), as it does to-day among the Hindus and Chinese. With some Teutonic peoples, like the Heruli, the practice of suttee prevailed, and there is evidence of it in the sagas.

4. sic...quo modo unum, etc. The wife takes her husband 'as a single body, a single life,' i.e. realising that he will be her one and only husband. The words cannot mean 'as a body and life *one with her own*,' which would involve a Christian (cp. Matt. xix. 5), not a pagan, idea. The passage is a protest against the constant divorces and remarriages of Roman society, where 'ladies reckoned their age not by consuls but by the number of their husbands' (Sen. *de ben.* III. 16. 2).

ne, sc. *sit*, cp. 13. 3.

ultra, beyond the first marriage, an idea repeated by *longior*.

ne tamquam, etc., 'so that she may love, so to speak, not the husband but the marriage state,' or perhaps 'may love him not as a husband but as an embodiment of the marriage idea' (Schwyzer). The wording of § 4 is forced and the sense by no means clear.

5. finire, 'to limit.'

adgnatis, in Roman legal phraseology applied to children born after the father had made his will and settled on his heirs, Cic. *pro Caec.* 25. 72, *de orat.* I. 57. 241. Cp. *Hist.* V. 5 (of the Jews) *necare quemquam ex adgnatis nefas.* Though the Germans did practise infanticide, it appears to have been mainly in cases of deformity or illegitimacy or in times of stress. At Rome the exposure of children was very common under the Empire, though actual infanticide was prohibited by custom except where the child was deformed or weakly (cp. Seneca *de ira* I. 15).

bonae leges, such as Roman laws for the encouragement of marriage and the rearing of children. See on *Agr.* 6. 3. For the sentiment cp. Hor. *Od.* III. 24. 35 *quid leges sine moribus | vanae proficiunt?*

CHAPTER XX

1. in omni domo, rich as well as poor.

nudi, 'scantily clothed,' or perhaps literally 'naked'; cp. Mela III. 3. 26 *nudi agunt antequam puberes sint...viri sagis velantur aut libris arborum.*

in hos artus, etc. Allusions to the great stature of Germans are frequent; cp. 4. 2.

nec...delegantur, sc. *infantes* from *quemque.* For the common Roman practice see on *Agr.* 4. 2.

2. educationis deliciis, 'refinements of upbringing.' Civilis' notion of juvenile military education is interesting; *ferebatur parvulo filio quosdam captivorum sagittis iaculisque puerilibus figendos obtulisse, Hist.* IV. 61 (quoted by Schwyzer).

dignoscas. For the subjunct. cp. *Agr.* 11. 4.

virtus adgnoscat, a strong personification; 'till valour recognises them as her own.' The slaves did not bear arms.

3. sera, etc. Cp. Caesar, *B. G.* VI. 21. Acc. to him they did not marry before 20.

nec...festinantur, i.e. are not hurried into marriage, like Roman girls, cp. on *Agr.* 9. 7. Later, German girls were regarded as marriageable at 15.

eadem iuventa, i.e. they show the same vigorous youth as the young men.

pares validaeque miscentur, 'well matched, strong girls are mated.'

referunt, 'reproduce.' Cp. 43. 1.

4. sororum filiis, etc. Tacitus' words imply that the relationship between a man and his sister's son was considered as close as that between father and son, or in some cases even closer. Thus Vannius, a king of the Suevi, was displaced by two of his sister's sons (*Ann.* XII. 29—30), Civilis assigned commands to two of his sister's sons (*Hist.* IV. 33, V. 20), and, to take a Gallic example, Ambigatus in the time of Tarquinius Priscus appointed two of his sister's sons to lead an army into Italy (Livy V. 34). Pictish kings too were succeeded not by their own but by their sisters' sons. These instances point to a system of tracing descent through the mother, which obtains among many primitive peoples (cp. Herod. I. 173 for its existence among the Lycians), and frequently involves the predominance of the maternal uncle over the father. Many scholars deny the occurrence among the Aryans of 'matriarchal' institutions with the rule of succession by which rank and property descend in the female line, but the German and Gallic evidence is difficult to controvert. Prof. Chadwick finds further evidence in the *lex Salica* (*op. cit.* p. 328). As acc. to § 5 a man's property passed to his own, not to his sister's, children, it may be surmised that a transition was taking place in Germany from a system where succession was reckoned through females to one where it was reckoned through males (see *op. cit.* 327).

ad, instead of *apud,* for variety.

sanctiorem, sc. than that of father and son.

exigunt, sc. *hunc nexum.* They demand a man's sister's sons rather than his own sons.

tamquam, cp. 12. 2; 'with the idea of getting a firmer hold over their feelings and a wider grasp on the house,' wider because the mother's and the uncle's family would both be interested in the hostages.

5. tamen, in spite of the uncle's importance.

liberi, more correctly *filii.* Daughters could not inherit till a later period.

nullum testamentum, for inheritance depended entirely upon blood relationship. The Romans seem to have been unique among contemporary Aryans in permitting testation, and there is reason to suppose that in the earliest times even they did not allow it.

possessione, 'seisin.'

propinquorum...adfinium, blood relations and relations by marriage respectively.

gratiosior, 'more respected.'

pretia = *praemia,* cp. *Agr.* 1. 2. Wealthy Romans who had no children were eagerly courted with presents and attentions by legacy hunters. Cp., among other references in Tac., *Ann.* XV. 19 *satis pretii esse orbis quod...gratiam honores cuncta prompta et obvia haberent*; Seneca, *ad Marc. cons.* 19 *in civitate nostra plus gratiae orbitas confert quam eripit.*

CHAPTER XXI

1. suscipere, etc. Feuds and friendships are inherited as well as property. The idea that blood revenge is a moral obligation (cp. *necesse est*) upon the kindred of the slain is very widespread: it survived until quite modern times in the Scotch Highlands and is found even to-day in Corsica, Albania and Montenegro. The victim's relations may kill either the slayer himself or some other member of his family or clan.

nec, 'but...not,' cp. *Agr.* 8. 3.

durant, sc. *inimicitiae.*

luitur, etc. Originally the dead man's kindred might refuse to accept compensation (wergeld) and insist upon taking personal vengeance, but public opinion and legal enactment gradually prohibited the latter course. In Wessex we find hereditary classes actually named from the amount of their wergelds, e.g. *twelfhynde*, with a wergeld of 1200 shillings. In Anglo-Saxon England we find too a regular scale of payments for bodily injuries.

universa domus, for the feud concerned the whole family of the slain.

in publicum, 'as regards the community.'

iuxta, 'side by side with,' cp. 30. 3. See 11. 3 for German *libertas.*

2. convictibus et hospitiis, 'social gatherings and hospitality.'

quemcumque, etc. See Caes. *B.G.* VI. 23 for the sanctity of a guest in German eyes.

pro fortuna, etc., ' with well-furnished entertainment in proportion to his means.'

cum defecere, sc. *epulae* ; 'when the entertainment is over.' The later Germans, like the South Slavs, Moors and Moslems, set three days as the extreme period for which hospitality could be expected (Westermarck, *op. cit.* I. 595).

monstrator hospitii, etc., i.e. directs and escorts his guest to another host.

3. nec interest, sc. that they come uninvited.

quantum ad, as in *Agr.* 44. 3.

moris, sc. *est* ; cp. *Agr.* 33. 1. So the Homeric Greeks made valuable presents to guests, *Od.* XIII. 13, XIX. 197. Sociologists tell us that kindliness to strangers does not rest altogether upon altruistic sentiment. A visiting stranger is often regarded not merely as a potential benefactor but as a potential source of evil (*op. cit.* I. 584). The curse or the evil eye of a stranger may involve particularly formidable consequences.

data imputant, ' make a merit of their gifts.' For *imputare*, ' put down to an account,' cp. *Agr.* 27. 2. Here the givers do not ' book ' their gifts on the credit side of their own or the debit side of the recipients' account.

victus inter hospites comis. This flat ending to the section on hospitality cannot possibly stand. It looks like a scribe's marginal title accidentally introduced into the text. Lachmann reads *vinculum inter hospites comitas*, but the passage ends much better with *obligantur.*

CHAPTER XXII

1. in diem extrahunt. The Roman rose at on before day-break.

saepius calida, sc. *quam frigida.* We have no other evidence of this practice. Caesar speaks of the Germans washing in rivers, *B.G.* IV. I, VI. 21.

plurimum, sc. *temporis.*

separatae, etc., again unlike the Roman practice. The custom of a separate seat and table for each person may possibly be a survival of a widespread savage superstition that eating and drinking are acts which should be performed privately, because attended with special danger from the evil eye, bewitchment, etc. Among the African Warua every person must actually cook for himself and light his own fire. It is often death to see, even unwittingly, a savage king at his meal. Furneaux points out that separate tables and seats were used by the Homeric Greeks. We do not hear of the practice in later Germany.

armati, the emphatic word of the sentence. Even to banquets they habitually go armed.

2. continuare, 'connect together,' so 'spend continuously.' Cp. *Ann.* XIV. 20 *ne...dies totos ignavia continuaret.* The Roman did not begin his dinner till the late afternoon.

transiguntur, 'are settled,' cp. 19. 3. There is little exaggeration in Tacitus' description. In a German hero it was considered the sign of a mild temperament not to massacre his mates (see Schwyzer).

3. in vicem =*inter se, Agr.* 16. 1.

iungendis, etc., 'contracting marriage alliances and adopting chiefs.' The formal election of chiefs would presumably take place at the regular *concilia,* cp. c. 12, with which indeed such banquets seem to have been associated.

de...bello. Civilis hatched his rebellion at a feast, *Hist.* IV. 14.

tamquam, 'in the idea that,' though the idea is rather that of Tacitus himself. Cp. note on 12. 2.

simplices cogitationes, 'frank deliberations.'

4. non astuta nec callida, 'not cunning nor sophisticated.'

adhuc. They had not 'as yet' learned the art of concealment. Cp. the Greek proverb τὸ ἐν καρδίᾳ τοῦ νήφοντος ἐπὶ τῇ γλώσσῃ τοῦ μεθύοντος. and Hor. *Sat.* I. 4. 89.

retractatur, sc. *res.*

salva, etc., 'the proper account is taken of either time.' Cp. Quint. IV. 2. 75 *salva ratione causae.* Acc. to Herodotus I. 133 the Persians first debated matters of importance when drunk. The decision then reached they reconsidered on the next day when sober, and adopted it if again approved.

dum fingere nesciunt, i.e. when they are in liquor.

CHAPTER XXIII

1. potui, dative expressing the purpose served, cp. 46. 3.

frumento, here 'wheat.' Beer was early in common use in Egypt, Armenia, Spain, Gaul and most European countries except Greece and Italy, where wine was the national beverage.

corruptus, 'decomposed,' so 'fermented.'

proximi ripae, cp. 17. 2.

. **agrestia poma**, wild fruits like crab-apples, berries and nuts.

recens fera, 'fresh game.' The Romans kept meat before cooking. Mela's statement, III. 3. 28, that the Germans ate raw flesh, fresh or dried, is quite probable, at least in the case of the less civilised (cp. Tylor, *Anthropology*, p. 264).

lac concretum, 'curdled milk.' Tacitus' account of German food and drink is somewhat sketchy. He omits, e.g., cheese (Caes. *B.G.* VI. 22), bread, porridge, vegetables, cider and mead.

apparatu, 'luxury,' Cp. Hor. *Od.* I. 38. 1.

blandimentis, appetisers, sauces, pickles, etc.

2. non eadem, cp. on 4. 3.

haud minus facile, etc. The literal meaning of the epigram must not be pressed. The Germans were of course not easy to 'conquer by arms.' See 37. 2. Tac. mentions two cases of the destruction of German troops while in a state of intoxication, *Ann.* I. 50, *Hist.* IV. 79.

CHAPTER XXIV

1. nudi, as though for battle, cp. 6. 2 ; see also on 20. 1.

infestas, 'levelled.' The dance seems to have mimicked the motions of actual combat.

se...saltu iaciunt, a lively variant for *saltant.*

2. artem, 'skill,' cp. *Agr.* 36. 1.

in quaestum, etc., 'though not with a view to profit or pay.' The sword-dancers were not paid like, for instance, Roman gladiators, though later it was customary for the spectators to present them with small gifts (Schwyzer).

quamvis...pretium, 'however reckless the sport, its only reward....'

3. quod mirere, appositional, 'a surprising fact.'

inter seria, 'as a serious occupation.'

extremo ac novissimo, 'last and final.' Cp. *Agr.* 34. 3.

corpore, 'their persons.'

4. iuvenior, sc. than the winner.   The form is post-Augustan and rare for *iunior*.

pervicacia, 'perverse obstinacy.' *prava* is ablative.

per commercia tradunt, 'dispose of by traffic.' Cp. *Agr.* 28. 5.

se quoque.   Even the winner would feel shame, if he kept the loser as a bondsman in his own establishment.

CHAPTER XXV

1. ceteris, other than those who had gambled away their liberty.

descriptis...ministeriis, 'with defined duties through the household,' as in the case of a Roman establishment.   Still the Germans did employ domestic slaves, as is shown by the evidence of language; see also **20. 2** and § 3 below.

suam quisque, etc., 'each one is master of his own abode, his own home.' Acc. to Seebohm these *servi* or serfs lived in the *vici* of **16. 2.**   But see note *ad loc.*   Like the Roman *coloni* they had their own homesteads, crops and cattle, paying rent to their lord in kind.

vestis, 'cloth,' made by the *servi*.

colono.   The Roman *coloni* were at the outset tenant farmers to whom the great Italian landowners let their estates in *fundi* on lease at a monetary rent.   Later, though still sometimes called *ingenui*, freemen, they became little better than serfs, attached to the soil (*adscripti glebae, servi terrae*) and rendering to their lords (*patroni*) as rent a definite proportion of the produce of the lands which they farmed.   They were liable to corporal punishment and were often ill-treated by the lords.   These later Roman *coloni* thus correspond very closely with the German serfs.   But it is uncertain when their change of status took place.   Our evidence for their later condition is mostly of the fourth or the end of the third century A.D.   From this passage it seems that the change must have begun in the first century, as the free Roman *coloni*, paying a monetary rent, present no analogy to the German serfs (see W. T. Arnold, *Roman Provincial Administration*, p. 177 f.).

hactenus paret, i.e. his obedience goes no further than this, viz. rendering a proportion of his produce to the lord. For *hactenus* cp. *Agr.* 10. 6. Tacitus understates the case. The lord required personal service from his *servi.*

cetera in strict logic qualifies only *officia,* not *domus officia* ; 'the rest, the household duties' (Furneaux). Greek often uses τὰ ἄλλα in a somewhat similar way, e.g. Herod. I. 193 καρπὸν ἐκφέρειν. τὰ γὰρ δὴ ἄλλα δένδρεα, 'for *on the other hand* trees,' corn not being a tree. *cetera* might be thus translated here.

uxor, sc. of the lord.

2. opere, 'hard labour,' 'task work.' T. is thinking of the Roman practice of consigning unruly slaves to an *ergastulum,* 'workhouse,' or *pistrinum,* 'pounding mill' (Furneaux). For *vinculis* here cp. Plaut. *Most.* I. 1. 19 (addressed to a slave) *augebis ruri numerum, genus ferratile,* i.e. 'fettered.'

disciplina et severitate...impetu et ira, two instances of hendiadys, 'sternness of discipline,' 'impulse of anger.'

nisi quod, 'the only difference being that,' cp. on *Agr.* 6. 1.

3. liberti, etc. Having no free kinsmen to defend their interests or take up a blood feud on their behalf, they had to rely for protection on their previous lord, so that they were still in a dependent position (Schwyzer).

raro, etc. 'rarely any influence in a household, never in a state,' in strong contrast to the Roman freedmen, who were sometimes the most important personages in the empire. Cp. *Hist.* I. 76, *Ann.* XIV. 39.

exceptis dumtaxat, 'with the exception, that is to say, of.' *dumtaxat* is properly an old legal word, 'so far as relates to,' hence 'strictly speaking,' 'at least.' Cp. Hor. *Sat.* II. 6. 42 *Maecenas me coepit habere suorum | in numero, dumtaxat ad hoc, quem tollere reda | vellet.* See Conway on Livy II. 61.

regnantur. See also 44. 1 for this intrans. verb used personally in the passive,—a poetical construction. For tribes ruled by kings see on 7. 1.

ibi, etc. The predominance of freedmen in such tribes was due to mutual jealousy and distrust between the king and his nobles, which prevented the latter from being offered or from accepting the high offices of state.

inpares libertini, 'the inferiority of the freedman class.' The name *libertinus* calls attention to a freedman's relation to the state and society, *libertus* to his relation to his former *dominus.*

libertatis argumentum, just as the ascendancy of freedmen in Rome was a proof of servitude.

CHAPTER XXVI

1. faenus agitare, etc., 'to operate with capital and spread it out at interest (*in* = 'with a view to' or 'in the direction of'). *faenus*, which generally means 'interest,' has here its less common sense of 'money lent at interest.' It is difficult to see how *in usuras extendere* can mean 'increase by *compound* interest,' as some editors hold.

ideoque, etc., 'and consequently it (sc. *faenus* NON *agitare*) is more carefully observed than if it were forbidden,' apparently a piece of cynical humour. For *servatur* we should have expected a word meaning 'guarded against,' and even then to say that a wholly unknown practice is avoided seems an abuse of language. Contrast the striking epigram in 19. 5. Apart from the internal difficulties of the passage, the abrupt transitions from freedmen to usury and from usury to land tenure are very unlike the usual studied sequences of the *Germania*.

agri, etc., 'lands in proportion to the number of cultivators are taken up in turn by the whole body of them; these they next divide among themselves according to their rank.' Each community appropriated an amount of land proportionate to the number of its freemen (the *cultores*), and then distributed this land in accordance with differences of rank, the chiefs and nobles getting larger shares than the mass of the freemen.

in vices (for which some read *vicis*, 'by villages as communities,' an excellent sense) probably means that when one part of the community's land or 'mark' was worked out a new piece was put into cultivation. Or it might possibly refer to the taking up of hitherto unappropriated lands *one after another* by the community, as it increased in numbers.

facilitatem, etc., 'the wide extent of open ground renders partition easy.'

2. arva, etc., 'their plough lands they change every year, and there is always land to spare.' Each occupier ploughs a different strip each year, leaving last year's arable waste. This is possible owing to the extent of their holdings. "Nothing could describe more clearly what is mentioned in the Welsh triads as 'co-aration of the waste.' The tribesmen have their scattered homesteads surrounded by the lesser homesteads of their 'servi.' And the latter join in the co-tillage of such part of the grass land [i.e. the *ager*] as year by year is chosen for the corn crops, while the cattle wander over the rest." Seebohm, *op. cit.* 344.

The German land system described by Tacitus must be distinguished from that mentioned by Caesar, *B. G.* VI. 22, cp. IV. 1, who says that no one had any private land of his own, but the magistrates and chiefs every year assigned to tribes and clans as much land and in such place as they thought fit, compelling them the next year to move somewhere else. Caesar is describing the practice of migratory tribes, in particular the Suebi, but Tacitus' Germans are a settled race.

nec enim, etc., 'nor indeed do they compete with the richness and the extent of the soil by labour, that is to say (lit. so as to) by planting orchards, enclosing grass meadows (*separating* them from the unenclosed *ager*) and irrigating gardens,'—a rhetorical way of saying that their land is fertile and extensive enough to produce all that they want without their exerting themselves in the ways mentioned.

seges, etc., 'corn alone is requisitioned from the soil.' Cp. Cic. *de sen.* 15. 51 *terra nunquam recusat imperium* (C. and B.).

3. totidem, sc. as the Romans.

species, i.e. seasons.

intellectum, 'a meaning,' a sense frequent in Quintilian. The names *Sommer* and *Winter* are pan-Germanic, but the words for 'spring' vary greatly in different languages. Schwyzer thinks that T. may be wrong in denying to the Germans a name for 'autumn,' as *Herbst* (Anglo-Saxon *hearfest*, our *harvest*) is pan-Germanic. The probability is that the absence in Germany of the Italian *bona autumni*, the vintage and the fruit harvest, led the Romans to think that there was no German word for autumn, forgetting that an important feature of the northern autumn is the corn harvest, which in Italy came earlier.

CHAPTER XXVII

1. nulla ambitio, 'no ostentation,' in contrast with the costly parade of Roman funerals.

certis lignis. Remains of oak, beech, fir and juniper have been found in German barrows.

crementur. Cremation superseded inhumation in Germany during the later Bronze Age and remained the usual practice until it was gradually ousted by Christian influences.

2. struem rogi, 'the funeral pile.'

vestibus, 'cloths.' For the Roman custom cp. Verg. *Aen.* VI.

221 and *Ann.* III. 2 *trabeati equites...vestes odores aliaque funerum sollemnia cremabant* (at the funeral of Germanicus).

equus. Not only the chief's war horse, but sometimes his dogs, slaves and even his wife (c. 19. 3 note) were burnt with him, that their souls might accompany him to the other world.

sepulcrum caespes erigit, artificial for *s. caespite erigitur.* Cp. Seneca, *ep.* 8. 5 *hanc domum utrum caespes erexerit an varius lapis... nihil interest.* The reference is to the earth barrow or 'low' (Anglo-Saxon *hlaew*, Lat. *clivus*), which in England forms so common a suffix in place-names.

monumentorum, genit. of definition, cp. *Agr.* 40. 1 : 'monuments with their lofty and elaborate splendour' (C. and B.).

gravem, explained by the epitaph *sit tibi terra levis.* The reason given is of course Tacitus' own.

lamenta...meminisse, a wonderfully dignified and sonorous ending to the 'general' section of the *Germania.*

3. haec in commune...accepimus, 'such are the general facts that we have gathered,' mainly, it appears, from literary sources. For *in commune* cp. on 5. 1.

ritus, probably 'religious observances,' but see on 45. 2.

differant, sc. from those hitherto described.

Chapter XXVIII

1. validiores, sc. *quam Germanorum.*

summus auctorum, 'that highest authority.' Caesar, *B. G.* VI. 24, says that at one time the Gauls were better fighters than the Germans, made aggressive wars upon them and sent settlers across the Rhine, among them the Volcae Tectosages, who had occupied the most fertile parts of Germany round the Hercynian forest and still dwelt there. The faint resistance offered by the Gauls under Vindex to the legions of Germany seems to have brought them into contempt.

etiam. Not only did Germans migrate into Gaul (27. 3), but we may believe (contrast Caesar's definite statement) *even* that Gauls passed over into Germany.

permutaret, 'take in exchange.'

promiscuas, etc., 'still unappropriated and divided among no powerful kingdoms.' Note *et nulla,* 10. 4.

Most archaeologists think it improbable that there were any large migrations of Gauls eastwards across the Rhine. The tide of migration flowed the other way. The earliest home of the Gauls appears to have been the great forest belt of Central Germany (see note on § 2) and especially the region of the Upper Danube. From thence they spread on the one side into northern Italy, and on the other into north-western Germany between the Rhine and Weser, and crossed the former river into Gaul.

2. **Hercyniam silvam**, 'known by report to Eratosthenes and certain other Greeks' (e.g. Aristotle, *meteor.* 350ᵇ 5 ὄρη τὰ 'Ἀρκύνια), Caes. *B. G.* VI. 24. It is a general expression for the wooded mountains north of the Danube from the Rhine to the Carpathians. See *B. G.* VI. 25. If the Rauhe Alp (otherwise known as the Swabian Jura) is, as Mommsen suggests, the part of the forest here intended, the Helvetian area comprised the Black Forest and the basin of the Neckar.

Moenum, the Main. The object of *Helvetii tenuere* is the whole phrase *inter...amnes*, an awkward construction which Möller removes by inserting *citeriora* after *Helvetii*. The migration of the Helvetii into the modern Switzerland perhaps took place about 100 B.C.

Boii. They originally dwelt in what is now Bohemia, extending south to the Danube. Poseidonius ap. Strab. VII. 293 says Βοίους τὸν Ἑρκύνιον δρυμὸν οἰκεῖν πρότερον. Apparently about 60 B.C. they were expelled from this district and went to Noricum (Caes. *B. G.* I. 5), some of them subsequently joining the Helvetii in their Gallic expedition. The remainder were annihilated by the Getan king Boerebistas in the time of Augustus (Strabo VII. 304).

significatque, etc., 'and points to the old tradition of the place.' *Boiohaemum* means the home (Germanic *haim*, later *heim*) of the Boii. From about 8 B.C. the district was occupied by the Marcomanni. See on 42. 1.

3. **Aravisci**, settled near the Roman Aquincum on the right bank of the Danube a little below its great southerly bend.

Osis. The Osi lived almost due north of this bend, but some 150 miles away across the Carpathians in the modern Silesia.

Germanorum natione, a difficult phrase, as in 43. 1 Tac. definitely states that they are *not* Germans, because they speak Pannonian and 'submit to tribute.' It seems impossible to translate 'a tribe belonging to the Germans,' i.e. tributary to them. We must either convict T. of inconsistency, or bracket the words as a gloss expressing perhaps a scribe's private opinion. The second of Tacitus' two alternatives is the more probable.

quia, etc., 'for as in the past equal poverty and equal freedom prevailed there, the advantages (sc. freedom) and disadvantages (sc,

poverty) of either bank were the same. The suggestion is that had
one bank been richer or freer than the other, there would have been
good reason to conclude that the migration was towards the
former.

4. Trĕverī, on the Moselle. Their name survives in Trèves or
Trier (Augusta Treverorum).

Nervii, the fiercest of the Belgae (*B.G.* II. 4), living between the
Sambre and Scheldt.

circa, etc., 'actually take ostentatious pride in claiming.' *circa*
in the sense 'in regard to' is post-Augustan.

similitudine et inertia, hendiadys; 'from resemblance to the
Gauls in indolence.' For the *inertia* of the Gauls cp. *Agr.* 11. 5.
Most probably the Treveri and Nervii were not Teutonic peoples
but Gauls from across the Rhine. See notes on 2. 3.

haud dubie, attributively with *Germanorum.*

Vangiones, etc. These three tribes were settled in Upper
Germany. Taken in order from north to south, the Vangiones
lived round Worms (Borbitomăgus), the Nemetes round Speyer
(Noviomagus) and the Triboci round Brumat (Breucomagus). They
all took part in Ariovistus' expedition.

5. Ubii. When first heard of, they lived on the east bank of
the Rhine opposite Coblenz, in the Lahn valley and part of the
Taunus range. Their friendly relations with Rome began in
55 B.C. when they put themselves under Caesar's protection. In
38 B.C. Agrippa transported them to new territories on the west
bank of the river some 50 miles lower down. Their chief settle-
ment, known as *oppidum* or *ara Ubiorum,* in 50 A.D. became a
Roman military colony and was renamed Colonia Agrippinensis
(or Agrippinensium) after Claudius' wife Agrippina, who was born
there, *Ann.* XII. 27. It is now Cologne.

meruerint. For the subjunct. after *quamquam* cp. note on
Agr. 3. 1.

conditoris sui, Agrippina, notwithstanding the gender; cp. 7. 4
hi laudatores. The notion that Tacitus blunderingly intended
Agrippa by *conditoris sui* seems absurd;—Agrippa's derivative
would be *Agrippensis.*

experimento fidei, 'because they gave proof of loyalty.'
arcerent, sc. *hostes.*

CHAPTER XXIX

1. non multum ex ripa. The 'small part of the (Roman) bank,' occupied by the Bătăvi (rarely scanned Bătăvi), was the region between the Waal or southern branch of the Rhine and the Maas or Dutch portion of the Meuse.

insulam, bounded on the north by the northern arm of the Rhine, which then entered the sea near Leyden (Lugdunum)—or perhaps by an arm connecting with the Zuider Zee—on the south by the Waal and on the west by the North Sea.

In Caesar's time the 'Island' was already occupied by the Batavi.

fierent, 'were to become.'

2. insigne. A 'token' of the ancient alliance dating from Caesar (once broken however in the revolt of Civilis, 69 A.D.), still remains in the following immunities.

contemnuntur, 'are insulted.'

oneribus (dative), the regular burdens like tribute, requisitions of corn, etc. Cp. on *Agr.* 19. 4.

collationibus, nominally voluntary contributions on special occasions, but often in fact compulsory. After Germanicus' campaign *ad supplenda exercitus damna certavere Galliae Hispaniae Italia, quod cuique promptum, arma equos aurum offerentes, Ann.* I. 71.

tela atque arma, weapons and armour. The Batavi provided one *ala* of 1000 cavalry and nine *cohortes*, each of 1000 infantry. Cp. *Agr.* 36. 1.

3. Mattiăcorum, living between the Taunus range and the Main round Wiesbaden (Aquae Mattiacae). Their mention next to the Batavi is due not to proximity of position but to similarity of status.

veteres terminos, the Rhine which Domitian's *limes* (see on § 4) replaced as the frontier.

imperii, depending on *reverentiam.*

sede, 'in respect of position.'

agunt, equivalent to *vivunt* or *sunt*, cp. 19. 1.   Notwithstanding their general friendliness, like the Batavi, they revolted with Civilis.

cetera, cp. 17. 1.

adhuc, to be taken closely with *ipso terrae suae solo,* 'except that they are keener spirited through *still* enjoying the actual soil and climate of their own land,' unlike the Batavi who had left their original homes.   Furneaux boldly joins it with *acrius.*   It is interesting to observe that the Romans were alive to the effects of a bracing climate. Schwyzer refers to Cic. *de div.* II. 42. 89.

4. numeraverim, cp. on *Agr.* 3. 1.

decumates agros, 'the Tithe Lands,' an expression found only here. From the fact that *ager decumanus* means 'land paying tithe,' we may conclude that the territories in question were so called because leased by the Romans for a tithe of the produce. The difficult form *decumas* is probably to be explained by the frequency of the suffix *-as* in a topographical sense, cp. *cuias*, *infernas*, and especially collocations like *ager Ferentinas*, from which *ager decumas* might easily be formed by false analogy. These 'Tithe Lands' apparently extended from the Main to the Danube, comprising the valley of the Neckar, the Black Forest and adjacent districts to the east.

levissimus, 'least respectable.' Note the combination of super-lative and positive here. Cp. the similar usage noted on *Agr.* 4. 5.

dubiae, because of constant danger from the Germans.

limite. Domitian's frontier line which ran along the eastern side of the *decumates agri*. For an account of it see on *Agr.* 41. 2.

praesidiis, the military posts on the *limes*.

sinus, 'a corner,' cp. 1. 1.

habentur, understand as subject the inhabitants of the *decumates agri*. They were regarded as belonging to the province of Germania Superior.

Chapter XXX

1. ultra hos, sc. *decumates agros*, really to the north of them. The Chatti occupied the upper part of the Weser basin round the Eder, Fulda and Werra, north-east of the Taunus range. Drusus subdued them in 10 B.C., but they recovered their independence after the disaster of Varus in 9 A.D. They gave trouble to Claudius in 50 and Domitian's expedition of 83 was directed against them.

initium sedis...incohant, 'begin the frontiers of their territory.' For the pleonasm cp. Livy III. 54 *prima initia incohastis libertatis vestrae*; so *initium oriri, principium incipere*, etc.

Hercynio saltu, here the hills east of the Taunus.

effusis, 'extended,' so 'broad,' 'level.' The ablatives are local.

durant, sc. *Chatti*; 'they continue so long as the hills (continue) and gradually die out with them (sc. *siquidem colles rarescunt*), and thus the Hercynian forest accompanies its native Chatti and finally sets them down,' i.e. the Chatti cease where the forest ceases on the plain (though as a matter of fact the Chattan territory did not extend as far as the north German plain). Others make *colles* the subject of *rarescunt*; 'the Chatti continue as the hills gradually die out.' Others again translate, 'since (*siquidem* being in anastrophe and introducing an explanation of *non ita effusis*, etc.) the hills continue, then gradually die out, and the forest,' etc. *simul atque* is not infrequently put by Tacitus for *et...et*. The picture of the forest 'accompanying its children' all through their territory is very striking.

2. stricti, 'well-knit.'

animi vigor, 'vivacity of mind.'

multum, etc., 'for Germans, they show a great deal of judgment and sagacity.' The following infinitives are in explanatory apposition with *multum rationis*, etc.

electos, emphatic, '*only* chosen leaders.'

nosse ordines, in a military sense, 'to know their ranks' or 'to understand orderly formation.' Livy XXIII. 35 has *signa sequi et in acie agnoscere ordines suos*.

intellegere, etc., 'to see their opportunity, to reserve their attack, to portion out the day (each part for a definite duty,—a frequent post-Augustan phrase), to entrench the night' (picturesque for *noctem vallis tutam reddere*, in formal antithesis to *diem disponere*).

3. ferramentis...et copiis, 'with tools (for engineering work) and rations,' such as Roman soldiers carried.

videas. Cp. on *Agr.* 11. 4.

ad bellum, 'to a campaign,' as opposed to a battle, for which alone other Germans, carrying only arms, were prepared.

excursus, 'sudden rushes.' With *fortuita pugna*, supply *rara est*.

equestrium, etc., 'it is of course characteristic of cavalry troops to win a quick victory and beat a swift retreat; but (adversative asyndeton) fleetness is close to panic, deliberate movements are more akin to steadiness.' The passage justifies the Chattan preference for infantry, which though less dashing than cavalry, is steadier and less liable to panic. For *iuxta* and *propior* cp. *Ann.* VI. 42 *populi imperium iuxta libertatem, paucorum dominatio regiae libidini propior est*.

CHAPTER XXXI

1. et aliis, etc., 'a custom adopted by other nations (dat. of agent), of Germany also (*et = etiam*), though but rarely and in consequence of individual hardihood, among the Chatti has become general, namely to....' For the appositional participle cp. on *Agr.* I. I. *audentia* is an uncommon post-Augustan word.

adoleverint, subjunct. of indefinite frequency.

submittere, for the earlier *promittere.*

votivum, etc., 'an aspect of face assumed by vow and devoted to valour,' i.e. which betokens their devotion to valour. For *habitus* cp. *Agr.* II. I, *Germ.* 4. 2. Civilis, a Batavian (cp. 29. 1), *barbaro voto, post coepta adversus Romanos arma, propexum rutilatumque crinem patrata demum caede legionum deposuit, Hist.* IV. 61. The custom was common among ancient peoples. Cp. the Nazarite vow, *Numb.* vi. 5, ' he shall let the locks of the hair of his head grow long '; *Acts* xviii. 18 ' having shorn his head in Cenchreae ' (of St Paul on the fulfilment of a vow). Julius Caesar let his hair grow long till he had avenged a defeat, Suet. *Caes.* 67.

2. super sanguinem, i.e. over the bleeding foe.

revelant frontem, by cutting off the mass of hair and beard.

pretia nascendi rettulisse, ' have repaid the price of their birth,' i.e. the debt which they owed their parents and country for their existence.

dignosque, sc. *esse.*

ferunt, 'they declare.'

squalor, 'unkempt condition.'

3. insuper, in addition to the long hair.

ferreum...anulum, worn on the arm (others say on the finger), a sign of thraldom, cp. *ignominiosum id genti.* Here it indicates that the wearer had devoted himself to the service of the war god.

4. plurimis = *permultis,* cp. 18. 1. A large number, T. means, wear the ring and the long hair and beard not only till they have slain an enemy but throughout their fighting days.

iamque canent, etc., 'and there are men already greyheaded distinguished in this way and conspicuous to both friends and foes.' For *monstratus* cp. *Agr.* 13. 5 with note.

haec, by attraction for *hi.*

nova, 'strange,' ' startling,' cp. 43. 6 *novum ac velut infernum aspectum.*

nam, etc., giving the reason for their prowess and startling appearance ; they never ' make themselves soft by a milder manner of life.' Others take *cultu* to mean 'aspect,' 'fashion,' like *habitus* above.

5. cura, 'occupation.'

exsanguis senectus, as in Lucan I. 343. Cp. Stat. *Theb.* XI. 323 *exsangues anni.*

CHAPTER XXXII

1. certum iam alveo, i.e. 'now with a well defined channel.' As T. is here enumerating the German tribes roughly in order from south to north, these words seem intended to contrast the lower course of the Rhine from Bingen, where the great gorge begins, northwards past Coblenz, with the upper part of the river where the valley is much broader and the channel liable to alter. The words are held to be a reminiscence of Mela III. 2. 24, *Rhenus Alpibus decidens prope a capite duos lacus efficit. mox diu solidus et certo alveo lapsus haud procul a mari huc et illuc dispergitur.* (In *Ann.* II. 6 *Rhenus uno alveo continuus* is contrasted with the bifurcation of the Rhine at the frontier of the Batavian territory.)

Rhenum, loosely put for *Rheni ripam.*

quique terminus, etc. From a few miles north of Coblenz, where Domitian's *limes* ended (see on *Agr.* 41. 2), the river formed the boundary between Roman and German territory.

Usipi ac Tencteri. In 55 B.C. these tribes crossed the Rhine under pressure from the Suebi but were almost annihilated by Caesar, who treacherously attacked them while he detained their chiefs who had come to negotiate. The remnant settled on the Lippe in the northern part of the territory of the Sugambri, and when the latter were transplanted by Tiberius in 8 B.C. to the left bank of the Rhine, occupied the southern part of their territory as well (see Schwyzer's note). At this time the Usipi (also called Usipii and Usipetes) appear to have lived between the Ruhr and the Lippe or perhaps the Yssel, and the Tencteri between the Ruhr and the Lahn.

2. solitum, usual among the Germans generally.

equestris disciplinae, 'horsemanship.' Caesar found their cavalry very formidable, *B. G.* IV. 12.

3. hi, sc. horsemanship.

4. inter, etc., 'along with the slaves, the home and the rights of succession (including the right to a portion of the community's land, 26. 1) the horses are bequeathed: to these last succeeds not the eldest son, as he does to the rest of the property, but the son who shows himself brave and superior in war.' The passage is interesting for its allusion to primogeniture, the exclusive, or almost exclusive, succession of the eldest son to property. Though the practice is by no means uncommon in various parts of the world, it was unknown to the Greeks and Romans (Maine, *Early Hist. Inst.* 197 ff., cp. *Ancient Law* 229) and is not mentioned elsewhere as an early Germanic institution. Since Tac. cannot be reading a southern European into a Germanic custom, there seems no reason to doubt the literal accuracy of his statement, at least as regards the disposal of the bulk of the property. We may suppose that the father, or perhaps a family council, decided the destination of the horses.

prout, etc., lit. 'according as (a son) is....' *bello* goes with *melior* as well as with *ferox*.

CHAPTER XXXIII

1. iuxta Tencteros Bructeri. The Bructeri were formerly settled north of the Tencteri and east of the Usipi, occupying the territory between the Lippe and the Ems and the upper and central portions of the Ems basin. Some ancient writers distinguished the Bructeri minores from the B. maiores, the latter of whom seem to have dwelt east of the Ems. In 4 A.D. Tiberius received the submission of the Bructeri. They took part against Varus and in the revolt of Civilis. See on 8. 3.

occurrebant, 'ran up.'

Chamāvos, once settled in the district subsequently occupied by the Tubantes and the Usipi (*Ann.* XII. 55), i.e. east and south east of the Yssel. They migrated into the part of the Bructeran territory between the Lippe and the Ems, where their name survived in the mediaeval district of Hamaland. Later they spread across the Rhine to the Maas.

Angrivarios, living on both banks of the Weser, south of Bremen. Their defeat of the Bructeri led to their extension in a south-westerly direction towards the Teutoburger Wald. Enger, near Herford, is thought to preserve their name.

pulsis. We have no other record of the event, which must have occurred between 70 and 98 A.D.

penitus excisis. Nevertheless the tribe maintained a separate existence. Pliny, *Ep.* II. 7, mentions that the Roman general Vestricius Spurinna *Bructerum regem vi et armis induxit in regnum ostentatoque bello ferocissimam gentem...terrore perdomuit.*

spectaculo, either dative (the earlier constr.) or ablative (of the thing in respect of which). For the latter cp. *Ann.* I. 22 *ne hostes quidem sepultura invident*, with a similar omission of *nobis*. Quintilian IX. 3. 1 describes the ablative constr. as a modern conceit.

2. oblectationi oculisque, datives of purpose, 'to gratify our eyes.'

urgentibus imperii fatis, 'while the doom of the empire presses hard upon it,' cp. Livy V. 22 *iam fato quoque urgente*, V. 36 *iam urgentibus Romanam urbem fatis*. These ominous words are remarkable in view of the restoration of public confidence brought about by the reign of Nerva and the accession of Trajan (*Agr.* 3. 1). But the fact that at the very time of the publication of the *Germania* Trajan was away strengthening the defences of the Rhine and Danube frontiers must have kept the Romans alive to the reality of the northern danger, which indeed had been impressing itself upon them for the past two centuries.

nihil...discordiam. Cp. *Agr.* 12. 2, *Ann.* II. 62 *haud leve decus Drusus quaesivit illiciens Germanos ad discordias* (C. and B.).

CHAPTER XXXIV

1. Dulgibini, only mentioned here and in Ptolemy II. 11. 17, who calls them Δουλγούμνιοι. They seemed to have lived on the Aller in Hanover, east of the Angrivarii.

Chasuarii, 'dwellers on the Haase' (cp. Ampsivarii, 'dwellers on the Ems,' *Ann.* XIII. 55), settled between the Ems and Hunte, behind the original territories of the Chamavi.

cludunt, a form not infrequent in T. and due to the influence of compounds.

haud perinde memoratae, 'not particularly celebrated,' cp. 5. 3.

a fronte, on the side towards the sea.

Frisii, between the Zuider Zee and the Ems, in the modern Friesland. Schwyzer thinks that the Frisii minores may have lived either between the Yssel and the Rhine or west of the outlet of the Zuider Zee. The Frisii were subdued by Drusus in 12 B.C. Oppressive tribute produced a revolt in 28 A.D. which was with difficulty suppressed, *Ann.* IV. 72, 73. They joined the rebellion of Civilis.

utraeque nationes, loosely put for *utraque natio*.

insuper. Not only are they 'fringed by the Rhine,' but they 'live around vast lakes *as well*,' sc. the Zuider Zee (*lacus Flevo*) and other salt lakes of Friesland which were anciently more numerous than now.

Romanis classibus, the fleets of Drusus in 12 B.C. and of Germanicus in 15 and 16 A.D.

2. illa, 'in those parts.'

temptavimus, 'ventured on,' 'explored.'

superesse adhuc, 'still awaited discovery.'

Herculis columnas. T. clearly has in mind something resembling the southern Pillars of Hercules or Straits of Gibraltar. Probably some rocky strait or fiord gave rise to the rumour. Prof. Chadwick would have us believe that the pillars of which Drusus heard were early examples of the Irminsul, "the name of an immense wooden shaft or pillar worshipped by the Old Saxons at a place called 'Eresberg,' now Marsberg on the Diemel. It was cut down in the year 772 by Charlemagne." There is other evidence for the existence of these sacred pillars, which were a kind of glorified Maypoles. The historian Widukind mentions 'pillars of Hercules,' apparently with reference to the Irminsul (see Chadwick, *op. cit.* pp. 226—229, and note on 9. 1). But it seems simpler to regard Tacitus' report as a piece of garbled geography.

consensimus, rarely construed with the infinitive.

3. Druso Germanico. The latter name was only given him after his death (9 B.C.).

obstitit, here construed with the infinitive on the analogy of *prohibeo*, apparently a unique instance.

mox nemo temptavit. These words convey a false impression. Drusus had reached the Ems or possibly the Weser in 12 B.C. So far from 'no one venturing after him,' in 5 A.D. Tiberius' fleet penetrated to the Elbe and ten years later Germanicus got at least as far as Drusus.

de actis, referring to § 2. The pious epigram is intended as a sarcasm upon Drusus' successors for their lack of scientific curiosity.

CHAPTER XXXV

1. hactenus, etc., 'up to this point we have a good knowledge of Germany towards the west,' a concise union of two statements, (1) that this is the limit of western Germany, and (2) that we know more of the western than of the northern and eastern districts of Germany about to be described. Cp. the introductory words of 44. 1 for a similar condensation.

in septentrionem...recedit, 'northwards it sweeps away in a vast bend,' a reference to the Cimbric Chersonese (Schleswig Holstein and Denmark); cp. 37. 1 *eundem Germaniae sinum. recedit* is Heraeus' emendation for *redit* of the MSS. and gives excellent sense, though its correctness is far from established by Mela III. 1. 8 *ab his promontoriis in illam partem quae recessit ingens flexus aperitur* (of the Spanish coast). C. and B. tr. the manuscript reading ' it runs up northwards and returns southwards with a vast sweep.' But could even Tacitus have been capable of such short-hand, involving as it does the separation of *in septentrionem* from *redit* ?

Chaucorum, dwelling between the Ems and Elbe and parted by the Weser into minores and maiores, the former to the west, the latter to the east of that river. They were loosely dependent upon Rome, helping Germanicus in his expedition of 15 A.D., *Ann.* I. 60. They gave trouble in 47 A.D. (*Ann.* XI. 19), and they joined in the revolt of Civilis. Pliny's dismal picture of them as poor fishermen living on earthen mounds among the fens, in constant danger from the sea (*H. N.* XVI. 1. 1), is only applicable to the Chauci of the coast. Contrast Velleius' account quoted on § 3 below.

omnium quas exposui, since c. 30. The Usipi and Tencteri, however, must be excluded.

donec...sinuetur, 'until it makes a curve right to the Chatti.' On the south the Angrivarii and the Cherusci came between the Chauci and the Chatti, unless indeed the victorious Chatti (cp. 36. 2) had forced their way down the Weser valley through Cheruscan territory and touched the Chauci where the river enters the north German plain. For the subjunct. after *donec* see on 1. 3. There is some authority for *sinuatur* here ; see note on text.

3. inpotentia, 'lawlessness,' lit. ' want of self-control' ; cp. *inpotens,* in the sense of *inpotens sui.*

secreti, 'secluded.' Cp. Velleius' account of the Chauci, II. 106. 2 *omnis eorum iuventus, infinita numero, immensa corporibus,* situ locorum tutissima.

4. ut...agant, 'their superiority,' dependent upon *adsequuntur.* For *agant* cp. 29. 3.

exercitus, ' a regular army,' explained by the appositional phrase *plurimum virorum equorumque.* (The Germans were not generally strong in cavalry, 6. 4, 30. 3, 32. 2.) Others bracket *exercitus,* which certainly comes in awkwardly.

eadem fama, sc. as in war. Even in peace they are regarded as superior to their neighbours. T. is fond of elliptical uses of *idem,* cp. 4. 3.

CHAPTER XXXVI

1. in latere, etc. The Chērusci lay south-east of the Chauci and north-east of the Chatti, stretching from the left bank of the middle Weser to the Elbe along the northern slopes of the Harz mountains. Cp. Caes. *B.G.* VI. 10. Subdued by Drusus and Tiberius, they later became very powerful, thanks to their leader Arminius, who in 9 A.D. destroyed Varus' legions and in 17 crushed the philo-Roman Maroboduus, the head of a large Suevic confederacy. After Arminius' death in 19 their power declined owing to internal dissensions. In 47, having lost all their nobles in civil wars, they asked the Romans for a king, and Italicus, the sole survivor of their royal house, who lived in Rome, was given them, *Ann.* XI. 16.

nimiam...nutrierunt, 'free from attack have long fostered an exaggerated and languid (i.e. enervating) peace.' In *Ann.* XII. 28 T. admits that they were perpetually at feud with the Chatti, but their relations with Rome had been peaceful since Arminius' day.

inpotentes, cp. 35. 3.

falso quiescas, 'it is a delusion to be peaceful.' For the subjunct. cp. on *Agr.* 11. 4.

ubi manu, etc., 'where matters are decided by the strong hand (cp. *Agr.* 9. 2), forbearance and goodness are names applied to the more powerful,' the weaker being called e.g. *inertes ac stulti*. The manuscript reading *nomine superioris sunt* seems too difficult to stand, though Schwyzer interprets it 'exist only with reference to (cp. 8. 1) the stronger,' i.e. only the stronger can afford to be forbearing and just; the weaker earns merely contempt by such qualities.

2. olim, sc. *vocati sunt*, cp. 2. 5.

Chattis victoribus, perhaps in 84 A.D., when the Chatti expelled the Cheruscan king Chariomerus (see Mommsen, *Provs. of R. E.* I. 146).

in sapientiam cessit. The Chatti's good fortune 'came to be reckoned as wisdom.' Cp. Curt. III. 6. 18 *temeritas in gloriam cesserat*.

3. Fosi, not mentioned elsewhere. It is suggested that their name survives in that of the river Fuse, a tributary of the Aller. If this is so, they lived in Hanover, north of the Cherusci.

ex aequo socii, 'equal sharers.' For *ex aequo*, 'on equal terms,' cp. *Agr.* 20. 3.

Chapter XXXVII

1. eundem...sinum, referring to *ingenti flexu,* 35. 1; cp. 1. 1.

proximi Oceano, 'nearest to the open sea,' πάντων ἀρκτικώτεροι Κίμβροι, Ptol. II. 11. It is to be remembered that the ancients thought Scandinavia an island; cp. 44. 2, note on 1. 1. The Cimbri lived in Jutland, *Cimbrorum promontorium*, Pliny IV. 27. 96, part of which was once called Himmerland or Himbersyssel, apparently preserving their name. Mela III. 3. 32 places them on the *Sinus Codanus,* by which he probably means the bay between the Jutish peninsula and the Prussian coast. Strabo locates them in a peninsula (VII. 292 *ad fin.*) between the Rhine and the Elbe (VII. 294), an obvious error. They are mentioned in the Monumentum Ancyranum: *classis mea per Oceanum ab ostio Rheni ad solis orientis regionem usque ad fines Cimbrorum navigavit, quo neque terra neque mari quisquam Romanus ante id tempus adit.*

gloria, ablative.

utraque ripa, on either side of the Rhine and Danube.

castra ac spatia, hendiadys, 'spacious camps.' The Pannonian place-names Cimbriana and Teutoburgium (the latter close to the Danube) may be relics of the great invasion, while the words *Mercurius Cimbrianus* and *civitas Toutonorum* occurring on inscriptions of our era found at Miltenberg near Aschaffenberg indicate that remnants of the Cimbri and Teutones were still settled there (see Schwyzer). Note that T., like the Mon. Ancyranum, does not mention the Teutones.

molem manusque gentis, 'the might of the race and the hands at work.' Cp. *Ann.* I. 61 *castra lato ambitu...trium legionum manus ostentabant.*

tam magni, etc., 'the credibility of so vast an exodus.'

2. sescentesimum et quadragesimum annum, really the 641st year or 113 B.C., when the Cimbri invaded Noricum and at Noreia routed Carbo's army which had been guarding the passes of the Alps.

alterum...consulatum, 98 A.D. Note the 'mixed' conditional sentence, *si...computemus...colliguntur.*

3. multa in vicem damna, sc. *fuerunt. in vicem* = 'mutual,' 'on both sides'; cp. *Agr.* 24. 1.

admonuere, 'have given warnings.' Note the collocation of sing. and plur., people and country, for stylistic effect.

Arsacis. Arsaces founded the Parthian empire, long Rome's formidable eastern rival, about 250 B.C. The name was dynastic rather than personal.

4. quid enim, etc., very concise Latin ; 'for what else can the East fling in our teeth except the slaughter of Crassus, the East which itself lost Pacŏrus and was cast down beneath the feet of Ventidius?' *et ipse,* referring to the personified *Oriens,* goes closely with the ablat. absolut., the phrase standing for *cum et ipse Pacorum amiserit.* Cp. note on *Agr.* 25. 4 *ad fin.* In 53 B.C. the army of Crassus was almost annihilated by the Parthians at Carrhae in Mesopotamia, Crassus being murdered at a subsequent conference. The Parthians were themselves defeated by P. Ventidius Bassus in 38 B.C., when Pacorus, son of the Parthian king Orodes, was amongst the slain. This Ventidius, during the Social War, was brought as a prisoner from his native Picenum to Rome, where he practised the trade of a mule-driver. Thanks to Caesar's favour he had a successful political career and ultimately became consul in 43 B.C. The aristocratic Tacitus implies that the obscurity of Ventidius' origin renders the Parthian defeat at his hands all the more ignoble.

5. Carbone. See on § 2. Tac. omits the disaster to Junius Silanus in the Rhone valley in 109 B.C.

Cassio. In 107 B.C. L. Cassius was defeated and slain by the Tigurini in the country of the Gallic Nitiobriges, north of the Garonne. The Tigurini were not Germans, but a branch of the Helvetii, with whom the Cimbri appear to have allied themselves on their westward march from Noricum, after they had defeated Carbo.

Scauro...Mallio. In 105 B.C. the pro-consul Servilius Caepio and the consul Mallius Maximus commanded armies on opposite banks of the Rhone, while Mallius' legate Aurelius Scaurus was with a force in advance of the main armies. The Cimbri first routed and slew Scaurus, and then at Arausio almost annihilated the armies of the two generals-in-chief, whose mutual jealousy prevented them from helping each other. After this the Germans moved into Spain, but returned to Gaul in 102 B.C. (As Scaurus commanded only an outpost, Tac. is not justified by his own enumeration in speaking of the loss of *five consular* armies.)

simul, in eight years, 113—105 B.C.

Varum, destroyed with about 20,000 men in the depth of the Teutoburgian forest (9 A.D.). Cp. on 36. 1.

Caesari, Augustus. His constant lament, *Quintili Vare, legiones redde,* is well known.

impune, 'without loss.'

C. Marius. In 101 B.C. he exterminated the Cimbri on the Raudine Plain near Vercellae in north Italy. The previous year he had destroyed the Teutones at Aquae Sextiae near Marseilles.

divus Iulius. Julius Caesar defeated the German Ariovistus in 58 B.C. and drove back the Usipetes and Tencteri across the Rhine in 56 B.C.

Drusus, brother of Tiberius (see below). He operated for four years in Germany, 12—9 B.C., dying from the effects of an injury received in his last campaign.

Nero. Tiberius Claudius Nero, son of Augustus' consort Livia by her previous husband, was the name of the future emperor before his adoption by Augustus in 4 A.D., when he became Tiberius Caesar. Tac., *Ann.* II. 26, quotes him as saying *se noviens a divo Augusto in Germaniam missum plura consilio quam vi perfecisse.* His first campaign was in 9 B.C., his last in 11 A.D.

Germanicus, son of Drusus. He conducted three German expeditions, 14—16 A.D.

mox, in 39 A.D. For Caligula's sham operations (which Mommsen does not condescend even to mention), see note on *Agr.* 13. 4.

6. donec, etc., referring to the revolt of Civilis in 69 A.D., when the Batavians and numerous other tribes took the opportunity of the civil war between Vitellius and Vespasian to rise against Rome, though at first nominally espousing the cause of Vespasian. After a long siege they captured Castra Vetera on the Rhine near Xanthen (*expugnatis...hibernis*) and massacred the garrison.

adfectavere, 'aspired to the possession of.'

inde, out of Gaul.

proximis temporibus, 'in recent times,' the reference being to Domitian's expedition, for which see *Agr.* 39. 2 with note.

triumphati. *triumpho,* properly an intransitive verb, is not uncommonly used in the passive by poets and later prose writers. Cp. *regnantur* 25. 3.

CHAPTER XXXVIII

1. Suebis. Tac. uses the term Suebi in a far wider sense than other authors, applying it indiscriminately to all the peoples of eastern Germany. In its ordinary application it is a group name for the Semnones, Hermunduri, Marcomanni, Quadi and Langobardi (Strabo p. 290), who seem to have been connected into some form of political and religious union. These Suebi all dwelt in the basin of the Elbe. Tacitus' extension of the term may be due to the fact that the Marcomannic Maroboduus incorporated into his Suebic empire a number of non-Suebic tribes, though by no means as many as Tac. includes under the name. Certainly the worshippers of Nerthus, c. 40, the east and north Germans of cc. 43—44, and the non-Germanic Aestii and Sitones, c. 45, were not Suebi (see Schwyzer's note and Chadwick, *op. cit.* pp. 216—218).

adhuc, 'still.' Others translate 'besides.'

2. insigne, etc., 'a distinguishing characteristic of the race is to draw the hair sideways and to bind it below in a knot,' on the right temple over the ear, a practice established by existing representations (cp. Schwyzer). Other Roman writers seem to regard the custom as common Germanic rather than distinctively Suebic, cp. Sen. *de ira* III. 26, *ep.* 124. 22.

servis. Their hair was cut close.

rarum, sc. *est*; i.e. the custom is found, but rarely, and it is confined to youth.

3. horrentem, 'in a shock.'

retro agunt, suggested by Schwyzer, who compares Quint. XI. 3. 160 *capillos a fronte contra naturam retro agere*, for the meaningless *retro sequuntur*.

ac saepe, etc., 'and often it is bound back in a knot on the very top of the head,' a practice also depicted, though infrequently, on the monuments.

et ornatiorem, 'even more elaborately dressed.'

4. ea, etc., 'in this, it is true, attention is shown to personal appearance, but it is innocent'; for the motive is not amatory but warlike.

in altitudinem, etc., 'but (antithetic asyndeton) to give an appearance of tallness and to cause terror, when about to go to war, they adorn themselves more finely for the eyes of the foe.'

CHAPTER XXXIX

1. Semnŏnes, extending from the east bank of the middle Elbe to the Oder. They are first heard of in 5 A.D. Maroboduus included them in his empire, but in 17 A.D. they revolted and joined the Cherusci against him.

fides antiquitatis, 'the belief in their antiquity.'

religione, 'by a religious ceremony.'

2. auguriis...sacram, 'hallowed by ancestral rites and reverence of old.' Note the hexameter. As it contains Virgilian reminiscences, Tac. was probably alive to its rhythm. Other hexameters, apparently accidental, occur in Tac., e.g. *Agr.* 10. 4 *ad fin.* (a bad one).

auguriis patrum, the auspices taken by their ancestors, either at the original dedication or in the ordinary service of the place.

omnes eiusdem sanguinis, perhaps all the Suebi proper, see on 38. 1.

legationibus, 'by means of representatives.'

caeso, not prior in time to *celebrant*, cp. *vectam* 40. 3 and *ictus*, *Agr.* 29. 1 (note).

primordia, 'inauguration,' a more impressive word than *initia*. See on 9. 1 for human sacrifice.

3. ut minor, 'as an inferior openly confessing the majesty of the divine power.'

attolli, in a middle sense, 'to raise himself.'

4. superstitio, Tacitus' regular word for a foreign religion. For *eo...tamquam*, with which supply *sint*, cp. 12. 2 with note.

inde, from the forest, where a divine ancestor was probably supposed to have sprung into existence.

regnator omnium deus, commonly identified with Tiu (cp. on 9. 1), because the Suebi or Schwabians of later times were called Ziuvari, worshippers of Ziu or Tiu. Tiu was a cosmic deity as well as a war god.

fortuna, 'the good fortune,' 'prosperity,' as distinct from their religious supremacy.

centum pagis habitant. Caesar, *B. G.* I. 37, IV. 1, gives the same account of his Suevi collectively. He is not aware of, or at least does not mention, their separate tribes.

magnoque corpore efficitur, 'the result of their being so large a body is.' *corpus* is common in the sense of 'corporate body,' 'body politic.'

Chapter XL

1. Langobardos, dwelling south-east of the Chauci on the lower Elbe, mainly to the west of the river, where their name survived in Bardanwik near Lüneburg, but also extending to the eastern bank. Their name apparently means 'Long-beards.' Vell. Paterc. II. 106 describes them as *gens etiam Germana feritate ferocior.* They were defeated by Tiberius in 5 A.D. Like the Semnones they became subject to Maroboduus and revolted from him. Towards the end of the fifth century they suddenly rose to importance and in 568 under Alboin invaded northern Italy, which they ruled with Pavia for their capital till 774. They are commonly known as Lombards.

paucitas, in contrast with the large numbers of the Semnones, 'their fewness lends them lustre.'

Reudigni deinde, etc. These seven tribes lived next to (*deinde*), i.e. north of, the Langobardi, but their relative positions are very obscure. It seems well established that the Anglii, who invaded Britain in the fifth or the sixth century, were at this time settled in the centre of Schleswig-Holstein, though Ptolemy II. II. 15 strangely places his Soueboi Angeiloi on the middle Elbe, apparently between it and the upper Ems. The Varini, possibly the Οὐίρουνοι of Ptolemy, and the Suarines are thought to have lived in Mecklenburg, the former in the north-eastern and the latter in the western part, in which districts the river Warnow and the town of Schwerin may perhaps preserve their names (Chadwick). The Reudigni, Nuithones (both probably corrupt names), Aviones and Eudoses do not appear to be mentioned elsewhere, though some would read Eudusii for Sedusii in Caesar *B. G.* I. 51 and thus find Tacitus' Eudoses in the army of Ariovistus. Aviones is said to mean 'island-dwellers.' The positions assigned to these tribes on the maps may well be mistrusted. On the whole question see Chadwick, *op. cit.* pp. 198 ff.

2. Nerthum, id est Terram matrem. Terra mater, equated by Tac. with the Ingaevonic goddess Nerthus, is the Magna Mater Idaea or Cybele, whose worship was introduced into Rome from Phrygia in 204 B.C. This identification indicates that Nerthus was a goddess of fertility, presiding over the increase of animal and vegetable life and bringing plenty and prosperity to men. Support is lent to this view of Nerthus by the functions and attributes of the Scandinavian god Niördhr, a name identical with Nerthus, and of his family, the god Frey and the goddess Freyia. Thus Niördhr ruled the waves for the benefit of travellers and fishermen and was generally a god of plenty. Frey produced abundant harvests and like Nerthus used to travel about in a car among his people. Freyia was among other things a goddess of love and marriage and also travelled in a car, drawn by cats.

invehi populis. It seems more probable that the tribes which worshipped Nerthus came to the island for the festival than that the goddess was carried across the sea to the mainland. The cult of Nerthus is fully discussed by Prof. Chadwick, *op. cit.* pp. 234—268.

insula, almost certainly in the Baltic, but hardly identifiable. Some believe it to be Alsen; Prof. Chadwick pronounces for Sjaelland (Zealand), which was the home of a goddess Gefion, a being similar to Freyia and hence to Nerthus.

castum, unprofaned by secular uses.

veste, cp. 27. 2.   The cloth veiled some fetish or symbol of the goddess.

uni sacerdoti, 'to the priest alone.'   A priest for a goddess, a priestess for a god (as for Frey) was the common rule, the minister being commonly regarded as married to the divinity.

3.   penetrali, 'the sanctuary,' the wood's holy of holies where the *vehiculum* was kept ; cp. *templo* below.

vectam, cp. on 39. 2.

bubus feminis, a ritual phrase for *vaccis*.

festa loca, sc. *sunt* ; 'every place where she deigns to visit and accept entertainment makes holiday.'

4.   clausum omne ferrum.   Iron is often regarded with superstitious fear by primitive peoples, especially by their priests and kings, apparently because it is an innovation.   See J. G. Frazer, *Taboo* etc. pp. 232 ff.

templo, 'sacred enclosure.'   Etymologically the word means 'a part cut off' (Greek τέμενος, √ τεμ = cut), and does not *necessarily* imply a building (*aedes*).   The Germans acc. to Tacitus did not build temples, cp. 9. 3.

5.   velis, see on *Agr.* 46. 3.

numen ipsum, implying that the object in the car was believed to be 'the divinity herself,' not a mere representation of her (cp. 9. 3).   Tac. would have found nothing strange in the washing of an image ; cp. *Ann.* XV. 44 *simulacrum deae* (sc. *Iunonis*) *perspersum est*, a ritual sprinkling which no doubt took the place of an earlier washing.   Zernial refers to Amm. Marc. XXIII. 3. 7.   For the Greek custom of cleansing a polluted statue in the sea cp. Eurip. *Iphig. in T.* 1157 ff.

illud, etc., the contents of the car.

CHAPTER XLI

1.   secretiora Germaniae, i.e. the far north.

Rhenum, sc. *secutus sum*.   In cc. 32—34 he followed the course of the Rhine by enumerating the nations roughly from south to north.   Now he will proceed from west to east.

Hermundurorum, living between the Werra and the Elbe and extending southwards towards the Danube, but not touching it. They settled in this district with the consent of the Romans about 2 B.C.   They are occasionally heard of during the first and second centuries but then practically disappear till the fifth, when they revive as the Thuringi. (*thur* represents the older *-dur-*, *ing* being a patronymic. *hermun* is for *irmin* = great. Schwyzer.)

non in ripa, 'not simply on the bank of the Danube.'

penitus, i.e. far within the province.

colonia, Augusta Vindelicorum, the modern Augsburg, founded by Augustus, but only as a *municipium*. Cp. the inexact use of *coloniae* in *Agr.* 5. 3. For Raetia see on 1. 1.

2. passim et sine custode, in contrast with less favoured tribes like the Tencteri, who complained that the Romans did not allow them to gather in Colonia Agrippinensis except unarmed, under the eye of sentries and on payment of dues (*Hist.* IV. 64).

cum, 'although,' 'while.'

non concupiscentibus, 'without their coveting them.'

Albis. The Hermunduran territory does not contain the source of the Elbe, which rises further east in northern Bohemia. But it does contain the sources of several important tributaries of the Elbe.

inclutum et notum olim. L. Domitius Ahenobarbus, about 2 B.C., starting from Vindelicia, 'crossed the Elbe with an army and penetrated further into Germany than any of his predecessors,' *Ann.* IV. 44. See also on 34. 3.

CHAPTER XLII

1. Naristi, by some identified with the Οὐάριστοι of Ptolemy II. II. 23, hence the reading Varisti. The maps place them south of the Hermunduri and west of the Marcomanni.

Marcomani, more commonly spelt Marcomanni, are mentioned by Caesar, *B. G.* I. 51, as forming part of Ariovistus' army. At that time they appear to have dwelt on the Main. Their nearness to the Rhine frontier may have perhaps given rise to their name, 'men of the marches.' Shortly before the Christian era they migrated into Bohemia (see on 28. 2) under the leadership of Maroboduus, who established a powerful kingdom and extended his sway over the Langobardi, Semnones and other Suebic tribes, as well as over several non-Suebic tribes such as the Lygii and Gotones (Strabo p. 290). In 17 A.D. his empire fell before the assaults of the Cherusci (see on 36. 1). Later the Marcomanni recovered some of their power and in the time of Marcus Aurelius waged constant war with Rome, 166—180 A.D.

Quadi, to the south-east of the Marcomanni on the river Marus in the modern Moravia.

pulsis olim Boiis, 'by driving out the Boii in days gone by.' There is good evidence to show that the Boii had been expelled from Bohemia long before the immigration of the Marcomanni, so that Tac. seems to be in error. It is of course possible that a small body of the Boii remained behind.

ea, i.e. the tribes just mentioned. With *frons* contrast *retro*, 43. 1.

quatenus, etc., 'so far as it is bordered by the Danube.' *praecingitur* is generally accepted for the almost untranslatable *peragitur* of the MSS.

2. Marobodui. He had spent his youth as a hostage in Rome, where he won the favour of Augustus. After his fall (see on § 1) he flung himself upon the protection of Tiberius and lived in honourable captivity at Ravenna until his death.

Tudri, presumably a Quadian, but the name does not occur elsewhere. When Maroboduus' empire broke up, a Quadian, Vannius, ruled over both tribes. See *Ann.* II. 63. Nothing is known of the 'foreign' kings mentioned below.

nec minus valent, 'nor are they (sc. the kings) less powerful for that.' Cp. 15. 3 *ad fin.*

CHAPTER XLIII

1. Marsigni, etc. The Marsigni are only mentioned here and cannot be located. As iron was found among the Cotini, their settlements are perhaps to be placed in north Hungary on the upper Gran, and thus south-east of the Quadi, but this situation does not agree very well with *retro*. The Osi (see on 28. 3) seem to have lived between the Carpathians and the upper course of the Vistula. The Buri (Ptolemy's Λούγιοι Βοῦροι) dwelt round the sources of the Vistula. They fought in the Marcomannic War.

cultu, 'by their appearance,' for which cp. 38. 3.

et quod, etc., another subject to *coarguit*.

2. Sarmatae. See on 1. 1.

quo magis pudeat, for with iron in their territories (cp. 6. 1) they might have forged weapons with which to free themselves.

pauca, etc., 'a small amount of level country but mainly mountain valleys.'

3. continuum montium iugum, i.e. the Riesengebirge and the Sudetic Mts, forming the ancient Asciburgius Mons ('Ash Mountains').

S.							13

Lygiorum nomen, 'the nation of the Lygii,' also spelt Lugii, a religious confederacy extending from the above mentioned mountains north-eastwards to the Vistula. It is generally supposed that the later Vandals (cp. 2. 4), who invaded Italy and Spain in the fifth and Africa in the sixth century, are lineal successors of the Lygii. We have no further evidence as to the separate Lygian tribes mentioned by Tacitus. The Helvecones are thought to be identical with Ptolemy's Ἀιλουαίωνες. The shorter form Naharvali seems as well supported as Nahanarvali.

4. **antiquae religionis,** probably genitive of description, 'of ancient sanctity.' Furneaux trans. ' of an ancient worship ' (possess. genit.), supplying *religioni* with *praesidet.*

muliebri ornatu, explained by Müllenhof as referring primarily to the mode of dressing the hair. He connects the priest with the later Vandal priest-kings, the Hasdingi, who, as their name indicates, wore a feminine *coiffure.*

sed deos, a somewhat forced contrast. The gods were male, despite the feminine appearance of their priest.

Castorem Pollucemque. Germanic mythology tells of two twin gods or heroes, youthful knights in shining armour, who more or less resemble the Roman Castor and Pollux and the Indian Asvins. These and similar pairs in other European mythologies clearly have a common Indo-Germanic origin. The Germanic pair are called the Hartunge. Tacitus' name, the Alci (*Alcis* being presumably dative plural), is puzzling. Grimm (*Teutonic Mythology*, Eng. Trans. p. 66) suggests that *alx*, which he equates with the Gothic *alhs*, ' temple,' may have been the name of the sanctuary, not of the divinities themselves. Another derivation is from the root *alk-* in ἀλκή, 'strength' or 'courage.' Lithuanian legends tell of a giant Alcis (Grimm, *op. cit.* p. 1390).

memorant, with vague subject ; 'people say.'

ea vis numini, ' such is the character of their godhead.'

5. **peregrinae,** i.e. other than German, such as the worship described in 9. 2 and cults associated with images, 9. 3.

tamen, although without images.

6. **ceterum,** ' for the rest,' ' to resume.'

super vires...truces, 'savage in addition to being strong above all the peoples just enumerated.'

lenocinantur, lit. 'pander to,' hence 'make the most of,' 'exaggerate,' a post-Augustan sense. Cp. *dial. 6 ipsa sollicitudo lenocinatur voluptati.*

tincta, perhaps with soot, says Schwyzer, who points out that

tattooing is not meant, though the existence of the practice in
ancient Germany is proved by the numerous discoveries of tattooing
instruments. With *nigra scuta* contrast 6. 2.

ipsaque, etc., 'merely by the awe-inspiring and shadowy appearance of their spectral host.' *feralis*, 'belonging to the dead'
(hence the common meaning 'fatal'), seems here used in the sense
of 'death-like,' 'ghostly.'

novum, etc., 'their strange and almost hellish aspect.' The
sentence is a striking example of Tacitus' wonderful power of
words.

CHAPTER XLIV

1. Gotōnes. This famous nation, according to Pliny, *H. N.*
XXXVII. 11. 35, was mentioned by Pytheas of Massilia (c. 300 B.C.)
as dwelling on an estuary of the ocean, i.e. of the Baltic, in an
amber-producing district. The 'estuary' must be the Gulf of
Danzig, whither, as the Gothic historian Jornandes (c. 552 A.D.)
tells us, his countrymen 'had migrated from the island of Scandza
(Norway and Sweden), which lies in the northern Ocean opposite
the mouth of the Vistula,' and which he describes as a 'manufactory
of nations,' *officina gentium.* The legends of the Gothic and other
Teutonic migrations from Scandinavia seem to have some founda-
tion in fact and may perhaps be explained, with Prof. Chadwick,
op. cit. p. 174, by supposing that a small but dominant element in
certain Germanic populations was of Scandinavian origin. At the
time of Tac. the Goths dwelt on the lower Vistula, perhaps
extending north-eastwards as far as the Pregel. From this district
they migrated about 200 A.D. to south Russia and soon began
making inroads upon the Roman Empire, in the affairs of which
they played an important part for several centuries. The Gothic
bishop Ulfilas (c. 311—381) translated the Bible into his native
tongue. The surviving fragments of his translation are the earliest
literary specimens of a Teutonic tongue which we possess.

regnantur. See 25. 3 for the transitive use and on 7. 1 for
German kings.

iam, i.e. now that we have reached this point, so far away from
the centre of freedom-loving Germany. Trans. 'here.' Cf. § 3
below *nullis iam exceptionibus*, and 46. 6.

adductius, 'more strictly.' Cp. *adducere habenas*, 'to tighten
the reins,' and *Ann.* XII. 7 *adductum et quasi virile* ('masculine')
servitium.

protinus...ab Oceano, 'immediately upon the Ocean,' i.e. the Baltic, on the coast of Pomerania. The Rugii probably lived at the mouth of the Oder, their name surviving in that of the island of Rügen, and the Lemovii, who are not mentioned elsewhere, east of the Rugii.

breves gladii. Swords found in eastern Germany measure from 16 to 30 ins. long and up to 2¾ ins. broad (Schwyzer).

2. Suionum, the inhabitants of Scandinavia, a land first mentioned by Mela III. 6. 54 and then by Pliny IV. 27. 96 *sinum, qui Codanus vocatur refertus insulis, quarum clarissima est Scatinavia incompertae magnitudinis.* See also on § 1 above. Other forms of the name Suiŏnes are Svear, Swear and Swede.

hinc, 'in this direction,' beyond the Rugii and Lemovii.

praeter viros, 'as well as in men.'

utrimque, used adjectivally, cp. *Agr.* 25. 1, etc. ; 'a prow at each end serves as a forepart always ready for running to shore.' *agit,* 'plays the part of,' a common stage metaphor, but used mostly with a personal subject. Similar boats are described in *Hist.* III. 47 and *Ann.* II. 6. The type still survives in Scandinavia.

nec velis ministrantur, 'nor are the ships provided with sails.' *ministrantur,* the unanimous reading of the MSS., is changed to *ministrant* by many modern editors who find an echo of *Aen.* VI. 302, X. 218 *velisque ministrat* (where *velis* is apparently dative, 'he attends to the sails'). The alteration seems unnecessary, as the change of subject with *adiungunt* (sc. *Suiones*) is tolerable enough.

in ordinem, 'in a row,' *in* with the accus. expressing the result intended. Cp. 46. 6, *Agr.* 8. 2, etc.

solutum, etc., 'the oars are free (i.e. not fixed to the side) and can be shifted from side to side.'

quibusdam fluminum. Writers of the Empire show a tendency to construe *quidam, nullus, omnis,* etc. with the partitive genitive, where a Republican writer would have placed such words in agreement with their nouns ; cp. *nullo hostium* 43. 6, *quidam bonorum Ann.* I. 49, *Macedonum fere omnes* Livy XXXI. 45.

3. et opibus, 'even for riches,' which the Germans as a rule did not value highly. See 5. 2 f.

unus, i.e. the wealthiest.

nullis, etc., 'no longer with any limitations but with an unquestioned claim to obedience.' For *non precario,* 'not resting on sufferance,' cp. *Agr.* 16. 5 *precario praefuit.* The use of *ius parendi* in the sense of 'right to obedience' instead of 'right of obeying' is very remarkable.

4. in promiscuo, 'at everyone's disposal.'

enimvero, 'and in fact.'   The clause explains why the arms were entrusted to a slave's keeping.

regia utilitas, 'a monarch's interest.'   The locking up of arms was probably not due to the reasons given by Tac.   It may well have had a religious significance, like the shutting up of iron during the festival of the peace-loving Nerthus, c. 40. 4.   The ancient Swedish king at Upsala appears to have been considered as a semi-divine being with magical powers and as *ipso facto* high priest of the great temple there ; "the neighbourhood of the king may have been regarded as a 'place of great peace.'" See Prof. Chadwick, *op. cit.* p. 321 ff., who remarks that when certain large barrows at Old Upsala were opened, though rich in gold ornaments they were found to contain no weapons.   The wealth of the monarch of the Suiones may have been due to the offerings of worshippers at the temple.

CHAPTER XLV

1. aliud, other than the ocean of 44. 2.

mare pigrum, etc., Pytheas' θάλασσα πεπηγυῖα, Pliny's *mare concretum* and the Celtic Morimarusa ('Dead Sea').   See *Agr.* 10. 6 and note there.   Reports of the frozen Arctic Ocean seem to have filtered through to the Greeks and Romans. (Plutarch, *de facie in orbe lunae* c. 26, p. 941, tells of 'a sea slow of passage and full of mud because of the number of streams which the great mainland discharges, forming alluvial tracts and making the sea heavy like land, whence an opinion prevailed that it is actually frozen.') (Prickard's Translation.)

hinc fides quod, 'it is believed from the fact that.'   For the perpetual daylight of the Arctic summer cp. *Agr.* 12. 4.   The earliest reference to this phenomenon occurs in *Od.* x. 84 where it is said that in the country of the Laestrygones 'a sleepless man might have earned a double wage ; the one as a neatherd, the other shepherding white flocks ; so near are the outgoings of the day and the night.'

emergentis, contrasted with *cadentis* above.   For noises connected in folk-lore and popular language with the dawn consult Grimm, *Teutonic Mythology*, Eng. Trans. pp. 741 ff., 1518.   The belief that the ocean hisses when the sun drops beneath it is mentioned by Poseidonius (ap. Strabo III. p. 138).

formasque equorum, etc. That the Sun-god, his head circled with a crown of rays, travelled in a horse-drawn chariot, is an idea found in Teutonic as well as in Roman mythology. The MSS. give not *equorum* but *deorum*, an improbable reading, as *radios capitis* clearly refers to the Sun-god. It is not improbable that we have here a confusion of the phenomena of an Arctic sunrise with those of the Aurora Borealis (with which crackling sounds are said to be sometimes associated).

persuasio, ' popular belief.'

illuc usque, etc., 'so far, and according to the true report only so far, does the world reach.' The words *fama vera* are best taken as ablatives, though Zernial regards *et fama vera* sc. *est* as a parenthetical clause. For *natura* sc. *rerum*, cp. *Agr.* 33. 6.

2. ergo iam. The force of the particles seems to be '*to return therefore* (as there are no peoples further north), we *next* find on the right shore of the Baltic the seabord nations of the Aestii.' With *adluuntur* supply *mari*, *dextro...litore* being a locative ablative. *dextro*, on the right of the districts hitherto mentioned, as one faces north, hence ' eastern.'

Aestiorum, stretching from the Pregel to the Gulf of Finland, on the southern shore of which the province of Esthonia preserves their name. Perhaps about 900 A.D. they were expelled from this district by the Finns, to whom the name Estii or Estones was wrongly applied. The Aestii were Indo-Germans and their language seems to have been the ancestor of Old Prussian (extinct two centuries ago), Lettic and Lithuanian.

ritus, ' practices,' a word not necessarily referring to religious rites in Silver Latin. For *habitus* cp. *Agr.* 11. 1.

lingua Britannicae propior, a remark only important as showing that their speech was not German and that therefore they could not be Suebi, among whom Tac. wrongly includes them (see on 38. 1). There can have been very little real likeness between the languages of the Aestii and the Britons.

3. matrem deum. Cp. on 40. 2.

formas aprorum. The boar, a common northern symbol, frequently appearing on Scandinavian and Anglo-Saxon helmets, is often associated with the worship of goddesses of fertility, e.g. Freyia, whom the goddess of the Aestii probably resembled, Cybele and the Greek Demeter. See Chadwick, *op. cit.* p. 248 f. With these *formas* cp. the *effigies et signa* of 7. 3.

omniumque tutela, ' protection against everything.' Others emend to *omnique tutela*.

fustium. A kind of wooden cudgel seems to have been used as a weapon by the Lithuanians even in the 14th cent. (See Zernial.)

4. solita inertia, cp. 14. 5, 15. 1, 26. 2. The transitive use of *laboro* is poetical until the Silver Age. The devotion of the Aestii to agriculture is the natural concomitant of the peaceful and settled character of their communities, a character celebrated by later writers.

sed et, cp. note on 6. 3.

sucinum, also known to the Romans by its Greek name *electrum.* This fossil resin, derived from certain species of pines, occurs in submarine formations in the Baltic, especially near Königsberg. Owing to its attractive appearance it was in very early times used for decorative purposes and had reached southern Europe as early as the Bronze Age. It occurs in tombs at Mycenae and is mentioned in the Homeric poems (see Tozer, *Anc. Geogr.* p. 31). The Homeric Greeks probably got their knowledge of the short Arctic summer nights (see on § 1) from amber-traders.

glesum, Anglo-Saxon *glaer* (cp. our 'glare'), a name given to amber because of its brightness. The Romans probably learnt the word from the Germans of the North Sea coast, which also produces amber, not from the Aestii, who may well have had a different name for it. Pliny, *H. N.* IV. 30. 103, speaks of *insulae in Germanicum mare sparsae Glesariae, quas Electridas Graeci recentiores appellavere, quod ibi electrum nasceretur.* Trustworthy accounts of the amber coast first reached southern Europe through Pytheas.

5. quae natura, sc. *sit.* *barbaris* is dat. of agent.

nomen, 'fame.' In spite of the early use of amber for ornament it cannot have reached Rome in any quantity until the Empire. Pliny tells how a Roman knight was sent by one of Nero's officers to the amber coast by way of Pannonia and came back with a large supply, *H. N.* XXXVII. 11. 45.

rude legitur, etc., 'it is gathered in a rough state and offered for sale in shapeless masses.'

6. sucum, hence the name *sucinum.* *tamen* refers back to *nec...compertum.*

terrena quaedam, etc., a favourite subject for epigram; see Martial IV. 32 and 59, VI. 15. Some 2000 species of insects, spiders, etc. have been found embedded in amber.

7. fecundiora, 'unusually rich.' *secretis* is neut. plur.; 'in the depths of the east.'

quae, very loosely constructed, its antecedent being not *nemora lucosque* but the exudations from the forests.

vicini solis. Tac. regards the north as nearer to the sun because of the phenomena mentioned in § 1. According to the story in Diodorus II. 47 the moon looked very near (παντελῶς ὀλίγον ἀπέχουσαν) from the island of the Hyperboreans.

8. naturam, 'natural properties.' For the subjunct. *temptes* cp. *Agr.* 46. 3, etc.

pinguem, 'oily,' 'heavy.' *ut in...lentescit,* 'softens into a kind of.'

9. Suionibus Sitonum gentes continuantur. As there was nothing to the north of the Suiones but the *mare pigrum* (44. 2), Tac. must have conceived of the Sitones as dwelling in islands to the east of the Suiones, between them and the Aestii. See note on text. Modern scholars generally regard the Sitones as Finns inhabiting northern Scandinavia, there being no good evidence for any Teutonic peoples beyond the Swedes. The name is supposed by some to mean 'magicians,' and this interpretation, if correct, agrees well with the Shamanistic worship of the Finns.

quod femina dominatur, hardly so unique a phenomenon as Tac. suggests it to be. He himself speaks of the power of the Bructeran Veleda who *late imperitabat* (see on 8. 3), and Prof. Chadwick points out, *op. cit.* p. 340, that 'Langobardic tradition begins with a woman, Gambara, who is represented, like Veleda, as both ruler and prophetess.' Moreover Tacitus contradicts his own brilliant epigram by the part which he assigns to Boudicca, *Agr.* 16. 1.

CHAPTER XLVI

1. Peucinorum. The Peucini, deriving their name from Peuce ('Pine-land'), part of the Danube delta, were not, as Tac. implies, coextensive with, but a subdivision of, the Bastarnae, whose territories reached from the upper waters of the Vistula along the basin of the Dniester to the mouth of the Danube. The Bastarnae first appear in history about 180 B.C. as allies of the Macedonian empire and later are found in the hosts of Mithradates. They are generally regarded as true Germans.

Venetorum. The Veneti, often spelt Venedi, cp. Wends, are identifiable with the Slavs. At this time they lived east of the Vistula, south of the Goths and the Aestii in the basin of the Bug. "Between the Slavs and the Germanic peoples constant overlapping has taken place. Their wide distribution over north-east Germany by the sixth century is attested by place-names" (Haddon). See Tacitus' view on § 2 below.

Fennorum, the Finns of the north-east coast of the Baltic. The idea that their name means 'flying ones' (cp. *penna*, 'a wing'), and was given them because of their snow-shoes, is pretty if not convincing.   The Finns entered Europe from beyond the Urals. They belong to what is known as the Finno-Ugrian race and have no connexion with either Germans or Sarmatae.

Sarmatis, widely spread in south Russia and Hungary and apparently an Iranian people. See on I. I.

cultu, 'manner of life.'   For *sede ac domiciliis* see c. 16. They were not nomadic like the Sarmatae.

sordes omnium ac torpor procerum, 'they are all filthy and their chiefs indolent.' The contrast seems abrupt and lacking in point, hence the commonly accepted emendation *sordes omnium ac torpor* : ⟨ora⟩ *procerum conubiis*, etc., an easy change palaeographically, though the collocation *torpor : ora* is not particularly graceful.

in...habitum foedantur, 'are degraded to the repulsive type.' For *habitum* cp. 45. 2.

2. moribus, sc. *Sarmatarum*.

quidquid...erigitur. The mountains exist only in the imagination of ancient writers.

domos figunt, 'they have fixed dwellings.'

scuta gestant.   Contrast *Hist.* I. 79 *inermem Sarmatam* (*neque enim scuto defendi mos est*) *comminus fodiebat*.

Sarmatis, dative, 'from the practices of the Sarmatae.'   For the abbreviated expression cp. *Agr.* 24. 2.

3. herba, 'herbs' not 'grass.'   It is implied below that they ate flesh as well.   Note that *non arma* is not contradicted by *solae in sagittis spes* below, *arma* being only used of weapons employed in close contest, as distinct from *tela*.

ossibus asperant, 'tip with sharp bones.'

comitantur, i.e. the women accompany the men.

4. ferarum...suffugium, 'protection against wild beasts.' For the genit. cp. *omnium tutela*, 45. 3, and contrast 16. 4 *suffugium hiemi*, where many wrongly alter to *hiemis*.

in aliquo ramorum nexu, perhaps a framework of boughs covered with brushwood or wickerwork.

5. inlaborare domibus, 'to labour at building houses,' a phrase modelled upon the poetical *ingemere agris*.   *inlaborare* does not occur elsewhere.

suas alienasque fortunas spe metuque versare, a difficult phrase, perhaps 'to handle (i.e. to speculate with) the fortunes of themselves and others amid hope and fear,' cp. Suet. *Galba* 9 *nummulario non ex fide versanti pecunias*; or else 'to subject...to the alternations of hope and fear' (C. and B.).

illis, emphatic (cp. the passage quoted below); herein they differ from everyone else. *illis* is correct rather than *sibi*, because the clause expresses a result noted by the author, not one aimed at by the Fenni. Schwyzer observes that Tac. intends an ironical allusion to the philosophical ideal of freedom from wants. Similar moralising in regard to the Scythians occurs in Justinus' epitome of Pompeius Trogus, a writer of the Augustan age; *haec continentia illis morum quoque iustitiam dedit, nihil alienum concupiscentibus; quippe ibidem divitiarum cupido est ubi et usus. atque utinam reliquis mortalibus similis moderatio abstinentiaque alieni foret*, Justin. II. 2. 10 (quoted by Zernial).

6. cetera iam fabulosa, 'everything beyond is fabulous.' For *iam* see 44. 1.

Hellusios et Oxionas, perhaps meaning 'deer-like' and 'ox-like.' Cp. the *monstra maris, ambiguas hominum et beluarum formas*, of which Germanicus' soldiers brought back tales, *Ann.* II. 24. Mela III. 6. 56 mentions northern men with horses' hoofs and others with ears so large and flexible that they used them as clothes to cover their bodies. Such marvellous stories were dear to the hearts of Greek and Roman geographers.

in medium, 'to be an open question,' *in* with the accus. giving an idea of purpose, cp. 44. 2. The fact that Gellius XVII. 2. 11 cites *in medium relinquere* as an established, though unusual, variant upon *in medio r.* should suffice to discredit the common alteration to *in medio* here.

INDEX OF PROPER NAMES

OCCURRING IN THE TEXT

INDEX TO THE NOTES

Map of Germany to illustrat

FENNI

MARE SUEBICUM

AESTII

(Pregel)

LEMOVII

GOTONES

Vistula F.

VENETI

(Bug)

HELVECONES?

NAHARVALI?

MANIMI?

LUGII

Viadus

HELISII?

BURI

Vistula F.

BASTARNAE

(Dniester)

OSI

Carpathus Mons

(Pruth)

Marus F.

COTINI

QUADI

Danuvius F.

(Gran)

Aquincum

ARAVISCI

SARMATAE IAZYGES

(Theiss)

ANNONIA

DACIA

SARMATAE

:e the *Germania* of Tacitus

Camb. Univ. Press

For EU product safety concerns, contact us at Calle de José Abascal, 56–1°,
28003 Madrid, Spain or eugpsr@cambridge.org.

www.ingramcontent.com/pod-product-compliance
Ingram Content Group UK Ltd.
Pitfield, Milton Keynes, MK11 3LW, UK
UKHW020308140625
459647UK00014B/1792